HERBERT SCHMIDT

SWORD FIGHTING

AN INTRODUCTION TO THE **SINGLE-HANDED SWORD AND BUCKLER**

Schiffer Publishing Ltd

4880 Lower Valley Road • Atglen, PA 19310

Other Schiffer Books by the Author:

Sword Fighting Volume I, ISBN: 9780764347924

Other Schiffer Books on Related Subjects:

Weapons of Warriors, ISBN: 9780764341168
The Heritage of English Knives, ISBN: 9780764326936
Guide to Knife and Ax Throwing, ISBN: 9780764347795

Originally published as *Schwertkampf Band 2* by Wieland Verlag © 2008.

Translated from the German by Dave Johnston

Library of Congress Control Number: 2015943706

Type set in ITC Garamond Std/Minion Pro

ISBN: 978-0-7643-4826-6
Printed in China

Published by Schiffer Publishing, Ltd.
4880 Lower Valley Road
Atglen, PA 19310
Phone: (610) 593-1777; Fax: (610) 593-2002
E-mail: Info@schifferbooks.com

Contents

	Foreword	5
1	Introduction	8
2	The Weapon: Model for Success	10
	2.1 The Sword	10
	2.2 The Buckler	15
3	The Sources: Historical Evidence	18
	3.1 I.33	18
	3.2 The Set-Plays of Andre Lignitzer	20
	3.3 Talhoffer's Set-Plays	20
	3.4 Kal's Set-Plays	21
4	General Principles: The Basis of the Techniques	22
	4.1 Holding the weapon	22
	4.2 Posture	22
	4.3 The Binding Position	22
	4.4 The Measure	25
	4.5 Footwork	26
5	The Techniques Contained in I.33: A Complex System	28
	5.1 The Guards and Counter-Guards	28
	5.2 The Triple Combination	46
	5.3 The Shield Strike and Thrust Strike	50
	5.4 The Protections	52
	5.5 The Half-Shield	59
	5.6 Fall under Sword and Shield	61
	5.7 "The Bound One Flees"	63
6	Tactics from the I.33: Opportunities from the Bind	66
	6.1 The Over-Bind and Under-Bind	66
	6.2 Taking the Arms	69
	6.3 Thrust from the Bind	75
	6.4 Nod from the Bind	77
	6.5 From the Bind Directly at the Head	78
	6.6 Change of Sword	78

7 Complex Combat Sequences: The Individual Plays 86
7.1 The First Guard and its Plays 86
7.2 The Second Guard and its Plays 118
7.3 The Third Guard and its Plays 128
7.4 The Fourth Guard and its Plays 146
7.5 The Fifth Guard and its Plays 150
7.6 The Sixth Guard and its Plays 157
7.7 The Seventh Guard and its Plays 159
7.8 The Priest's Hat and its Plays 166
7.9 The Fiddle Bow and its Plays 169
7.10 The Walpurgis and its Plays 174
7.11 Special Guards and their Plays 177
8 Further Advancements: The Pieces of Later Master Fencers 178
8.1 A Change in Concept 178
8.2 The Guards and Blows 180
9 A New Concept: Andre Lignitzer's Set-Plays 186
9.1 Lignitzer's First Set-Play 186
9.2 Lignitzer's Second Set-Play 189
9.3 Lignitzer's Third Set-Play 191
9.4 Lignitzer's Fourth Set-Play 194
9.5 Lignitzer's Fifth Set-Play 197
9.6 Lignitzer's Sixth Set-Play 200
10 Difficult Reconstruction: Hans Talhoffer's Set-Plays 202
10.1 Talhoffer's First Set-Play 202
10.2 Talhoffer's Second Set-Play 205
10.3 Talhoffer's Third Set-Play 206
10.4 Talhoffer's Other Set-Plays 208
11 The Long Sword and Buckler: Paulus Kal's Set-Plays 209
11.1 Kal's First Set-Play 210
11.2 Kal's Second Set-Play 212
11.3 Kal's Third Set-Play 214
11.4 Kal's Fourth Set-Play 216
12 Offensive Action: Blows with the Buckler 218
13 Safety First: The Equipment 222
13.1 The Sword 222
13.2 The Buckler 224
13.3 Protective Gear 227
14 The Most Important Part of Training: The Free Fight 228
15 Very Briefly: Tips and Tricks from Experience 230
Appendix 232

Foreword: About This Book

Combat with the sword and shield is part of many epics, novels, films, and other forms of entertainment in which knights play a part. In any medieval spectacle, one will see knights bashing each other with a wide variety of shields and one-handed swords. The Vikings had large round shields and fought with the sword and axe as well. The shield is therefore a requisite in the Middle Ages and any representations of that time. In fact, the shield was used in many forms for a very long time, both on foot and on horseback.

One does not realize how truly complex the subject of sword and shield is until one delves deeply into it. Each period and region had its shields and preferred weapons that were used with them. There is also the environment in which the shield was used: the fighting was different in a Roman shield wall than in a band of Vikings, who in turn fought differently than the Anglo-Saxons in England or the students in Heidelberg, for example.

The shield changed and the weapons used with them were completely different. We know a great deal about the development of shields and weapons thanks to depictions and archeological finds. But how were they really used in combat? Answering this question is much more difficult, not least because no techniques have been passed down concerning big and early shields. What we have are instructions in the use of the small hand shield, the buckler. These instructions are not very precise and comprehensive, but they are the earliest known instructions for sword fighting that we know. I am speaking of I.33—a sixty-four-page manuscript which, though written in Germany, now resides in the Museum of the Royal Armouries in Leeds, England.

I.33 is not only the oldest fencing manual (*Fechtbuch*), but also the most interesting. While it offers deep insight into the way of combat in its day, it also raises many questions. It depicts a priest and a student who is being taught to fence. Did priests fence in those days? Is the author an old soldier who spent his retirement in the monastery and passed on his knowledge? How could he afford the expensive parchment for this book, who illustrated it so well, and in particular, why does a woman appear on the last page? This woman (Walpurgis) fences with a monk, obviously following his directions. Did priests also instruct women in the martial arts? Is her presence in the manuscript merely symbolic, to simply depict a guard in keeping with the motto: "Even a woman can do it?" Or is there more behind it? Unfortunately we will never know; we are left to speculate.

If one is seriously interested in combat with the sword and shield, one cannot overlook I.33. It is in any case a source *par excellence* for using the sword and buckler. There are other sources, but the majority of them lack the scope, complexity, and depth of I.33. Not until Paulus Hector Mair do we again find a large number of techniques. I have not yet completed the interpretation of Mair, however, so I have excluded the system of Mair and Wilhalm (one can only be understood through the other) from this book. I.33 thus forms the main body of the reconstruction of this fascinating weapons combination.

In selecting sources, I limited myself to the German titles. As these sources differ greatly, I decided to also reflect this in the book. I.33 permits a systematic approach, while Lignitzer's set-plays must be worked out. Often Talhoffer and Kal have left us no more than snapshots without the text required to work out an entire technique, so less space is dedicated to Talhoffer and Kal, and accordingly, the interpretation of these snapshots is kept open. Thus, in this book we find a number of different approaches to interpretation. I hope that you will forgive me this lack of consistent methodology, but to me it seems better to seek the best approach depending on the source, even if the book loses some continuity as a result.

Referring to the interpretation of techniques, there are many fencers who have grappled intensively with and continue to grapple with the sources. Some of them have come to similar interpretations independently of one another while others have developed different interpretations. Some of these are so far from the sources that, while they can be recommended as an introduction to combat with the sword and buckler, they often have very little to do with the original manuscript. Other interpretations adhere very closely to the sources and nevertheless reveal other contents and processes.

As long as they conform to the sources, the different interpretations are of equal value. Which is better is impossible to say with certainty; one would have to ask the master fencer of the day. Comparisons in free fighting are only valid to a point, because the qualities and abilities of the individual fencers are often more important to the outcome than different interpretations. I have also mentioned differing points of view in this book to give the reader the opportunity to form their own opinion.

An interpretation is never anything more than a snapshot. Work continues on interpretation of I.33, and at some point I will probably interpret this or that technique somewhat differently. A book like this is not only an explanation and introduction to a system, but also a documentation of the level of research at a certain time. We all develop and only end this development when we die—but then it is too late to write a book. I am therefore happy to be able to make a small contribution to the development of historical fencing.

It is often tiresome to give boring explanations of certain sequences of movements when there are specific terms for them, even if they first appeared 100 years later. To avoid unnecessarily complicating the text, I will use many terms from the German School and the Liechtenauer tradition. I will not explain all of these terms on the spot, but you will find them in the glossary. All of the dedicated terms from fencing with the long sword are explained in my first book *Sword fighting—Combat with the Long Sword according to the German School.*

Developing such an interpretation requires a great deal of practice, experience, and testing, but this cannot be done alone. I would therefore like to thank all those who fenced and discussed with me and offered criticism. Without you I would not have gotten this far. Many opinions and ideas from others have flowed into this book. Nevertheless, the contents of the book are a representation based on my understanding and experience. This means that any mistakes in the book are mine alone.

While on the subject of mistakes: many of the photos in this book were taken with the subjects in static poses. For the sake of clarity movements have sometimes been exaggerated. One always fences vigorously, using the entire body. Part of this is taking advantage of the body's kinetic energy, which is almost impossible to capture in photographs. I therefore ask that you keep this in mind when training and never ignore it.

I would specially like to thank Dieter Bachmann. Without his patience in clarifying and processing the original Latin text I would not have been able to resolve many questions. Special thanks go to Roland Warzecha as well. Much became clear to me while answering his questions and critically examining his interpretation of I.33. He has contributed much to the interpretation of the manuscript. Some things in this book were inspired by him. His critical eye also turned up many errors.

I would also like to thank Dieter Kraft, Thomas Locker, Dave Rawlings, Harald Winter, and Chris Stride. None of this would have been possible without the regular training sessions at Ars Gladii, whose members patiently worked on my ideas and experiments.

I would also like to give special thanks to all of the members of the Ars Gladii forum. Their discussions enabled me to answer many questions and learn a great deal. Discussions in such a forum often reach an unbelievably high level. I hope that the scientific world will very soon turn its attention to these experts, who possess an enormous amount of knowledge without holding corresponding titles or positions. It is they who have done much pioneering work in this field of medieval studies.

I would like to give very special thanks to Bernhard Müller, who again made himself available to take photographs to illustrate this book, plus our other photographer, Frank Soens. The photography would have taken twice as long without the help of Arnold Hartmann—thank you very much! I am also grateful to Søren Niedziella of Albion Europe and Allan Senefelder of Mercenarys Tailor for generously providing photographs.

As with my first book, I have enjoyed working with the Wieland Verlag team. Through her confidence and charm, Caroline Wydeau in particular made the job a joy.

CHAPTER 1

Introduction: A Definition

Historical European sword fighting is generally understood to mean combat with the European sword according to the researchable fencing system of past epochs. In principle, all swords are included: epées, rapiers, long swords, and short swords. This book is dedicated exclusively to combat with the short sword—the sword that is wielded in one hand—and the buckler—a small shield held in the hand. As I adhere to verifiable sources, I will devote myself to the most important combat manual on this subject (the I.33 manuscript) and consider three other sources. From a geographical point of view, we will remain exclusively in the German.

There is a marked difference between historical sword combat and the stage or show battles we often see at medieval fairs, on stage, and not least in motion pictures. These show combats usually have nothing in common with true sword combat. The phenomenon of show combat is not new, for we have proof of such show fighters from the fourteenth century, whose acts were designed to appeal to the public. Then as now, serious fighters did not have a great deal of sympathy for these show fighters.

Historical sword fighting is not about amusing the public. It is all about winning a sword combat as efficiently and quickly as possible. To achieve this, we follow the masters from the time when such combats were a matter of life and death. Historical fighting is not appealing to the public, as it is often over too quickly. The spectator understands little of what is happening. Instead, the techniques are designed to overcome one's opponent with as few movements as possible and the least possible expenditure of energy.

In reconstructing the fighting system with the short sword I adhere to surviving sources. These in turn concern themselves only with unarmored combat, meaning the fighters wear no armor. This, of course, affects the techniques used. We must therefore also search in the civil realm—in particular in trials by combat, in which "right" was determined by the sword.

Although we have a plethora of illustrations showing fighters in full armor carrying bucklers, unfortunately, there are none that show how the buckler was used in this situation. Nevertheless, these illustrations clearly show how ubiquitous the buckler was in its heyday in the fourteenth and fifteenth centuries. We find it represented in everyday life and on the battlefield. It is carried by average people, as well as by mercenaries and nobles. A manuscript from the St. Gallen monastery from 1465 shows the buckler at the side of an oriental knight in the First Crusade. The Manesse Manuscript shows the buckler in a duel between two unarmored nobles and the buckler is also represented in Maximilian's *Triumphal Procession* by Dürer. It appears the buckler was very popular—and not just in Central Europe.

It is not feasible to describe every possible technique in one book. This also applied to the author of I.33 and the writers of later combat manuals. Many situations in I.33 permit additional techniques that unfortunately are not there. Some of these techniques function so well I was reluctant to omit them. I have therefore included them in the appropriate places, but characterize them as supplementary techniques. They expand the system of I.33 but are not part of the system imparted in this manuscript.

It is also almost impossible to produce modern photographs that show every detail. The interplay of photos and explanatory text is required to provide a sensible whole. We have tried to arrange the photos as effectively as possible. I ask for feedback where we have failed to achieve this. In places the text includes technical terms that are not explained until later. You can refer to the glossary at the end of the book at any time.

Illustration from the Book of Hours commissioned by Ètienne Chevalier about 1452.

Detail from the Oldenburger Sachsenspiegel of 1336. Trial by combat with the sword and buckler.

Depiction from Maximilian's Triumphal Procession by Albrecht Dürer (1520).

CHAPTER 2

The Weapon: Model for Success

From the earliest times it was customary in Europe to carry a shield with the sword. These shields came in a wide variety of shapes, sizes, and designs. The way one fought with a sword and shield likewise changed frequently. The so-called buckler was a special type of shield. The combination of a buckler with a sword or long knife was used for a very long time.

Small bucklers were known very early on and appear frequently in illustrations and texts. There are illustrations showing fencers with swords and bucklers from as early as 1230. If one goes back further, one even finds this combination in ancient Rome, as mosaics in the *Augusta Raurica* from approximately 200 BC show. Among the most well known are the illustrations in the Manesse Manuscript and appropriate places in Geoffrey Chaucer's *Canterbury Tales*.

2.1 The Sword

The sword wielded in one hand is the oldest form of sword. Greeks, Romans, and many other cultures used the sword almost exclusively in one hand. The one-handed sword was the rule until the High Middle Ages and everything else was the exception. The one-handed sword was also never completely superseded.

We are familiar with the archetypal sword of the Middle Ages—the knight's sword—from illustrations and books, films, and many other sources. They always depict a knight with a large shield and a sword wielded in one hand. Few are interested in the fact that this depiction mixes images from several eras and that the style of armor conflicts with the sword and shield that are used. It is a fact that the sword wielded in one hand was used for a very long time throughout the entire Middle Ages, but during that time it also underwent major changes. Its origins lie in the weapons used by the Vikings and Normans—swords with a relatively broad blade, a very small cross guard, and often very short grips. These swords were almost always carried with a large shield.

The classic "knight's sword" is usually depicted with a straight or slightly curved cross guard and a disc pommel. The blade is somewhat broader and is equivalent to an Oakeshott Type X. This type was very widely used but is one of the early forms. These swords were also used with various large shields. The sword later developed further, conformed to the armor in use, and became more elegant, faster, and changed its shape.

The sword was also always a weapon used to guarantee personal safety. The sword or "long knife" was often a life saver on trips and in everyday life. Numerous contemporary accounts tell of fights with the sword and buckler. The *Canterbury Tales* come to mind immediately, but even much later it was commonplace to go out armed for defense, as one can read in the biography of Benvenuto Cellini (1500-1571), for example.

The sword wielded in one hand was usually simply called a "short sword" (*kurzes Schwert*) by swordsmen. It is important to mention the term "short sword" has

Illustration from a crusader's Bible of 1250.

A reproduction Viking sword by Albion.

Sword by Albion modeled after an original in the Blade Museum in Solingen. Swords like this were typical of the period of I.33.

The hilt of a Viking sword. Reproduction by Albion

The Oakeshott typology: developed in the late 1950s, it has been generally accepted since about 1990.

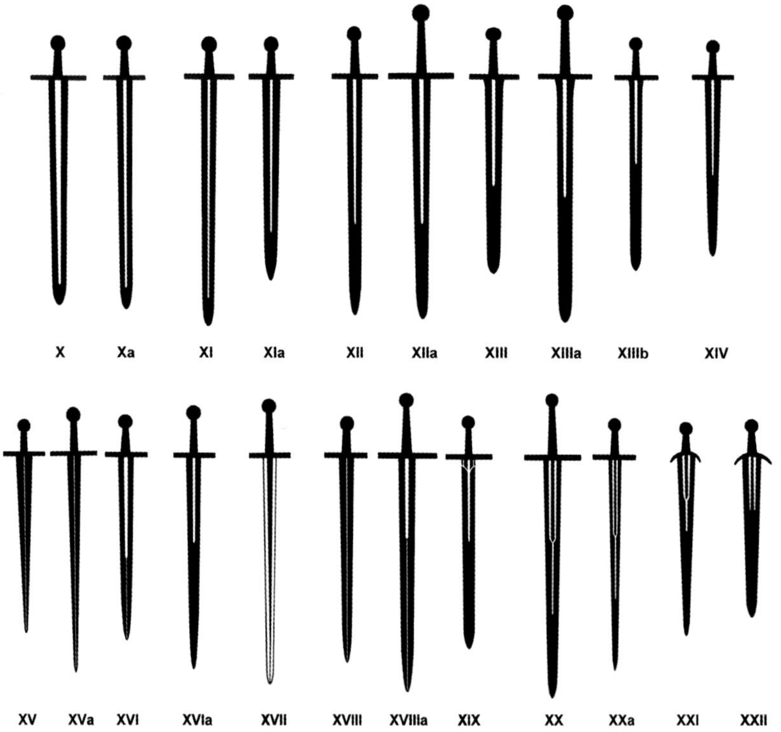

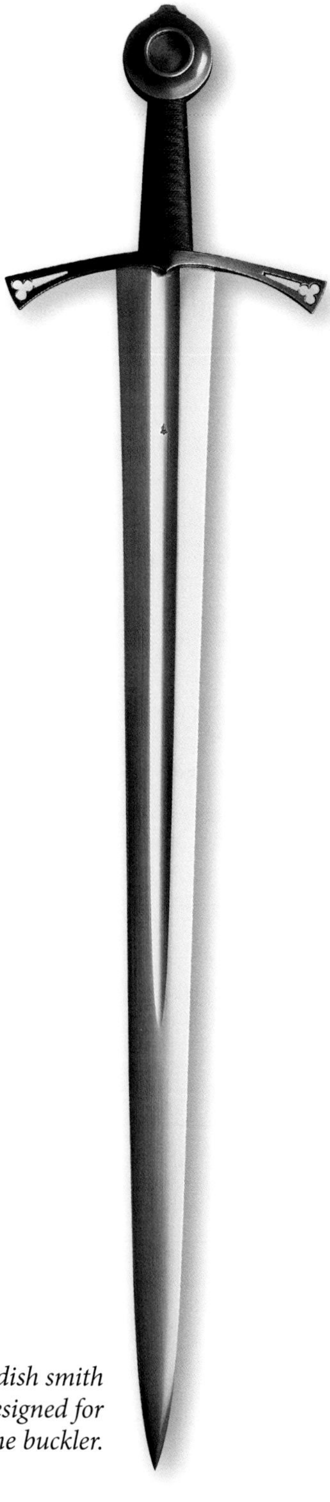

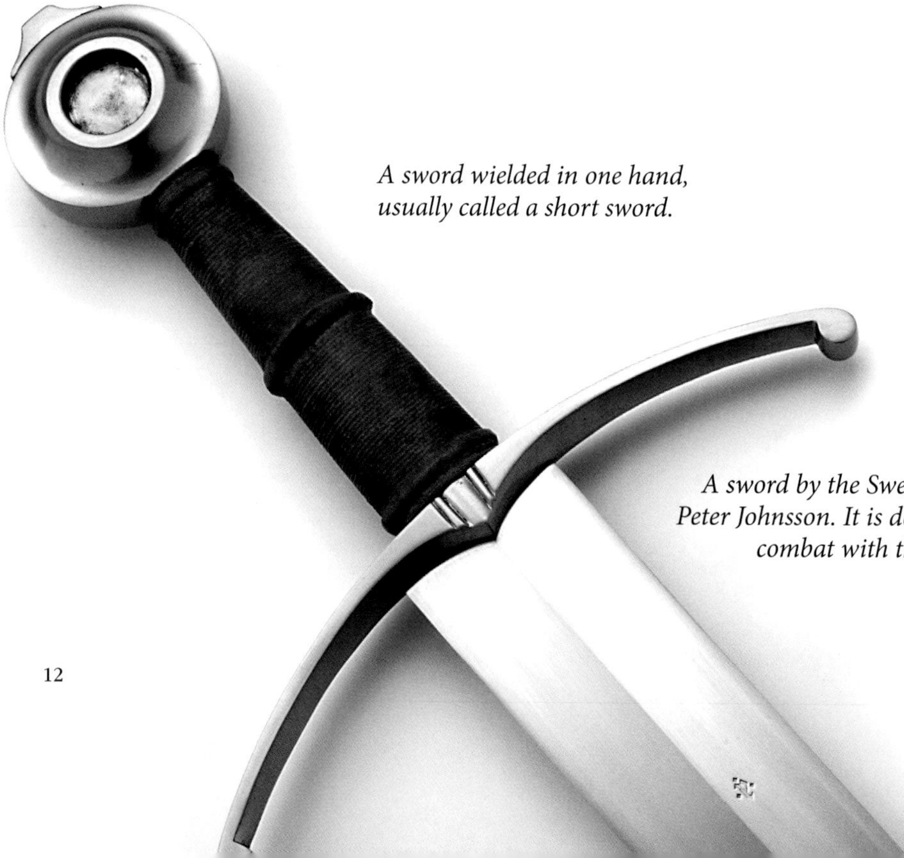

A sword wielded in one hand, usually called a short sword.

A sword by the Swedish smith Peter Johnsson. It is designed for combat with the buckler.

nothing to do with the "*Kurzschwert*" (shortsword), whose precise scope is not clearly defined. When I speak of the short sword here, I am referring to the sword wielded in one hand as used throughout almost the entire Middle Ages.

The short sword developed from the *spatha* used by the Celts. At about the end of the ninth century it received a longer cross guard and then, in the eleventh century, the disc pommel. Many other styles of grip were also used. The transition to the classic European short sword was thus completed in the tenth century. The blade form changed from very top-heavy blades primarily conceived for striking blows to narrow blades that were relatively broad at the base but tapered sharply toward the tip. Their balance made very quick fencing possible.

It is thus possible to understand a change in the art of fencing, even theoretically. One can assume that fighting style changed a great deal over the centuries. In combination with the *spatha*, the centrally-wielded shield was probably used in a strongly offensive role. Targeted work with the edge of the shield led to the sword being used to strike or thrust at resulting openings in an opponent's defense without endangering the sword hand. This style of fighting was not possible with later shields that were carried on the arm. The concept of binding blades became dominant in combats so the cross guard grew longer to offer more protection for the sword arm.

The earliest surviving combat manual (I.33) illustrates one such system based on the binding of blades. Fighting with an early blade in the style of I.33 would have been both exhausting and difficult—the sword lacked mobility. Consequently, even in the time of I.33 and later combat manuals that deal with the sword and buckler we find weapons that are suitable for this style of fighting and indeed made it possible.

When one looks around a museum one finds a large selection of short swords. All are different and have their special characteristics. Nevertheless, there are a few things that all of them have in common. A sword usually consists of a blade, a cross guard, the grip, and the pommel. The cross guard, grip, and pommel together form a unit called the hilt. The blade has various shapes and forms. It always passes through the grip and ends in (or after) the pommel, where it is riveted. The part of the blade that passes through the grip is called the tang. This tang should be as sturdy as possible, as it is subjected to great loads.

The blade is provided with a cross guard and pommel. Both are fitted as precisely as possible and fixed in place. The tang is then riveted. This ensures all parts are held firmly in place. Then a grip is added to the end. It usually consists of two half shells glued together. Then the grip is wrapped and covered with leather. This style of grip mounting is not only historically accurate, it is also the most durable and reliable version.

Every sword vibrates and this vibration is very important. If you hold a sword in your hand and strike the pommel sideways you can easily see the vibrations of the sword. You will notice that there is a point in the blade that does not vibrate. That is one of the so-called vibration nodes. A sword has two vibration nodes. The forward vibration node in the blade is also called the striking point, or point of percussion (POP). Ideally, this spot strikes the target when a blow is made because the blade vibrates the least there. The blow is smoothest, most stable, and thus achieves its highest efficiency. As well, the hand shock is much reduced. The second vibration node is in the grip, ideally under the swordsman's index or middle finger. This ensures the sword rests as quietly in the hand as possible.

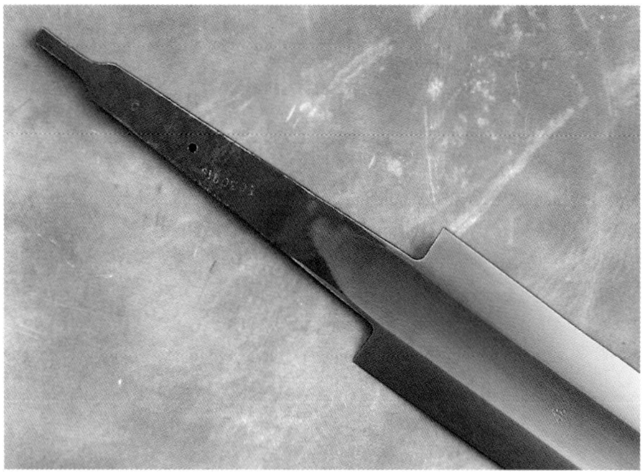

The tang of a blade. Clearly visible are the "rounded" shoulders where it meets the blade, designed to avoid the development of a pressure point at this location.

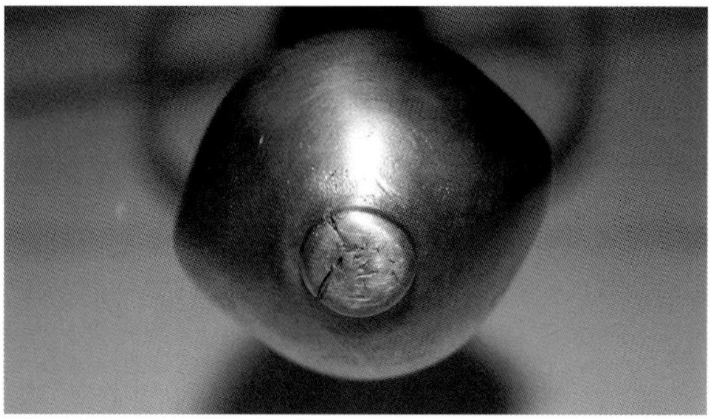

Riveted tang on an historical original.

Blade with mounted cross guard and pommel. The grip is still missing, as it is not fitted until the end.

SWORD NOMENCLATURE

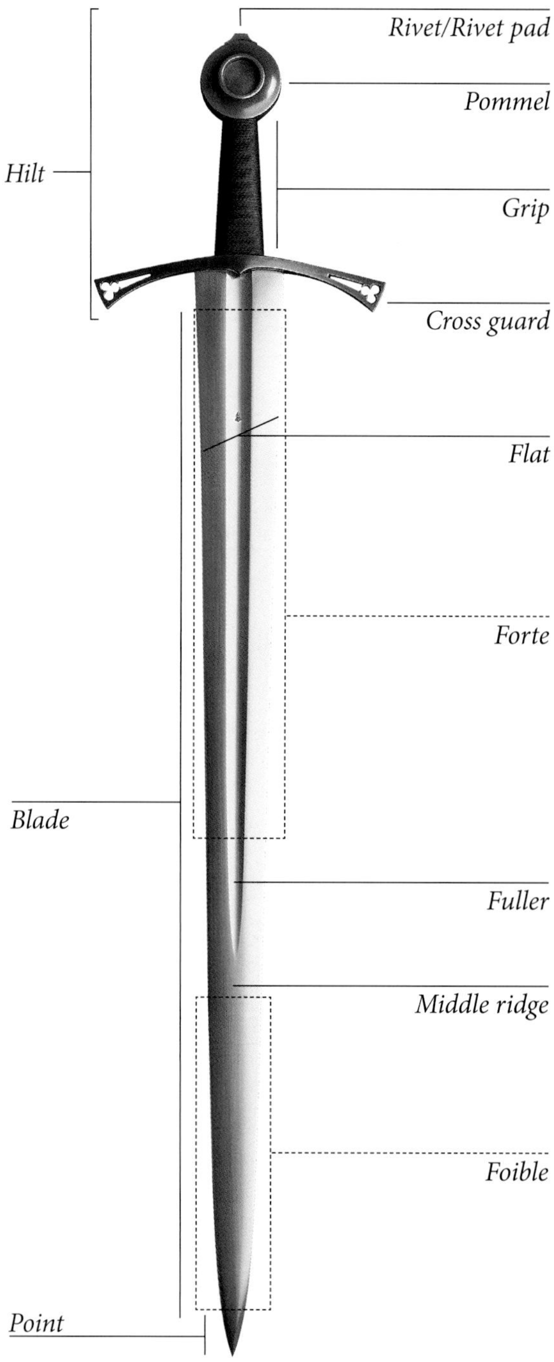

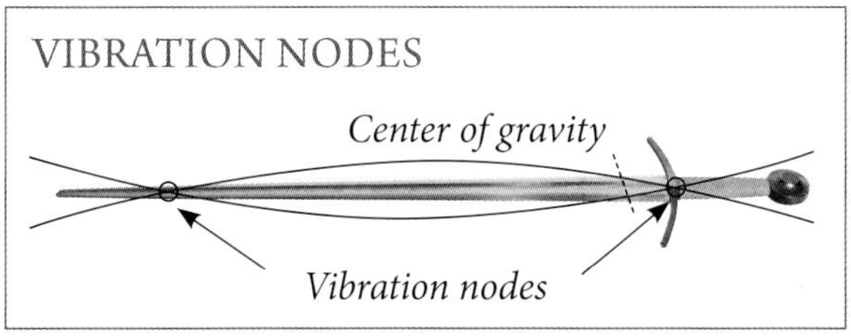

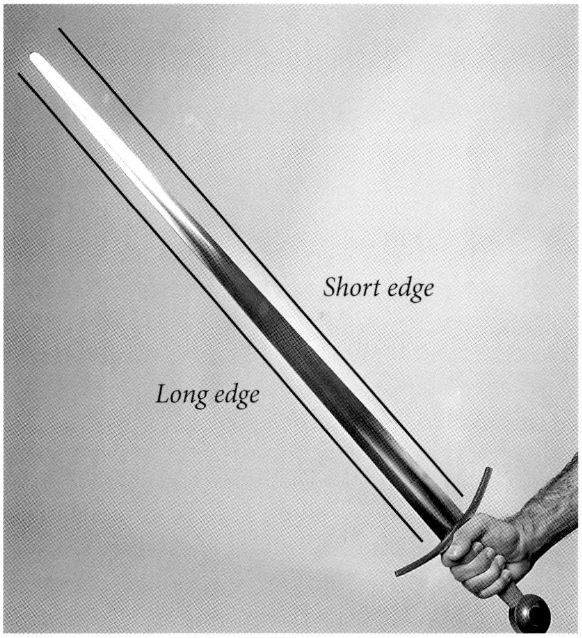

The long and short edges of a sword.

The author in the Blade Museum in Solingen. Working with surviving originals is indispensable in evaluating the quality of modern replicas.

There is also a center of gravity that can be found just in front of the cross guard. The center of gravity is not especially significant and its importance is usually exaggerated. Ultimately the feel of the blade is decisive. Pick up a sword, make a few movements with it, and feel how the blade behaves, how the sword can be wielded. With greater experience you will also be better able to evaluate a sword. The most important thing about a sword is that it suits your fighting style. Obviously it should not be too heavy, balance should be good, and the finish should be as good as possible.

A short sword usually weighs between 900 and 1300 grams (2 to 2.9 lbs.). Many training swords are too heavy. In general, one can say a short sword that weighs more than 1400 grams (3.1 lbs.) is too heavy and many would place the limit at 1200 grams (2.65 lbs.).

2.2 The Buckler

For a long time the buckler was ignored by art history, weapons historians, and even by martial artists. In the martial arts this changed several years ago, but there is still work to be done in the fields of archaeology and weaponry.

The origins of the buckler are shrouded in darkness. It is clear that various forms of the buckler were used in ancient Rome. These bucklers then seem to have been forgotten, for there is almost no evidence of them to be found. The buckler did not experience a second flowering until the High Middle Ages. There are many illustrations of the buckler from that period, including some on the battlefield. Suddenly it appears almost everywhere and is used in combination with the long knife, a short sword, or special sword types such as the falchion or malchus. The buckler was used mainly by combatants without armor: bowmen, simple foot soldiers, and other fighters on the battlefield are often depicted with a buckler. Warriors in full armor are also frequently shown carrying a buckler.

The typical buckler was usually made from steel, but also wood and hardened leather. The average diameter was between 25 and 35 centimeters (10 and 14 inches). They were usually round, but this could also vary greatly: there are depictions of square and oval bucklers, bucklers with faces, and adventurous forms with spikes.

Illustration from the Talhoffer Tafel. The dagger in the buckler hand is clearly visible.

The buckler was always held by a grip located centrally behind the boss of the shield. Many illustrations also depict a dagger held in the buckler hand that was obviously used for offensive fighting. This style is known mainly from Scottish warriors and their *targes*. The Scottish targe is a hybrid between the large shield and the buckler. It is rather larger than the buckler, but it is worn on the arm with two straps and not held centrally by a grip. It actually has nothing in common with the typical buckler, as its construction, manner of carriage, and use are completely different.

Combat with sword and shield changed over the centuries, as can be read about and followed through the development of the sword. With respect to the style of fighting, the shield was almost as important as the sword. Changes to the shield were always an indication of changes in fighting tactics and techniques. The buckler resulted in the development of an entirely new style of sword combat typified by special characteristics, including a very fast style of combat that led to success even in the most confined spaces. This may also be an important reason why the buckler enjoyed such popularity.

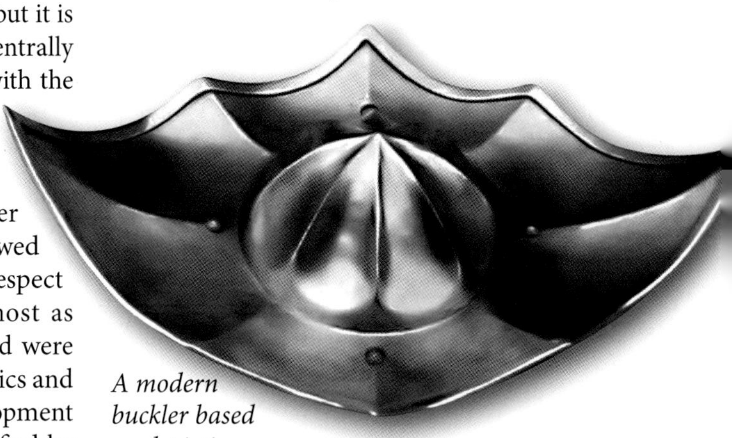
A modern buckler based on depictions in the Talhoffer Tafel.

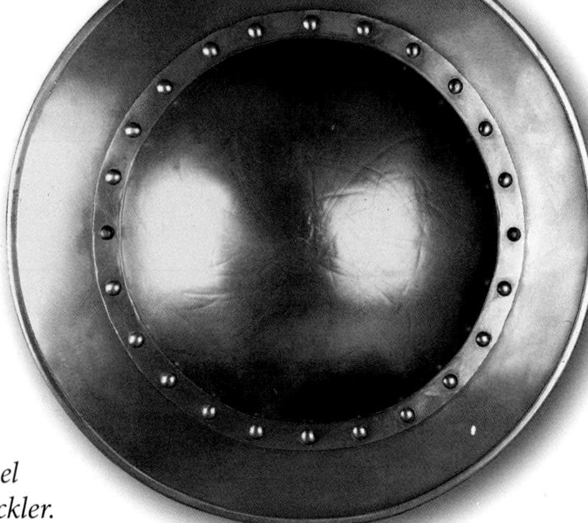
Steel buckler.

A border illustration from a Corpus Iurius Civilis (Body of Civil Law).

Illustration from the Thott Edition of Talhoffer, 1459. The different styles of buckler can be seen clearly. Here the combatants are fighting with long knives.

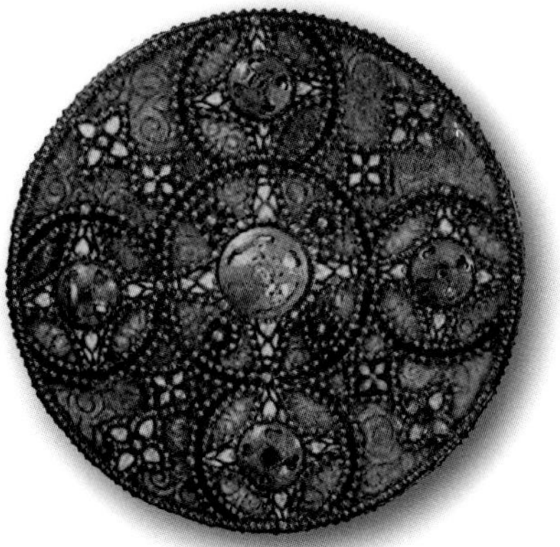

Targe from the Scottish National Museum in Edinburgh.

Historical Bible by Guyart des Moulins, a medieval monk of the late fourteenth century ("The Assassination of Gedaliah").

Illustration from the combat manual by Paulus Kal, late fifteenth century.

Buckler made of steel and wood. The central grip is a typical feature of a buckler. The rawhide edge banding is clearly visible.

Armed warriors with buckler on the battlefield from an English manuscript from 1473.

The Sources: Historical Evidence

The techniques described in this book were developed and reconstructed from surviving sources from the Middle Ages. In the process we span a broad spectrum. We begin with I.33 and then continue into the techniques of Andre Lignitzer and Paulus Kal, then touch on the set-plays described by Hans Talhoffer. The main part of this book concerns itself with the techniques contained in I.33. This manuscript is the most important source we possess on the sword and buckler.

There are other sources concerning combat with the sword and buckler. Worthy of mention are the works of Jörg Wilhalm and Paulus Hector Mair. Jörg Wilhalm—a hat maker from Augsburg—wrote several combat manuals in the first quarter of the sixteenth century. Entries in the manuals show that three of the five were in the possession of Paulus Hector Mair. Paulus Hector Mair was himself a colorful personality. He left us several outstanding combat manuals whose illustrations are among the most beautiful ever created. Mair appears to have copied Wilhalm, however. Identical techniques appear in both combat manuals, but they are described better by Mair. Many of Mair's techniques also appear in I.33 and in the writings of Lignitzer, Talhoffer, and Kal.

All of these sources teach the use of the sword and buckler in unarmored combat; the techniques were designed for combats in which the swordsmen wore no armor. When one evaluates the techniques, one must assume what was worn at the time as normal street clothing or prescribed attire for trials by combat. This is very important when assessing the effectiveness of various techniques.

The following brief description of the most important sources shows this book covers a span of a good 150 years; a long time during which much happened, as evidenced by sword fighting techniques.

3.1 I.33

I.33—also called the "Tower Fechtbuch"—is an extraordinary manuscript. It consists of thirty-two vellum folios about 23 by 30 centimeters (9" x 12"). It is preserved in the Royal Armouries in Leeds, England. The manuscript was written in southern Germany, probably in Würzburg. I.33 is the manuscript's designation in the Royal Armouries. The complete designation would be *Royal Armouries MS I.33*, the "I" being a Roman numeral. Its complete name, therefore, is "one-thirty-three." The name consists of MS (Manuscript), I (Class I), and the item number "33." This is simply the museum's internal cataloguing.

The illustrations were created from the text, so in some cases there are references to errors in the illustrations. It is often advantageous to keep this sequence of creation in mind during interpretation. The manuscript obviously went through some hard times. There are some holes in the vellum, and on several pages a child drew beards on the faces of the swordsmen, tried to paint out the bucklers, and also added a variety of other drawings.

A word about the page references: it is customary to number manuscripts either continuously with page numbers or number the individual pages (folios), indicating whether something is located on the front or back of the page. The front side is indicated with an "r" (*recto*) and the back side with a "v" (*verso*). In a manuscript the *recto* is on the right, the *verso* side on the left; "3v" therefore refers to the back side (*verso*) of the third page (Folio 3).

Jeffrey L. Forgeng has written an excellent book about I.33 which, in addition to full-page illustrations, contains a transcription and an English translation. To many, this book was and is a basis for working with I.33. Dieter Bachmann of Switzerland has now translated I.33, so today we have an English and a German translation. Forgeng used continuous page numbering (1–64), while Bachmann used the classic folio method (1r–32v). To do justice to both and simplify searching and finding, I have used both page numbering formats: "3v/6" therefore means "Folio 3 *verso* / Page 6." An odd page number always indicates a *recto* page while even numbers stand for *verso* pages.

In I.33 there appear three protagonists who illustrate the techniques. The first is a priest—probably the author himself. He explains the techniques and instructs the other two. The second person who is portrayed is a student of the priest. He is the counterpart who learns. These two demonstrate the techniques while reversing roles. Surprisingly, a woman also appears on the last two pages. This *Walpurgis* fences with the priest and even demonstrates her own guard and counter-guard.

The system depicted in I.33 is very complex and multilayered. It was not intended for beginners. The monk Liutger—to whom I.33 is attributed—frequently refers to the "ordinary swordsman," who would react quite differently than he should based on his instruction. He consciously elevated himself and his system above the usual level of the ordinary swordsman. Unfortunately, this "ordinary system" of the "ordinary swordsman" has been lost.

In I.33, the individual "set-plays"—the sequences of techniques—are referred to as "games." This is not an indication that these techniques—or I.33 in general—

A page from I.33.

were intended as pastimes or sport. The illustrated techniques are not only very effective, but also absolutely deadly, so a sporting character, especially with no armor, can probably be ruled out. Here the term "game" probably serves to indicate the individual techniques should be seen as related and self-contained. This is also suggested by the frequent depiction of sword and buckler on battlefields, in trials by combat, and civilian life, i.e., while travelling.

I.33 contains numerous illustrations of postures that can only be achieved through an extreme twisting of the wrist (for example 9r/17 or 25r/49). A corresponding posture is often possible without a limiting effect, for example the Priest Guard. In other cases it is almost impossible or absurd to assume the depicted postures. Why were they illustrated this way? In the

A page from I.33 with child's drawings.

Middle Ages there was a problem with illustrations, specifically perspective. This not only affected buildings and landscapes, but also people and their posture. Illustrators always tried to draw things from the side. In the entire I.33 there is not a single example of a sword drawn from the narrow side; instead, one always sees the flat of the blade.

As a result, when the observer is actually looking at the edge of the sword because it is pointing at him, in the drawing the sword is "flattened." This knowledge makes many techniques understandable. I have always tried out both versions—the original hand position and the alternative. I use whichever functions better as the basis for interpreting the technique.

3.2 The Set-Plays of Andre Lignitzer

Six set-plays with the short sword and buckler appear in several German language combat manuals. These six set-plays are usually attributed to Andre Lignitzer. According to Peter von Danzig's *Fechtbuch* (Cod. 44a8 of 1449), they come from him. They appear in very many combat manuals almost word for word, suggesting one copied from the other. I stick with the set-plays as they appear in Peter von Danzig's work.

They are opposite pole to the system in I.33. Lignitzer's set-plays are of a completely different nature: they originate from different basic principles and postures leading to a different fencing style. Combat tactics are also completely different. These differing systems could have existed in parallel, but perhaps they also developed and were adapted to changing times. We do not know.

3.3 Talhoffer's Set-Plays

Hans Talhoffer is a very famous name in the show- and sword fighting scene. This is curious, and certainly has to do with the earlier publication of a reprint of his work that appeared in 1998. Unfortunately, Talhoffer's true significance is not nearly as great. His combat manuals (1443, 1459, and 1467) lack the content of other *Fechtbücher*. For this reason he is often referred to as a supplement in reconstructions, and that is also the case in this book.

3.4 Kal's Set-Plays

Paulus Kal wrote his combat manual sometime around 1460. It is noteworthy in a number of respects, especially his chapter on the sword and buckler. The weapons used are unique. One of the bucklers is a grotesque face with the tongue sticking out. The sword itself is a long sword, not a short, one-handed sword.

The set-plays themselves are rather unimaginative and very simple. It appears he only included the sword and buckler in his book for the sake of completeness and paid little attention to this class of weapon.

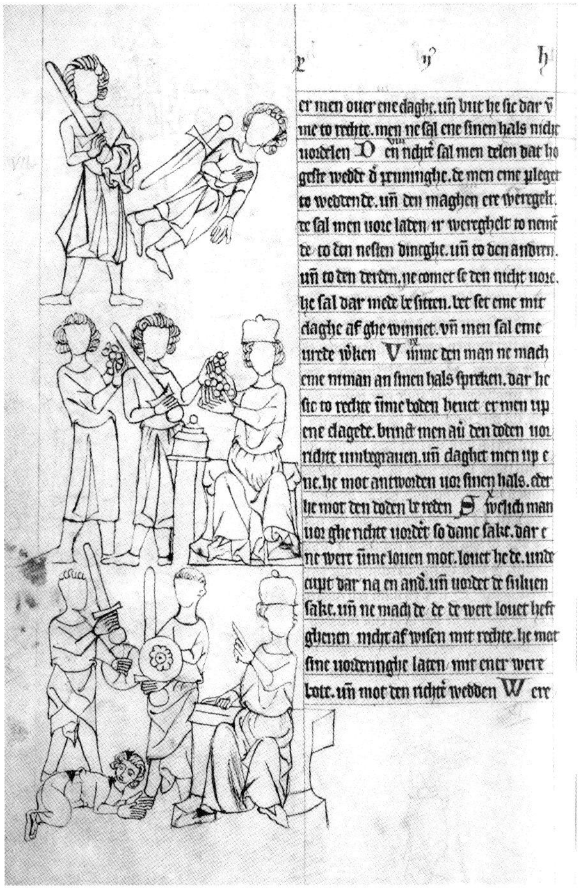

Illustration of a trial by combat from the Oldenburger Sachsenspiegel of 1336.

Capital in the Oviedo cathedral.

A page from the Thott Edition of 1459 by Talhoffer.

CHAPTER 4

General Principles: The Basis of the Techniques

4.1 Holding the Weapon

Before you practice combat with the sword and buckler, you must first know how to properly hold both.

HOLDING THE SWORD

For right-handers, the short sword is held with the right hand (all of the descriptions in this book are laid out for right-handers, the mirror view applies to left-handers). Depending on the length of the grip, there can be some distance between the hand and the cross guard and/or pommel. Exactly where you place your hand—at the cross guard or pommel—is a matter of taste. If you hold the sword at the cross guard then it is possibly easier to control, while holding the sword at the pommel lends more momentum to the blow. The differences are minor.

It often happens that you must somewhat turn the sword in your hand. Your grip should therefore be somewhat flexible, but obviously the sword should be held firmly in your hand when striking a blow or (even more so) when in a binding position. Sometimes it is an advantage if you place your thumb on the flat of the blade for better stability. In this "thumb grip," the sword is usually turned in the hand slightly so that you can rest your thumb on the blade without bending the wrist. This thumb grip is either not depicted in the combat manuals or only in connection with the long sword. I.33 makes no reference to this type of grip. It is often practical, but it does not conform to the sources.

HOLDING THE BUCKLER

In combat the buckler moves hither and thither. You will repeatedly turn the buckler in your closed hand: sometimes left, sometimes right. You should therefore practice this turning movement over and over. With time it becomes quite automatic. Always try to keep your wrist as straight as possible, otherwise very high forces can affect the wrist. It is better to turn the buckler in your hand than bend your wrist.

As far as possible the buckler covers the sword hand and is therefore moved concomitantly. With one exception, in I.33 the buckler is not used to directly intercept an opposing blow; however, the fighting masters who came later—Lignitzer, Kal, and Talhoffer—definitely used the buckler for direct parrying. There in particular it is important to hold the shield properly, for in certain circumstances one must absorb considerable force with the buckler. A straight wrist is a must here.

4.2 Posture

In the basic fighting posture the swordsman is bent forward slightly. In this way the fencer can more quickly execute the dynamic attacks typical of combat with the sword and buckler. It also virtually eliminates the legs as a target.

4.3 The Binding Position

The bind—the moment at which two opposing blades are against each other—is always of decisive importance in sword fighting. This moment is often brought about intentionally. The bind is of central importance in I.33. Subsequent techniques are often determined at the moment the blades bind. Through the bind one also gains control of the opponent's blade.

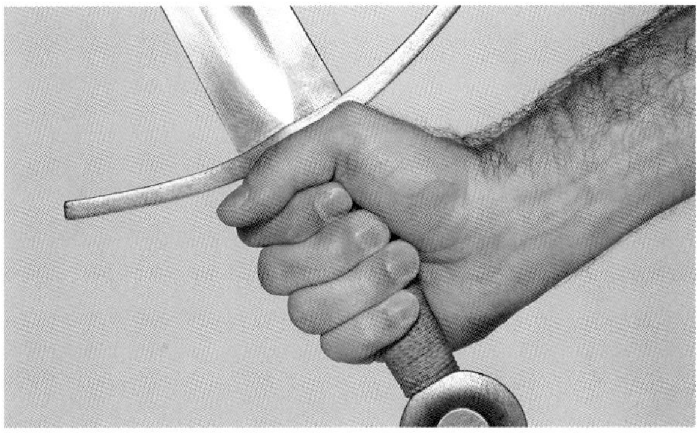

The correct way to hold the sword: as a beginner, be sure to keep your wrist as straight as possible. Wait until your confidence and strength improve before you begin working from the wrist.

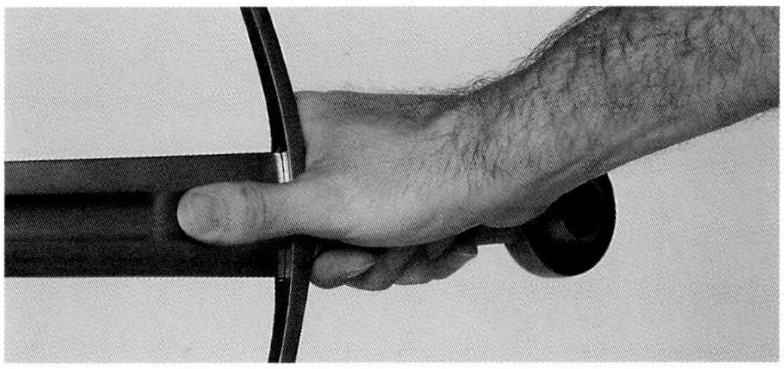

The thumb grip: place your thumb on the flat of the blade, with the sword turned slightly in your hand so that the flat is positioned transversely to you.

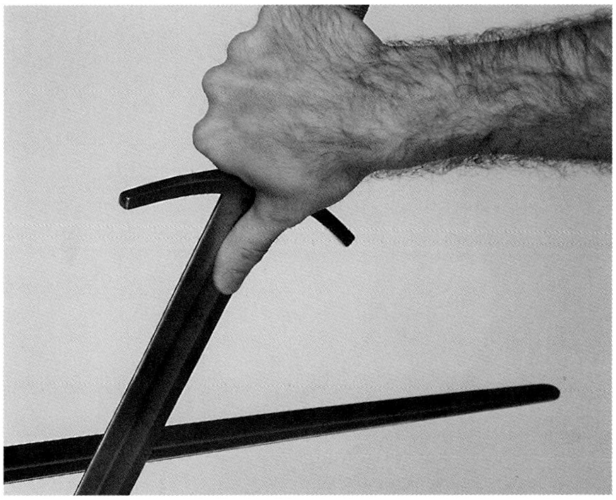

The thumb grip is used, for example, when you wish to allow the opponent's blade to slide off yours.

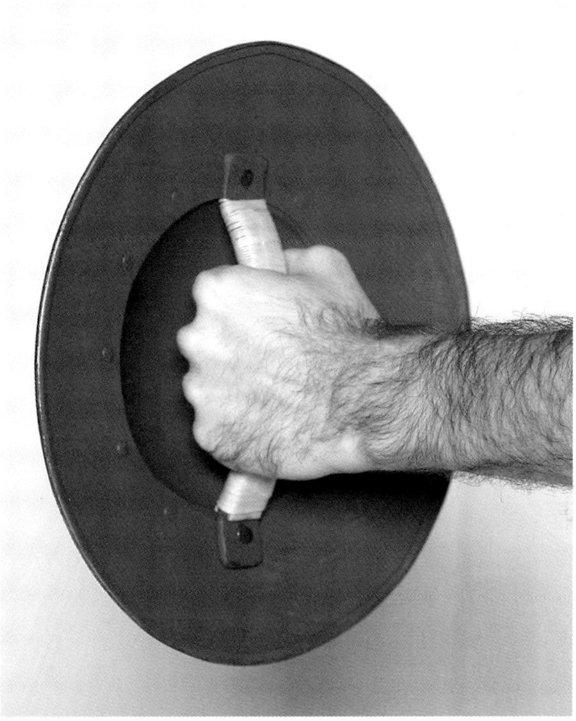

The buckler is always wielded with a straight wrist.

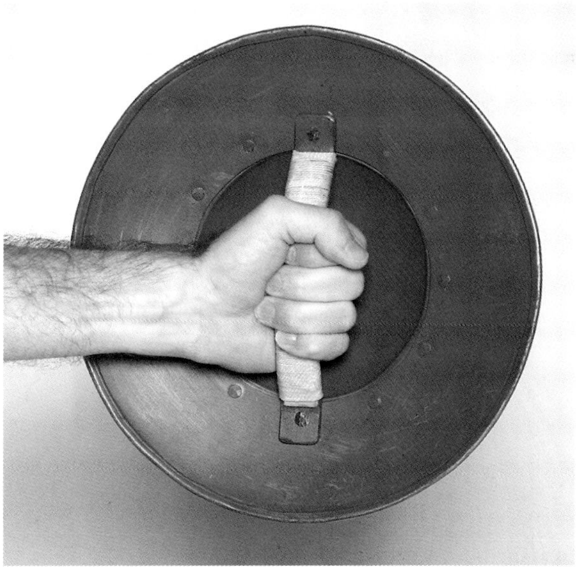

The buckler is turned in the fist while the wrist remains straight.

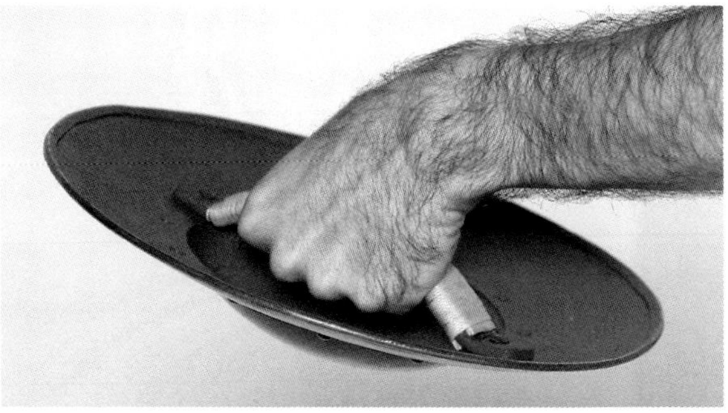

A wrist turned this way leads to painful injuries.

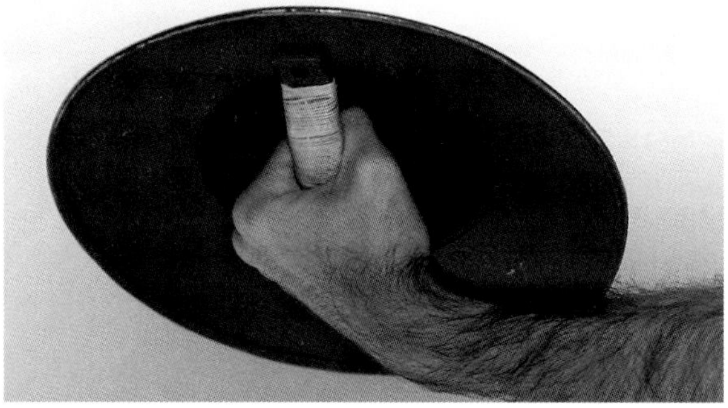

Turn the buckler in your fist and do not bend the wrist. You cannot develop any force with the wrist bent.

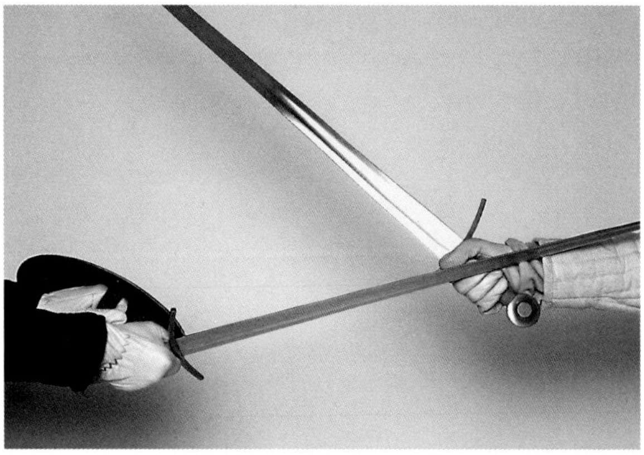

In the system in I.33 the sword hand is always covered by the buckler, otherwise the sword hand is the first and simplest target. This also results in an effective improvement in range. The buckler cover allows the fencer to fight closer to the opponent.

The rather forward-leaning posture in I.33 eliminates the legs as targets for attack.

When White tries to attack a leg ...

... Black simply moves his leg back and strikes at the head from above. Because of the longer range in the horizontal and the forward-leaning posture the blow strikes the head while the blow aimed at the leg misses. In combat with the long sword this technique is called running over.

Often enough the moment the blades bind is like a starting shot for the actions that follow. One must realize that by going into a bind one provides the opponent with impetus to move. That can be a disadvantage, but also an advantage. The correct tactics in this situation distinguish a good fencer. The bind often becomes the starting point of a tactic and is therefore consciously at the beginning of a sequence of actions. There are three types of bind:

- the bind at the forte (here one engages the bind in one's own forte)
- the bind in the center of the blade (here one engages the bind roughly at the middle of the blade
- the bind at the foible (here one engages the bind in one's own foible)

In a binding position, it is often advantageous to bind with the edge instead of the flat of the blade. A bind with the edge is more powerful. Due to the biomechanics of the wrist, you can usually develop more power from this position. If at the moment the bind is engaged you can generally read the opponent's next move from the direction of pressure, the direction of the opponent's blade, and his posture, this is called feeling. This feeling takes place in an instant and enables the fencer to react to their opponent with a minimum of delay and employ the best possible strategy. Effective fencing is almost unthinkable without feeling. It is particularly important in the techniques contained in I.33.

4.4 The Measure

The term measure means the distance between two fencers. Fighting with the sword and buckler usually occurs at a closer measure than with the long sword. This is because the weapon itself is shorter, but also because with the buckler, you can get closer to an

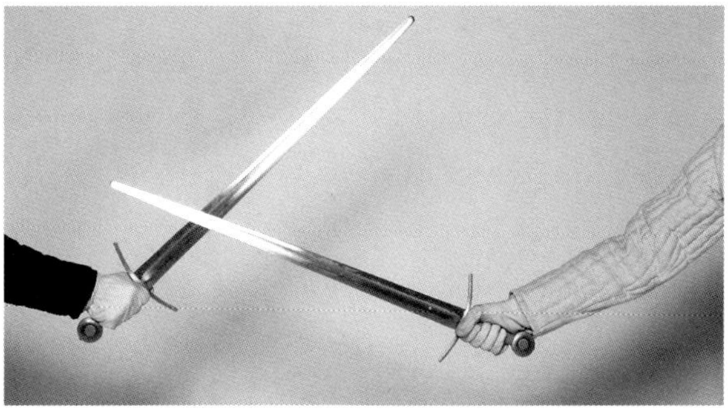

White's foible is against Black's forte.

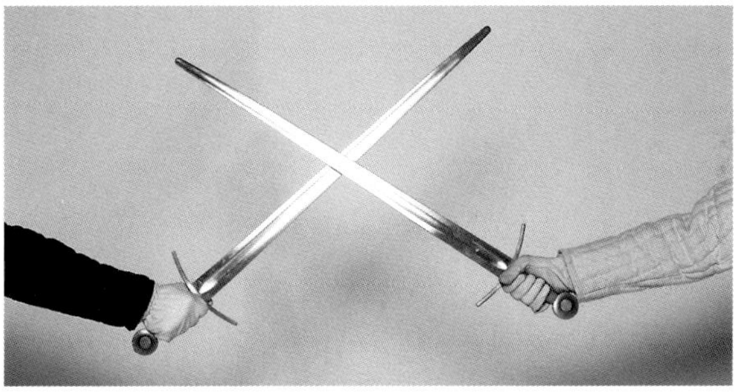

Both fighters are in a binding position with the middle of the blade.

Both fighters are in a binding position, forte against forte.

Both fighters are in a binding position, foible against foible.

Feeling: While in the bind, in a short moment the fencer analyzes the opponent's direction of pressure, the position of the blades, the opponent's balance and, if possible, his intentions. Accurate feeling makes it possible for the fencer to react very quickly.

Typical posture for I.33: the torso leans forward and the weight rests mainly on the front leg. Nevertheless, the fencer is flexible and can work in any direction.

opponent relatively safely. If one places additional emphasis on binding and controlling the opponent's blade then the measure chooses itself. This in turn makes the fencing very quick. Fencing with the sword and buckler is therefore typified by a closer measure and quick action.

4.5 Footwork

Almost every fighting system places great emphasis on footwork and there is a reason for this. Without good footwork many techniques are difficult or even impossible. Combat with the sword and buckler is of course no exception. Unfortunately, in I.33 which leg is in front, or how one should position the legs, is precisely indicated just once. The other manuscripts are also stingy with information, but the illustrations often permit better conclusions. Unfortunately, the illustrations in I.33 offer few hints as to the position of the legs, since it is practically impossible to determine which leg is forward and which one is back. Various attempts have been made to interpret the illustrations, but so far none are convincing, as they are all either inspired by wishful thinking or make no consistent sense. Nevertheless, one can derive certain postures from other illustrations, even if they are not clear in I.33. Clues from other manuscripts should at least be seriously checked.

In many techniques it makes little difference with which leg one begins. In some it is rather easier if one starts with the left leg forward. For this reason I have decided not to illustrate footwork, instead providing the relevant details, such as they exist, with various techniques. If, for example, the technique description indicates you should take a step forward, as a rule it makes no difference with which foot you do it. The objective is simply to cover distance. If which leg is moved is relevant then I will say so explicitly in the appropriate place.

What little information on posture and footwork there is in I.33 is a rather low stance with the torso bent slightly forward and acting on the balls of the feet. The basic posture therefore consists of the torso bent slightly forward with legs simultaneously bent slightly to obtain a low stance. Most of the weight is on the balls of the feet. The heels can still touch the ground, but contact should be kept light. This makes it possible to react quickly without first having to raise the heels and redistribute weight.

The techniques of the later fencing masters Kal, Lignitzer, and Talhoffer call for the torso to be upright and the posture is rather straight. I will go into this in more detail later.

FUNDAMENTAL TERMINOLOGY

As with everything else, when approaching sword fighting it is easier if certain fundamental terminology is defined. The master fencers realized this in the Middle Ages and used quite a number of technical terms. Others were added later and have since become established. The most important are:

Over-Cut: *Every blow that is struck from above. An over-cut usually strikes above the belt line, but even a blow on the leg from above should be seen as an over-cut.*

Under-Cut: *Every blow that is struck from below. Here it depends exclusively on the direction of the blow. An under-cut is struck from below and can strike the legs, but also the armpits or head.*

Middle-Cut: *The middle cut is struck horizontally with the long edge. Usually the striking plane is at belly or chest height.*

Opening: *An opening is an unprotected spot on a fighter. A fighter cannot move without exposing one or more openings. Openings can also be consciously employed as invitations to an opponent to begin an attack.*

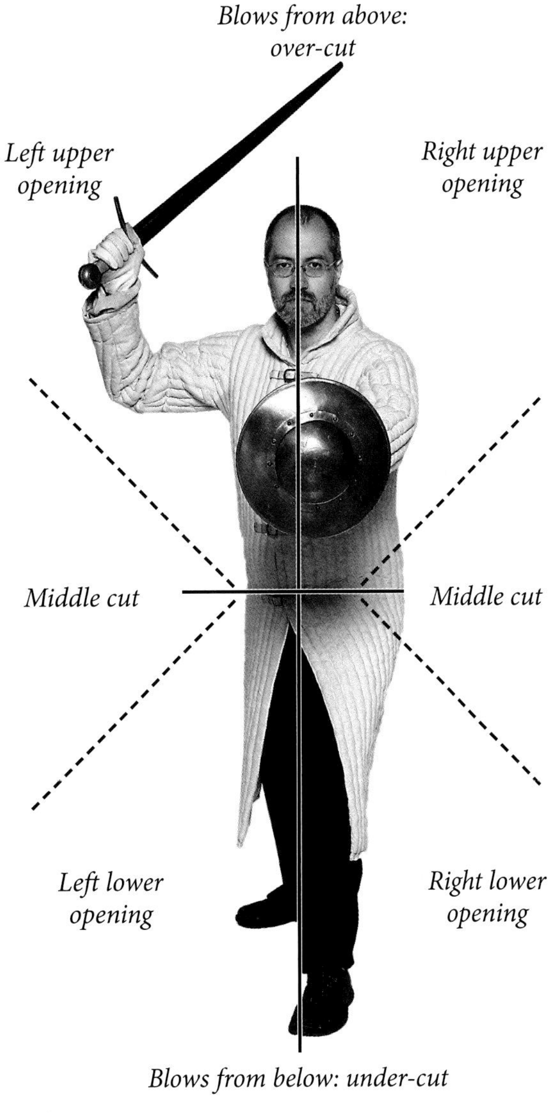

CHAPTER 5

The Techniques Contained in I.33: A Complex System

5.1 The Guards and Counter-Guards

I.33 built classically on certain guards. There are seven basic guards, a series of guards that expand these seven guards, and the counter-guards. The seven basic guards are numbered sequentially in I.33. In addition to special postures, it specifies the position of the sword in relation to the body. The seven guards cover all of the positions around the body so we have a corresponding guard for every place where one can hold a sword. In fact, all possible positions are roughly recorded.

THE SEVEN BASIC GUARDS

First Guard	Blade left under the arm
Second Guard	Blade right over the shoulder
Third Guard	Blade left over the shoulder
Fourth Guard	Blade over the head
Fifth Guard	Blade right below, pointing backward
Sixth Guard	Blade directly in front of the body, grip near the chest
Seventh Guard	Blade extended in front of the body

If you know the guards, you can also recognize when the opponent is in one. I.33 provides a guide as to how best to counter each guard and overcome it. The opponent's posture gives us an indication of how best to defeat him. As these postures are universal they can be used against anyone, even if he is not using the system in I.33.

The guards are not just used before a combat; instead, they are also employed during combat. Unfortunately, in combat it is not always possible to adopt a perfect posture that corresponds to the pure form of each guard. One should therefore become used to working from less than perfect guards, especially if standing with the wrong leg forward. One can execute almost every technique even if the starting position is not held exactly as depicted here. Even more important is recognizing the many variations of the guards during combat to be able to react as quickly as possible.

I speak of the guards frequently in the text and especially in the captions accompanying the illustrations. This is done purely for linguistic simplification. It is important to always bear in mind the following classification:

Guards: first to seventh guard
Obsesseos or counter-guards: Half-Shield, Crutch, Walpurgis, Priest's Hat, Fiddle Bow
Protections: Upper, middle, and lower protections, as well as the Half-Shield.

FIRST GUARD

Of the seven guards, the First Guard is used most often. The guard is taken as follows:

- right leg forward
- sword is held with the blade under the left armpit
- the sword hand grips the sword with the thumb downward, with the back of the hand facing right
- the elbow of the sword hand points downward
- the buckler shields to the left or right

The First Guard is used against threats from the left, from above, or against the threat of a thrust, but not against a threat from the right. The First Guard takes away distance optically and allows the opponent to

Pages 1r/1 and 1v/2 from I.33 with depictions of the seven guards.

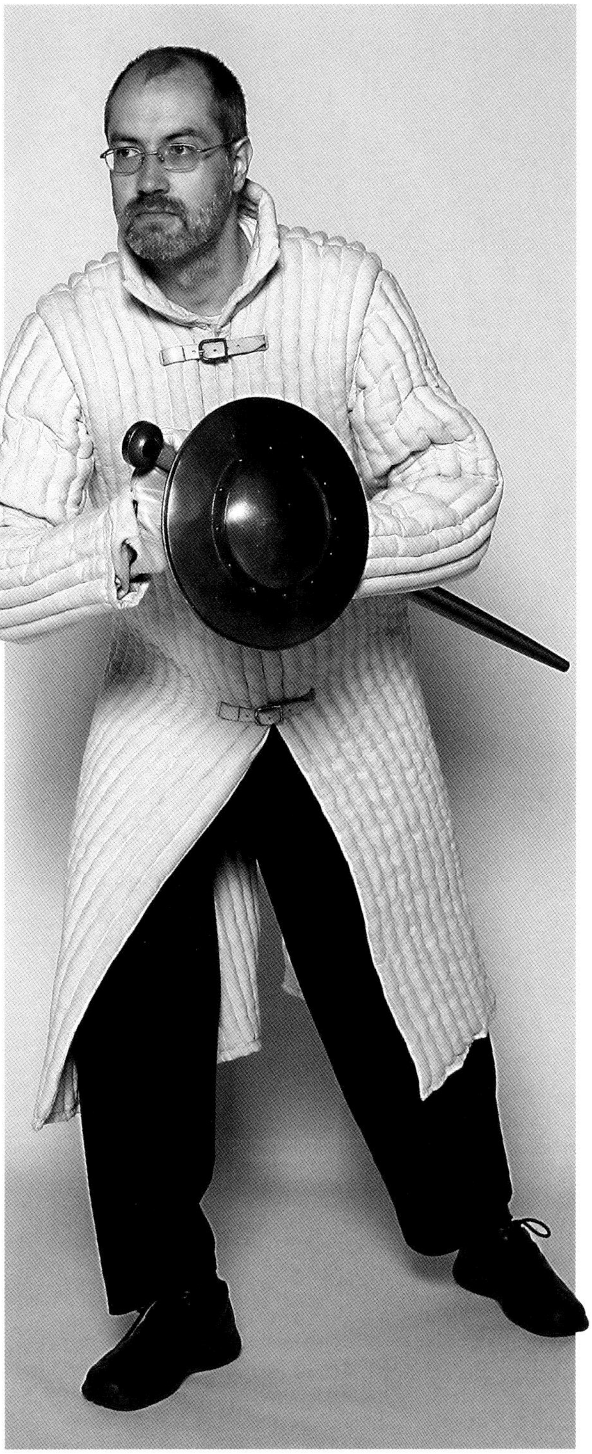

The First Guard.

move closer to the fencer. It does not look especially threatening; instead, it has a very defensive appearance. It can be countered with the Half-Shield, Crutch, Long-Point, the Fourth Guard, and the Walpurgis (more on this later).

SECOND GUARD
The Second Guard is taken as follows:

- left leg forward
- the sword is held over or on the right shoulder
- the buckler faces forward toward the opponent

If the sword is not resting on the shoulder, then it is held by the hilt above or very close to the shoulder. One can end up in the Second Guard if one makes an under-cut from the First Guard and follows through upward into the Second Guard. The Second Guard is countered with Protections and the Half-Shield. It appears threatening and the opponent expects a powerful over-cut. It is a very offensive guard. By holding the buckler forward you force the opponent to keep his distance. As well, the Second Guard is almost impregnable.

THIRD GUARD
The Third Guard is taken as follows:

- right leg forward
- sword held over or on the left shoulder
- the buckler points forward toward the opponent

If the sword is not resting on the shoulder, then it is held by the hilt above or very close to the shoulder. The Third Guard is also a possible end position from an under-cut from the Fifth Guard. The Third Guard can be countered with the Middle Protection, the Half-Shield, the Long-Point, and the Priest's Hat. The extended buckler creates space, forcing the opponent away like the Second Guard.

FOURTH GUARD
The Fourth Guard is taken as follows:

- left or right leg forward
- the sword is held over the head
- the buckler is extended in front of the body or in front of the breast

The Fourth Guard is countered by the Half-Shield, the First Guard, and the Priest's Hat. It also forces the opponent back optically like the Second and Third Guards. The sword held over the head also makes this guard seem difficult to attack while appearing rather aggressive.

FIFTH GUARD
The Fifth Guard is taken as follows:

- left leg forward
- the sword is held on the right side of the body
- the buckler points left or forward toward the opponent

A blow from the Third Guard naturally ends in the Fifth Guard. The Fifth Guard is countered with the Priest's Hat and the Half-Shield. It takes away space by holding the sword back, while the buckler keeps the opponent at a distance. The opponent sees the threat but can do nothing, as he cannot grasp the sword. He is confronted by the buckler, which is difficult for him to get past.

SIXTH GUARD
The Sixth Guard is taken as follows:

- left leg forward
- the sword is held by the pommel next to the chest
- the back of the sword hand faces downward
- the buckler points forward at the opponent
- the sword points directly at the opponent in a thrusting position

The Second Guard.

The Third Guard.

The Fourth Guard with left leg forward.

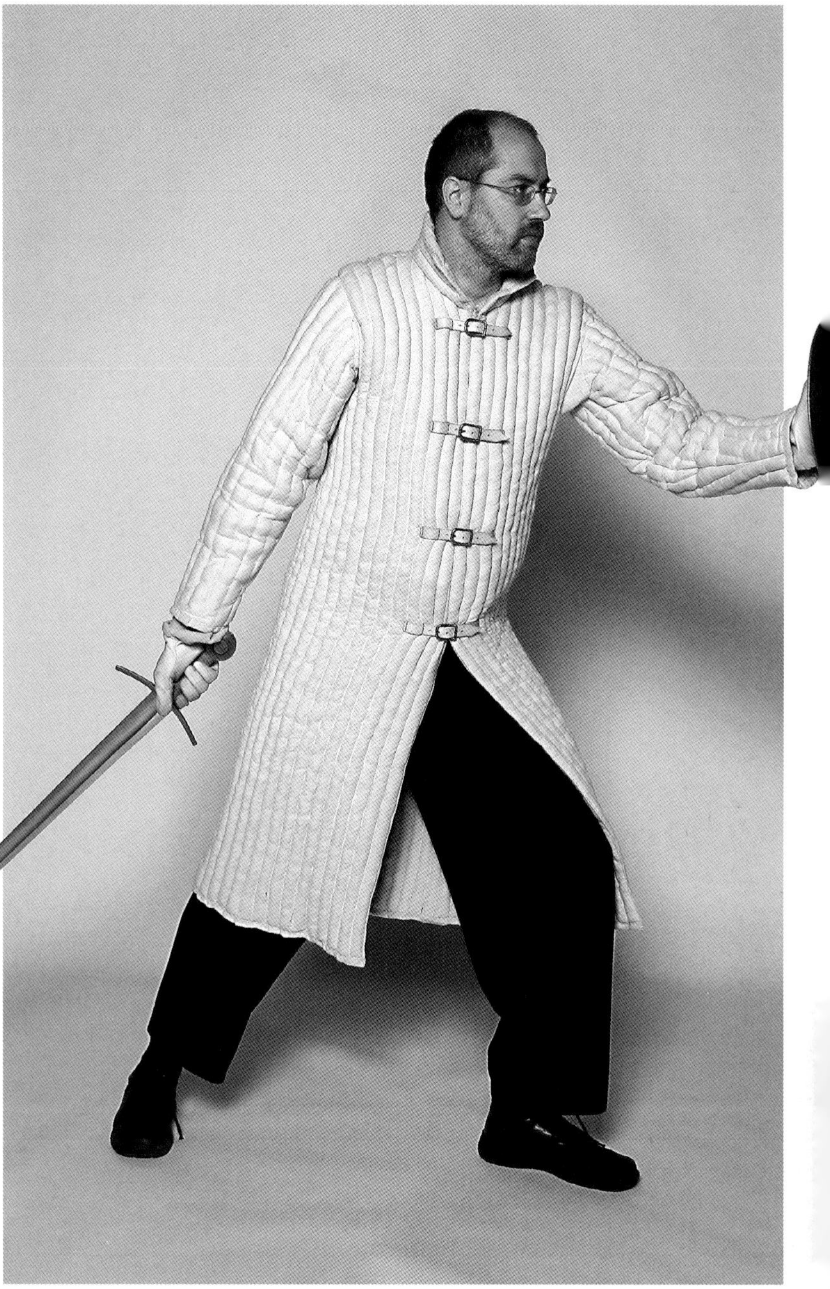

The Fifth Guard.

The Fourth Guard with right leg forward. As the Fourth Guard is a central guard, it makes little difference which leg is forward. This does not become important until the techniques that follow from the Fourth Guard.

The Sixth Guard. The posture illustrated here is very comfortable, but it does not conform to the sources. Here the sword is hidden behind the buckler, so to speak.

The same posture, but here with the blade held beside the buckler.

The Sixth Guard in a posture that conforms to the sources. Here the blade is held beside the buckler.

In this position one can also hold the sword behind the buckler.

The Long-Point is used against the Sixth Guard. It unsettles the opponent, as he can cannot see the sword. It forces him back and creates space. The Sixth Guard has a rather wait-and-see effect.

THE SEVENTH GUARD / LONG-POINT

The Seventh Guard is taken as follows:

- left or right leg forward
- the sword points forward
- the buckler covers the sword hand

In I.33, Liutger uses the term "Long-Point" for the Seventh Guard and the Long-Point as we know it from the long sword. More on this in the chapter on the seven guards and their set-plays.

There are two versions of the Long-Point: the lower and the middle. In the lower Long-Point, the sword is held downward in front of the body, similar to the Fool with the long sword. In the middle Long-Point, the sword is held in front of the body toward the opponent similar to the Long-Point with the long sword.

The Seventh Guard appears harmless. It lures the opponent while simultaneously keeping him at a medium measure. Experienced fencers know about the potential of the lower guards and often beginners do not take them seriously enough.

In I.33, the Seventh Guard is characterized as the "core of the entire art." This is true insofar as the seventh Guard represents the end of a powerful over-cut. The Seventh Guard is always shown bound in I.33, which one could understand as a suggestion to fall upon the opponent's sword before he completes his blow and take control. This is very similar to Travelling After, which appeared a good 100 years later in the Liechtenauer school. The big difference is that here the opponent himself is not attacked; rather, his blade is bound. This prevents further action by the opponent. Falling upon the opponent's blade during the last phase of his attack requires a good feeling for the measure.

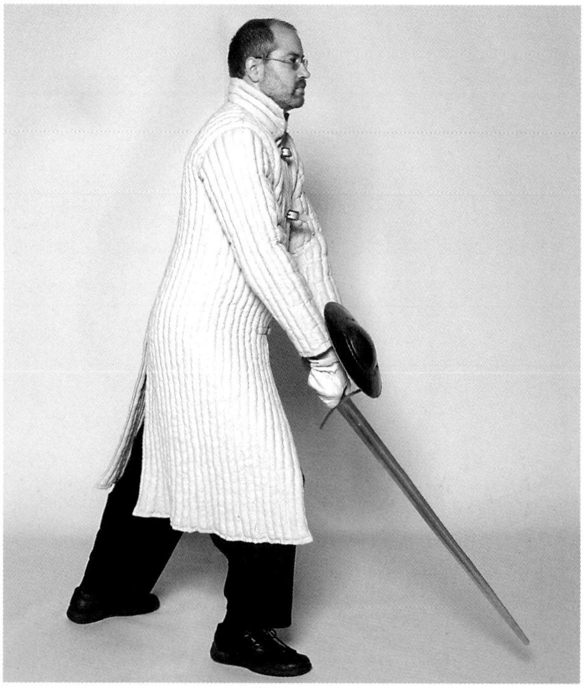

The Seventh Guard: as the Seventh Guard is a central guard, which leg is forward is only of concern with respect to the technique that follows.

Middle Long-Point.

Lower Long-Point.

The fencers are in their guards. White changes into the Seventh Guard …

… and is immediately over-bound by Black.

HALF-SHIELD
The Half-Shield is taken as follows:

- left or right leg forward
- the sword is held centrally in front of the body
- the arms are extended
- the buckler faces left, rests next to the sword, and covers the sword hand
- buckler and hilt are roughly at shoulder height or just below it

It is very important to hold the Half-Shield high enough. If you hold the Half-Shield at belly height then it is a simple matter for your opponent to break this guard. If you hold the Half-Shield too low then the foible of your blade is in front of your head. If your opponent now strikes hard from the side against the foible of your blade he will knock your blade away and then immediately and unhindered strike at your head. If he tries this against a properly-held Half-Shield then he will land on your forte and you will have no problem intercepting his attack and binding over.

The Half-Shield can be used against any of the guards, with the exception of the Sixth. It creates space and keeps the opponent at a distance; it has a wait-and-see effect and at the same time is difficult to attack.

CRUTCH (*KRÜCKE*)
The Crutch is taken as follows:

- left or right leg forward
- the sword is held at head level in the center of the body
- the buckler faces left

The Crutch lures the opponent into a too-close measure, as it is often not taken seriously enough by inexperienced fencers. The Crutch's potential is easily underestimated.

PRIEST'S HAT (*PRIESTERHUT*)
The Priest's Hat is taken as follows:

- right leg forward
- the sword is held diagonally over the right thigh so that the point is pointed toward the rear
- the buckler faces left, is held beside the sword, and covers the sword hand
- buckler and hilt are roughly at shoulder height or just beneath it

The Priest's Hat is used against the Half-Shield, the Third Guard, the Fourth Guard, and the Fifth Guard. It takes away distance and allows the opponent to come closer to the fencer. The Priest's Hat is itself a very powerful counter-guard and has a rather wait-and-see effect.

The Half-Shield. Be sure to keep your hands at shoulder height.

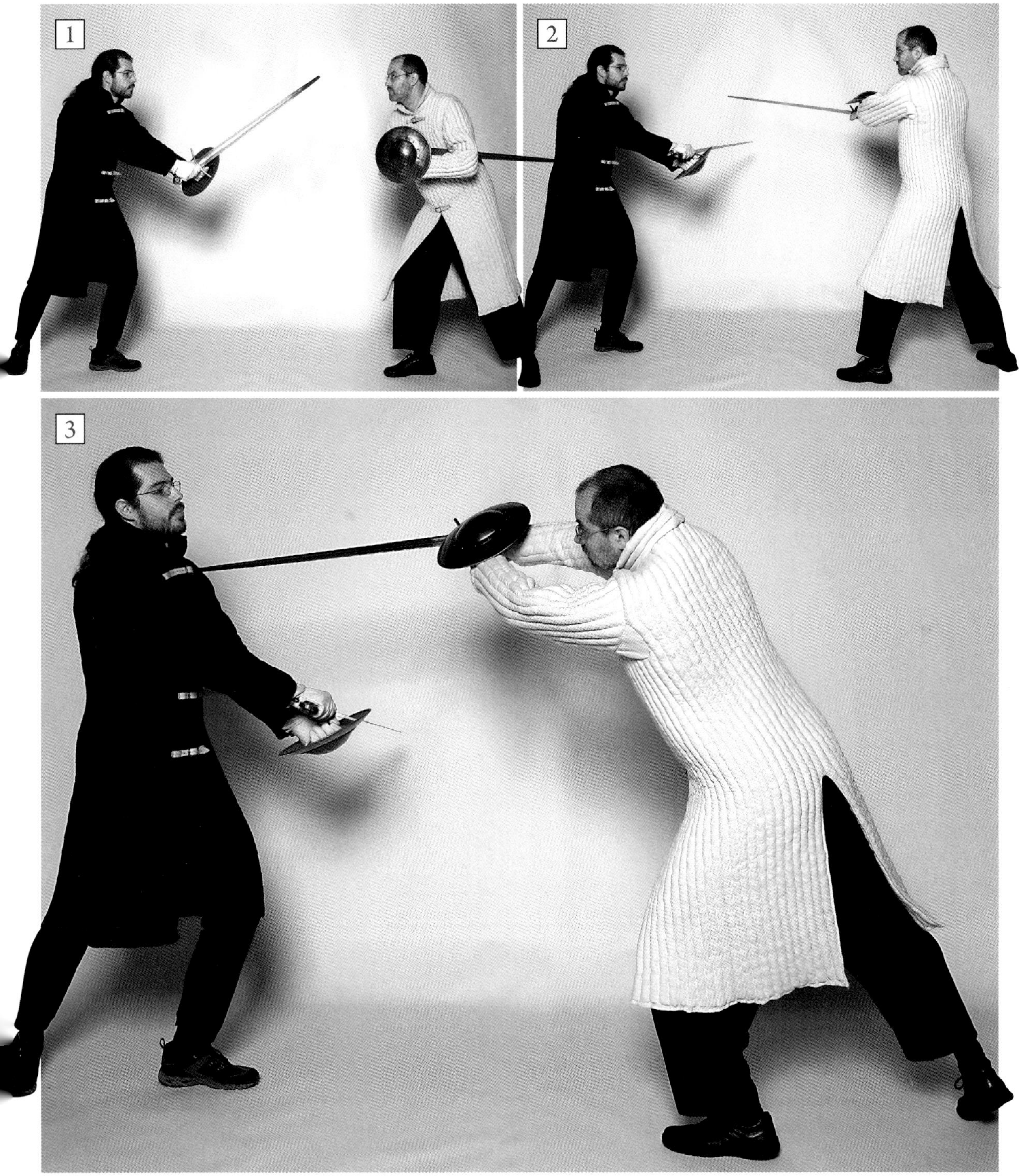

If the Half-Shield is held too low then it is an easy matter to knock the blade away and thrust into the opening.

If the Half-Shield is held correctly then the attacker strikes your forte and can easily be over-bound and defeated with a shield strike.

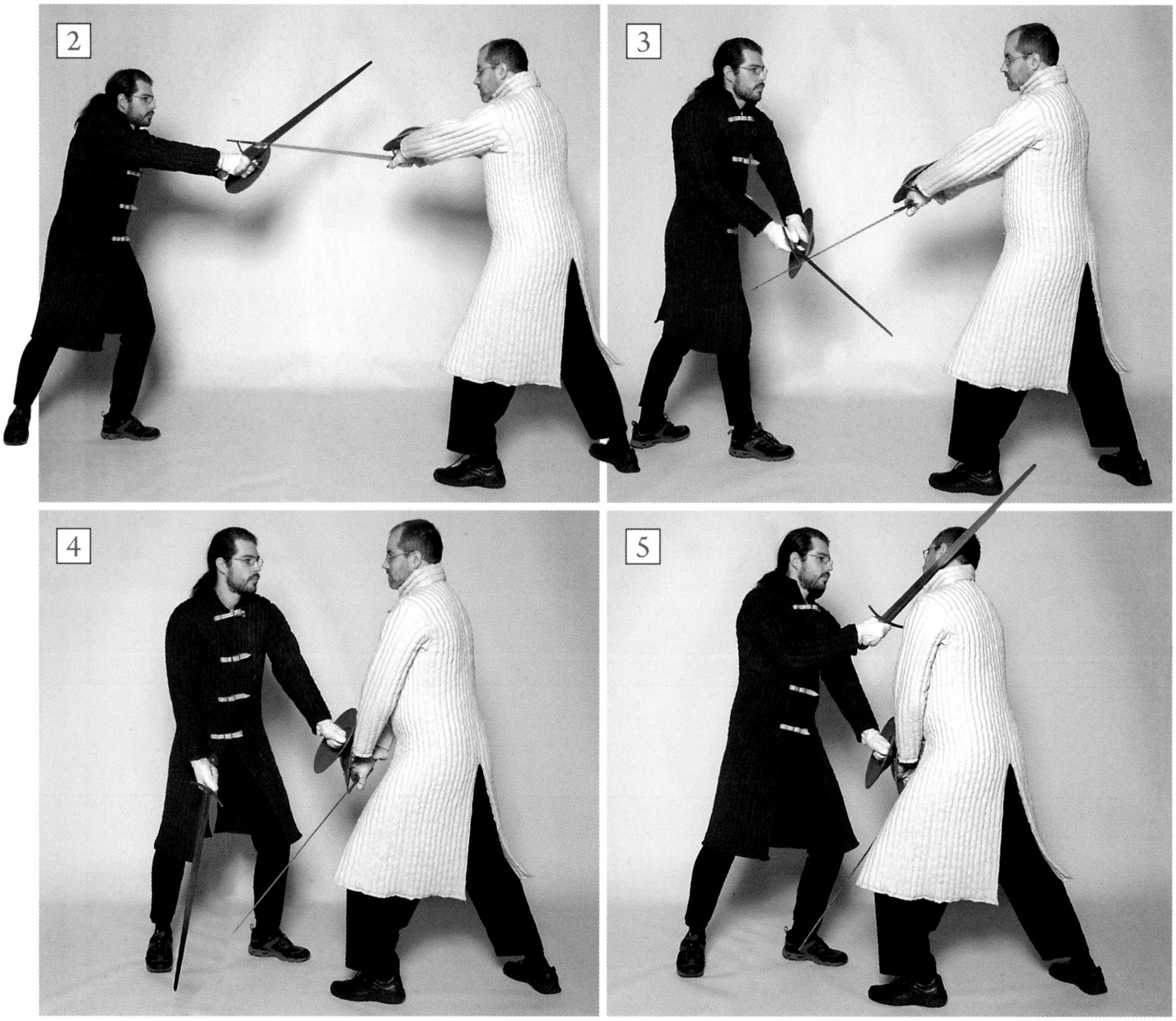

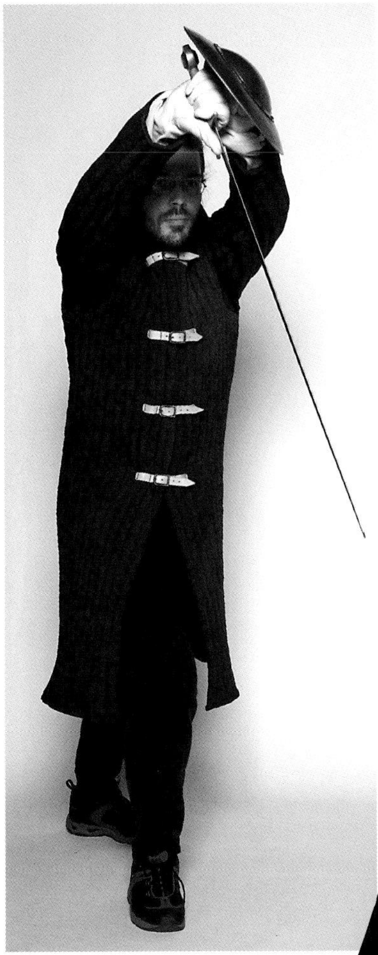

The Crutch. In this posture the thumb rests on the blade. The Crutch is held high enough for you to be able to look through under your arms.

Side view of the Crutch.

The Priest's Hat.

A variant of the Priest's Hat, the Obsesseo Rara or "Rare Blockage."

The Fiddle Bow.

In the Fiddle Bow your blade's forte rests on your forearm. At the same time the blade touches the buckler, forming a sort of "V" in which you can easily intercept the opposing blade.

VARIATIONS OF THE PRIEST'S HAT

These variations of the Priest's Hat are taken as follows:

- right leg forward
- the sword is held diagonally over the right thigh so that the point is pointed down or forward. You can also take the right elbow upward and back as described in I.33 to achieve a greater "preload." As a result you can react even faster.
- the hilt is held rather higher than the hip
- the buckler faces forward and with it the left shoulder

These variations of the Priest's Hat are used against the Fifth Guard. It creates more space thanks to the buckler, which is held forward.

FIDDLE BOW (*FIDELBOGEN*)

The Fiddle Bow is taken as follows:

- right or left leg forward
- the sword is held with the forte placed on the left forearm, with the point facing up
- the buckler covers to the front

The Fiddle Bow is probably used against over-cuts, but this is not exactly clear from the sources.

WALPURGIS

The Walpurgis is taken as follows:

- left leg and left shoulder forward
- the sword is held on the right side with the point facing upward
- the buckler is held on the left side, likewise at chest height

The Walpurgis is used against the First Guard. It takes away a great deal of space and creates a very defensive, almost fearful impression, thus luring the opponent into a closer measure.

USING THE GUARDS

One can obviously see the guards as static positions. For example, a fencer stands in the First Guard, whereupon his opponent takes up the Half-Shield. At that moment, one of the two fighters immediately begins an attack, initiating combat. The techniques used decide themselves in the explosive moment of attack.

Movements during the combat itself are just as important as the beginning of combat. A fencer moves and also changes guards and postures during combat. This is where the tactics of guards and counters come into play. Many guards and counters—in particular the so-called Protections—develop their full potential in this environment. It is the reaction to a change of guards or to a movement in a particular guard that allows a properly timed counter to be so effective. The object is to see the entire system as dynamic, as a guide during combat.

As the guards also determine the position of the sword, they are a guide to behavior during combat. At all times we have a counter-guard or a technique in response to the opponent's current posture, even if he is not explicitly standing in one of the seven guards.

Because there is a protection, but often also an *Obsesseo* (opposition) or counter-guard for every guard, during combat one always has a guide to how one should attack. As soon as the opponent is in the position equivalent to one of the guards one knows what one has to do. If one pays attention to this, the result is a very dynamic combat in which one finds it very easy to react. It becomes possible to employ the techniques one has practiced without delay.

The Walpurgis.

COUNTER-GUARDS OR OBSESSEOS

If one fencer assumes a guard then his opponent responds by going into a counter-guard. This counter-guard covers the opponent's probable lines of attack and puts the fencer in his best possible starting position. If the fencer in the guard hesitates then the opponent can immediately attack from the counter-guard. The goal here is not to "rest" in a guard and remain there, but rather to fight explosively from a consciously created starting position. That is the characteristic feature of this system—the approach passes very quickly.

ALTERNATIVE INTERPRETATIONS

Fencers with sword and buckler appear in many manuscripts. These manuscripts were possibly created and illustrated by contemporaries with little or no knowledge of fencing. The illustrations often served as embellishments to enliven the text and make it clearer. Nevertheless, these illustrations are often astonishingly precise. Some of these illustrations depict fencers in one of the guards known to us, but they often show leg positioning that does not agree with my interpretation.

It is now open to question how seriously we should take these illustrations with respect to footwork. There are also combat manuals from the fifteenth century in which similar postures are depicted—and these sources are to be accepted as absolutely accurate. Consequently, there are alternative interpretations of leg positioning with respect to some of the guards.

The postures previously described were derived from body mechanics while working from the guards and also conform to guides for use of the long sword by fencing masters from the fourteenth and fifteenth centuries. Nevertheless, I do not wish to omit the alternative positions.

Depictions of the First Guard often show the fencer with his left leg forward. The guard can be assumed naturally this way. This leg positioning results in less range if one falls under sword and shield. I personally regard the First Guard with the left leg forward as feasible and practical, but only if a closer measure is adopted from the very beginning.

The Second Guard is also depicted with the right leg forward. First, I find this positioning rather cumbersome, for it only permits a half step with the blow. The body rotation and the force it generates are thus missing. Second, here the measure is again limited.

The Sixth Guard also appears in many illustrations with the right leg forward. Once again, there is a serious shortening of the measure.

Most of the alternative positions result in the fencer being in a shorter measure, as one can only take a half step with the front leg instead of a full one. Fighting in a closer measure is of course faster, which can be an advantage. One reaches this closer measure by properly employing the buckler.

In the described alternative positions, the body rotation during the blow is missing, making it less powerful. Nevertheless, blows struck with the arm also suffice to surely end a combat. Ultimately it is the fencer's decision how to take up the guards. No matter which leg is forward, both positions are verifiable and there are good arguments for both. In this case it is a decision of personal preference. The works of Roland Warzecha show unmistakably that these alternative leg positions are absolutely practical and lead to very intense combat. These alternative leg positions cannot and should not be seen as wrong or less effective.

The First Guard with left leg forward.

The Second Guard with right leg forward.

The Sixth Guard with right leg forward.

The fencers face each other.

White hesitates and does not react to Black's guard. As White fails to react, Black immediately attacks.

5.2 The Triple Combination

Direct attacks are rare in the I.33 system. The only attacks carried out without detours are executed when the opponent does nothing and only waits. Only then does Liutger advise a direct attack. The second possibility is to make a shield strike or long-point thrust directly in an attack.

In contrast to the direct attack, the fencer always seeks to gain control. Usually gaining control and the attack that follows always take place in three steps:

1. You bind the opponent's blade with your blade.

This gives you control over the opponent's blade. You immediately sense what the opponent is doing. This binding is executed actively when you seek the opponent's blade, but also passively when you parry an opponent's attack and end up in a binding position. This in turn means you never directly parry the opponent's blade with your buckler. If you are in a binding position you can over-bind the opponent's blade or push it downward. If you are in a low bind, you can still sense what the opponent is doing and have the opportunity to react immediately should he disengage the bind to attack.

2. You take control with your buckler.

You strike with the buckler at the spot where you can control both weapons—the opponent's buckler and his sword. If you have engaged in a bind with your buckler then your blade is free for an attack, as it is no longer needed for control. Precisely where this point is depends on the situation and technique. With time you will get a feeling for exactly where you should bind in order to gain control of the opponent's sword and buckler.

3. You attack with the sword while maintaining control with the buckler.

You can now attack with confidence for the opponent's weapon is briefly under your control, enabling you to strike his openings with no danger to yourself.

This triple combination is almost always executed. It is therefore essential. In combat, these three phases obviously merge into a fluid sequence of movements that is executed quickly. The faster and more fluidly you carry it out, the shorter the time you must retain control of the opponent's weapons. In an extreme case it is enough to interrupt and deflect your opponent's flow of movements. Of course this attempt to bind results in the combats in I.33 being fought at a very close measure.

In training, while executing the triple combination, the opponent is often in a position to strike your legs. That is a sure sign the buckler was not used forcefully enough. If the blow from above with the buckler to gain control is carried out seriously enough then the opponent can no longer strike your legs. If you find yourself in this situation then try to work more strongly and seriously with the buckler. But be sure to raise the opponent's buckler so high that a serious shield strike is no longer possible, then step to the side (usually to the left) and strike the resulting openings or his sword hand.

The fencers standing in their guards.

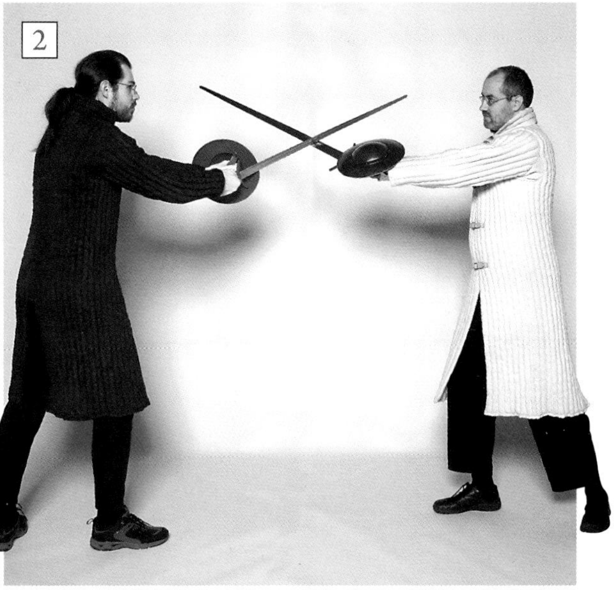

White has attacked; Black strikes into a bind and thus controls White's blade.

With his buckler Black takes control of White's hands and also his weapon. Black does not disengage from the bind until he has gained control with his buckler.

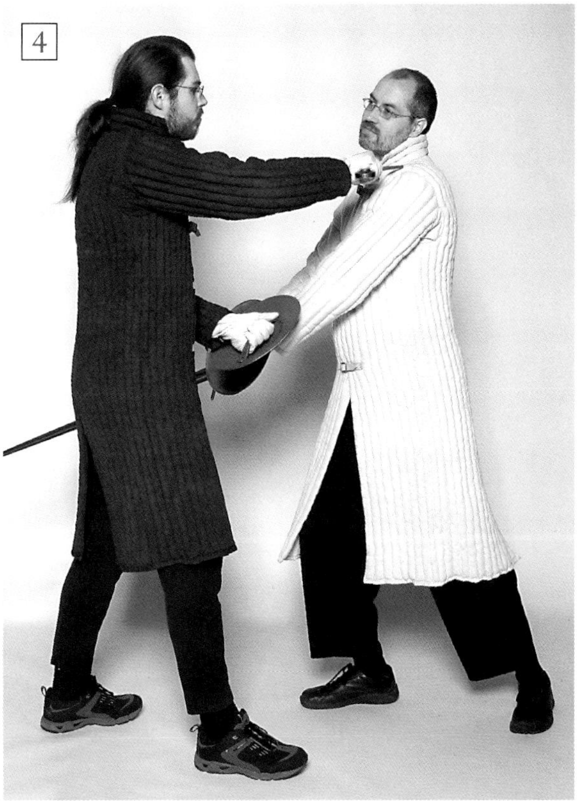

His sword now free, Black strikes at the head.

The fencers are standing in their guards.

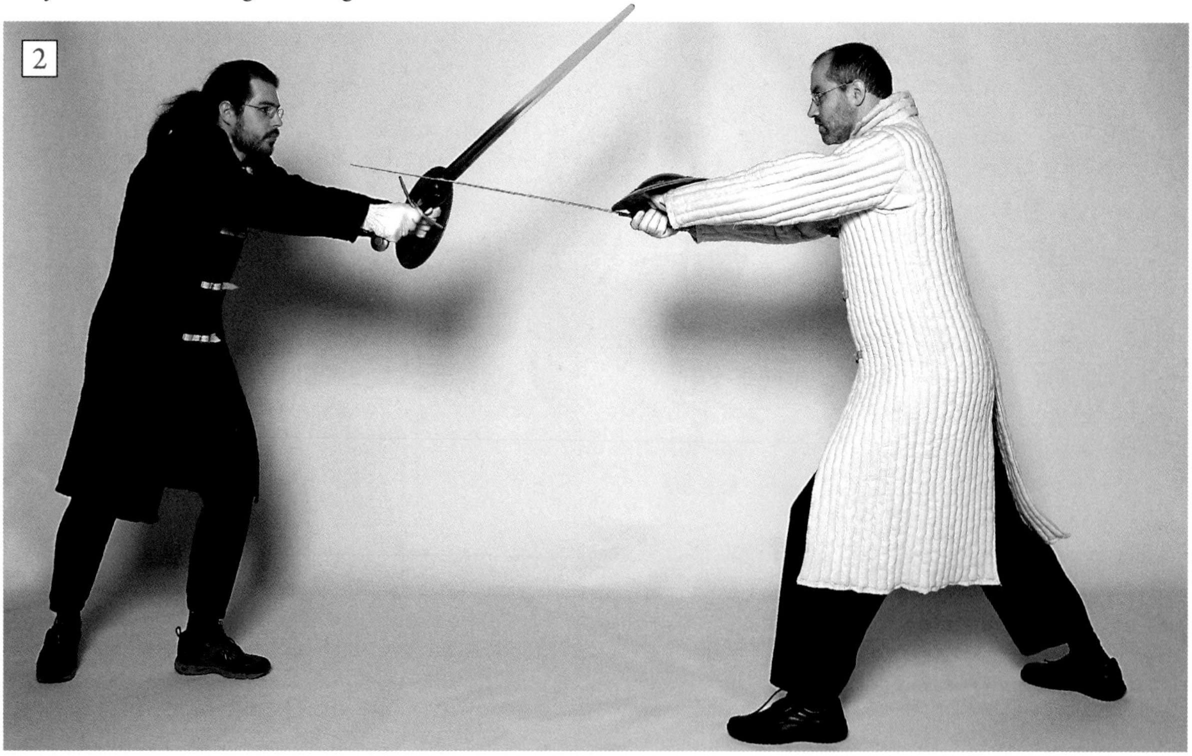

White falls under sword and shield and binds Black's blade.

Black over-binds, pushing White's blade downward. Black immediately takes control of White's hands with his buckler.

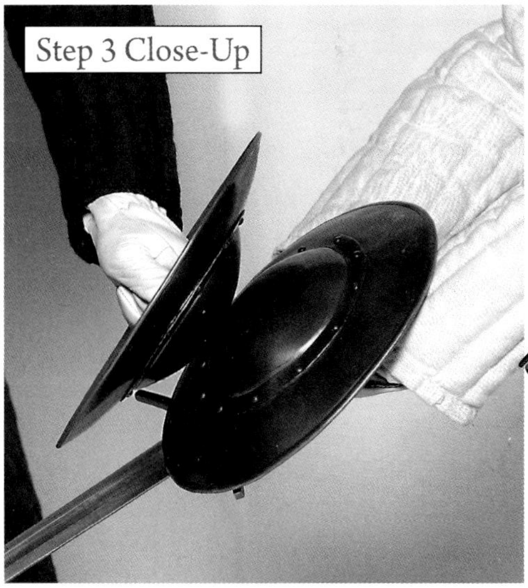

Positioning of the buckler is decisive here. It must be positioned in different places depending on movement and direction of pressure.

Black maintains control with the buckler and strikes the opponent's head.

5.3 The Shield Strike and Thrust Strike (*Schildschlag und Stichschlag*)

The shield strike is the most important technique in I.33. The term is perhaps confusing at first, for it means more than just a blow with the shield. The technique involves striking with the sword in combination with the buckler blow. If you thrust with the sword instead of striking a blow then it is a *Stichschlag*. Thus, the only difference between a *Schildschlag* and a *Stichschlag* is whether you execute a strike or a thrust with the sword. This combination of striking with the shield and simultaneously striking or thrusting with the sword makes the Shield strike very effective, but also difficult. In part, you must simultaneously move the arms in different directions. This takes some practice.

One can employ the *Schildschlag/Stichschlag* against a direct attack. Here you counter an opponent's attack simply by deflecting the opponent's blade (ideally the blade and buckler) with the *Schildschlag/Stichschlag* and then strike at the resulting opening. Basically it is the previously described triple combination with the binding of blades omitted. This is only possible if the measure is reduced quickly enough.

It is important that the blow with the buckler is made powerfully. It should put the opponent off his stride, obstruct his movement, and briefly divert him so that it takes time for him to collect himself and execute a movement. This is particularly important with respect to the triple combination.

The fencers are both in the Second Guard.

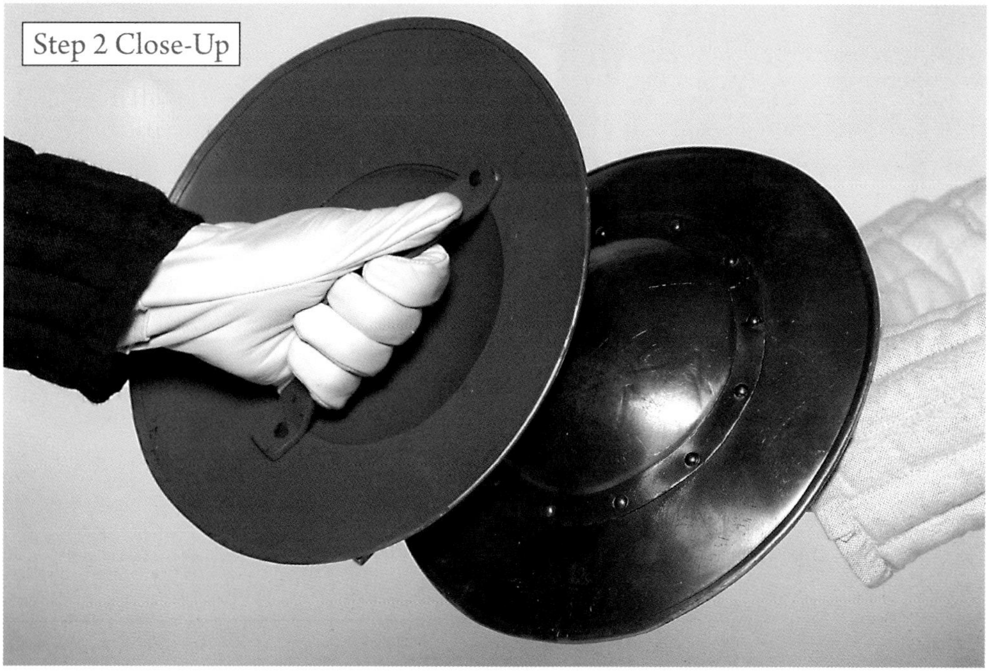

White attacks with an overcut, Black executes a shield strike. As he deflects the opponent's weapon, he strikes at the opening.

The buckler is bound at the place where White's sword and buckler touch.

5.4 The Protections (*Schützen*)

Some of the concepts in I.33 are very precisely explained and are therefore not all that difficult to reconstruct. Others are explained rather hazily. Unfortunately, this includes the Protections. For this reason when reconstructing them one must work from context.

Three different versions of the Protections are shown in I.33. The same thinking underlies all of them. For simplicity's sake I have named these three different variations "upper protection," "middle protection," and "lower protection." It has been found useful in practice to at least differentiate between the upper and lower protections.

The Protections combine several important strategic elements:

- One places his weapons between oneself and the opponent, thus impeding his attack.

- Because of the spatial advantage—your weapons are closer to the opponent than his to you—one achieves a time lead, because one has less distance to cover. One is practically halfway to the target of the attack.

- One offers the opponent a target that appears all the more enticing because you have deprived him of almost every other possibility. Should he in fact attack this target then you react immediately, usually with a sword thrust or shield strike.

As all of these qualities apply not just to the Protections but also fully to the Half-Shield (see next chapter), I also count the Half-Shield as part of the complex of Protections. It is used similarly, offers the same advantages, and uses the same tactics.

If you employ the Protections at the right time—namely in the first third of an attack by your opponent—then you can often halt the flow of his attack without making blade contact at all. The new situation, together with the obvious threat and the closing of the line of attack, causes many fencers to interrupt their attack and go over to the defensive, even if only briefly. The optimal sequence is therefore to go into a Protection as soon as the opponent launches his attack, cause it to stop, and at the moment the opponent hesitates attack via the shortest route—that is with a thrust.

It is also no problem if your opponent is difficult to shake and the Protections fail to put him off his stride: thanks to the Protection you are in a situation in which you can easily react to the attack. In the Protections you already have a distance and thus time advantage.

THE UPPER PROTECTION

The Upper Protection is carried out as follows:

- the right leg is forward
- your point is aimed up and forward
- your buckler hand is beneath your sword hand and supports it at the wrist
- you stand leaning forward

In I.33, the Upper Protection is only used against the Second Guard. The fencer gains an advantageous position by moving his sword and buckler forward. The high positioning makes it possible for him to counter almost all blows from above. If the fencer is attacked directly he only has to react with a thrust strike or shield strike.

The attacker can not attack directly; he must take another route. Obviously the hands are offered as a target. If he attacks them though, the fencer again reacts with a sword thrust or shield strike. All that is left to the attacker is to bind the blade of the fencer standing in the Protection. The resulting possibilities are examined in Chapter 6.

White is standing in the Upper Guard, Black in the Second Guard. Black ignores White's guard and tries to attack directly.

White simply strikes a shield strike against Black's attack. As White's arms were already forward in his guard he can react without rushing.

It is not as advisable to make a direct attack against the Middle Guard.

Here White answers the attack with a thrust strike.

The same principle can also be used from the Lower Guard.

Here a thrust strike ends the combat.

In the Upper Guard the sword hand rests on the shield hand (see close-up above).

THE MIDDLE PROTECTION

In principle, the Middle Protection is no different than the Upper Protection, except the sword is held with the point toward the ground. Here, too, the shield arm rests on the sword arm and the buckler covers to the right. The Middle Protection offers a number of advantages. By turning or bending the wrist the point can be brought forward. This not only makes a very quick thrust possible, but if often causes the opponent to stop in the middle of an attack because he is suddenly confronted with the point of your sword.

A shield strike is often carried out from the Middle Protection. It is also used against the Middle Protection; however, a shield strike against the Middle Protection is only possible if the protection is made low enough. If it is made high, with the buckler held at roughly the same height as in the Crutch, then it is impossible for the opponent to deliver a shield strike from the bind or subsequently attack the arms. The fighter in the protection alone determines the possibilities through his posture and can prepare himself accordingly. With the high-held protection a thrust into the lower opening is more likely. You can also effectively attack the arms from a high protection (see part 6.2). One must decide which makes more sense at the moment.

THE LOWER PROTECTION

The Lower Protection is assumed as follows:

- right leg forward
- the buckler covers to the left
- the sword is held with the point aimed downward and the back of the sword hand faces to the left

The Lower Protection is also used to displace (deflect) a thrust. Depending on the direction of attack and your own stance, the thrust can be deflected to the left or right. From this binding position one continues working with a *Schildschlag* or *Stichschlag*.

The Middle Guard: the blade is simply held downward from the Upper Guard.

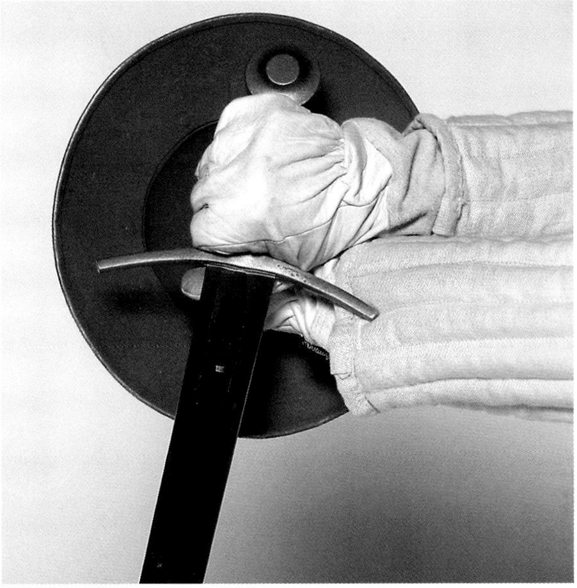

The sword hand also rests on the shield hand in the Middle Guard.

It is possible to thrust from the Middle Guard simply by rotating the wrist. The buckler can also be held facing left instead of right, as White is holding it here.

The Lower Guard from the left.

The Lower Guard from the right.

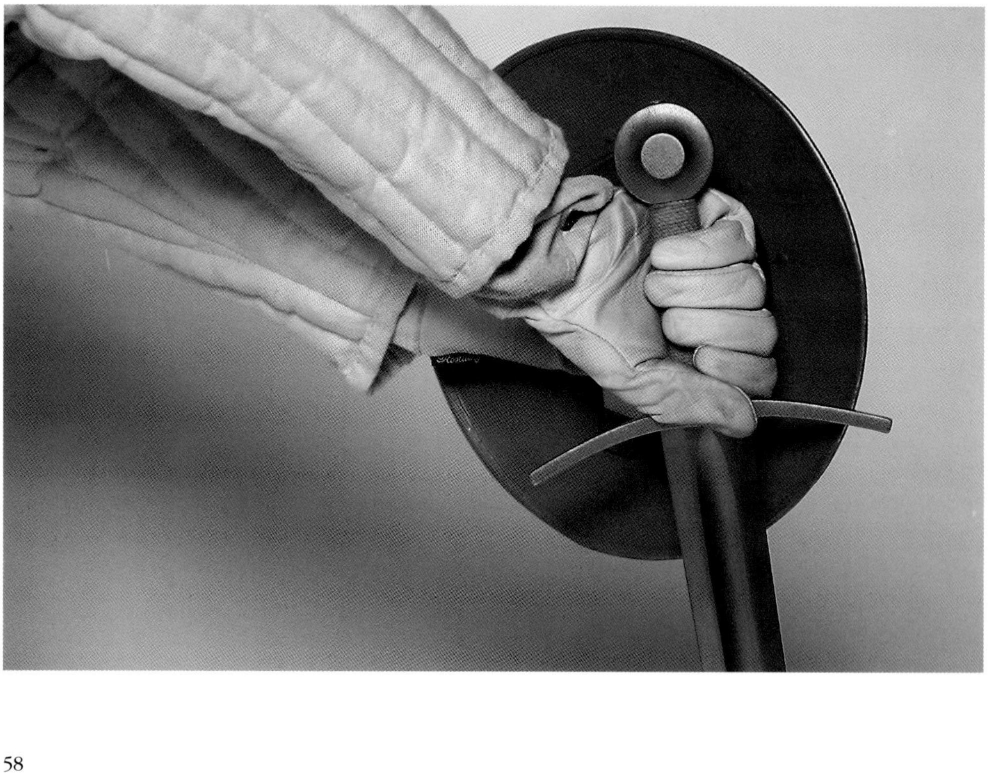

Position of the hands in the Lower Guard.

5.5 The Half-Shield

The Half-Shield is basically a static counter-guard and also the most-used counter-guard. It is used not just against upper guards—like the Second or Third Guard—but also against lower guards, such as the Fifth Guard. As the Half-Shield is used so often, it must obviously have special advantages that other counter-guards do not.

How the weapon is held reveals what makes the Half-Shield so versatile and universally employable. Because the fencer holds the weapon between himself and the opponent, the latter cannot attack directly. The opponent is not left many alternatives: he will try to bind or attack the arms. But for the fencer it is always an advantage if he can divine the opponent's reaction.

The way the weapon is held puts it halfway to the opponent. That means that any action—whether attack or parry—happens more quickly, as the distance to be covered is much smaller. This distance and time advantage should not be underestimated.

This combination of shortened distance, forward-held weapon, and limiting of the opponent's options make the Half-Shield a somewhat offensive posture. The Half-Shield is not intended for waiting. Instead, an attack or other action from the Half-Shield is executed as quickly as possible. This in turn forces the opponent to react to the Half-Shield as quickly as possible.

If one executes the Half-Shield from the correct measure this automatically initiates combat, for neither fighter can allow himself to wait long.

A direct attack on a fencer in the Half-Shield (left) is very easy to break.

The Half-Shield: be sure to keep the hands at shoulder height.

5.6 Fall under Sword and Shield (*Unter Schwert und Schild fallen*)

"If Half-Shield is carried out, fall under sword and also shield." This direction is frequently repeated in I.33. "Fall under sword and shield" is a central and important point. The Half-Shield is one of the most common counter-guards and for this reason alone it is important to know how to best counter it. If your opponent is standing in the Half-Shield then you should "fall under his sword and his shield." This means you should immediately establish a binding position so that you can feel what the opponent is doing. This way you can better control your opponent and achieve a good position from which to attack.

In falling under sword and shield, bind the blade of the opponent in the Half-Shield from the outside. If the Half-Shield is properly executed then you bind on the forte, directly above the hilt. Where you bind—your forte, middle of the blade, or foible—determines which techniques follow. More on this in Chapter 6.

In order to fall under sword and shield, step left out of line and forward. Bring your sword forward with a horizontal blow and bind the opponent's sword with your short edge. You are now standing in an excellent thrusting position. Thrust immediately. Your opponent will try to under-bind your blade and pull away down and to his right. Despite this, often enough you will be able to follow up and thrust following his action. To do this, you increase the angle somewhat and try to thrust behind his blade. Of course this all occurs smoothly. You simply carry through your intention to thrust.

1

If a fencer adopts the Half-Shield then you should fall under sword and shield.

2

You bind with the short edge. Step forward and to the left.

Binding with the short edge and stepping to the left places you in a good position from which to thrust. Your point should be aimed at your opponent. In a smooth movement thrust immediately at the opening.

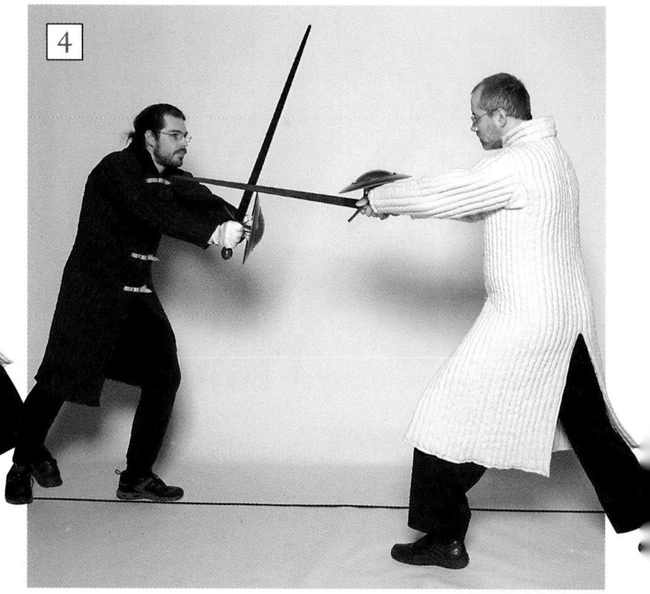

If your opponent deflects your thrust to the side …

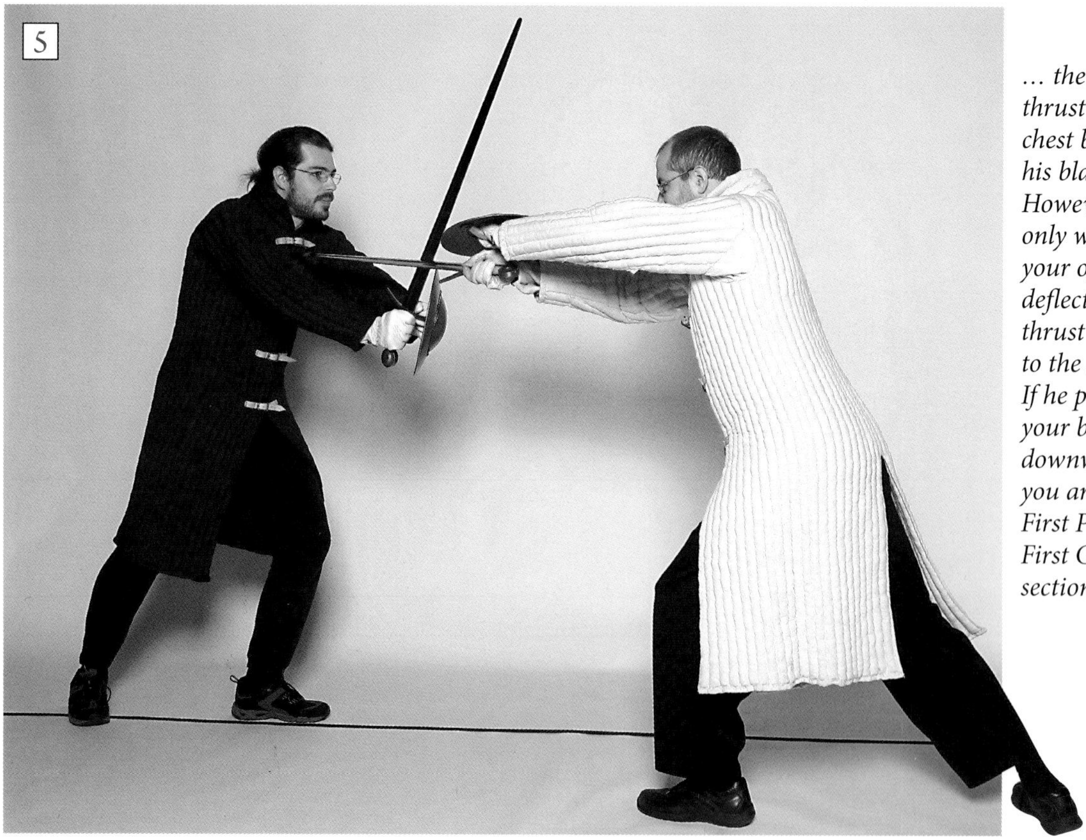

… then thrust at his chest behind his blade. However, this only works if your opponent deflects the thrust straight to the side. If he pushes your blade downward then you are in the First Play of the First Guard (see section 6.1).

5.7 "The Bound One Flees" (*Der Gebundene flieht*)

"Binder and bound are adversarial and angry. The bound one flees to the side, I try to follow." This mnemonic is found repeatedly in I.33. What is it all about?

In a binding position there is one fencer who binds (establishes the bind) and one who is bound. The passive one can dissolve the bind at any time by pulling back his blade (i.e., going into the First Guard) or increasing the measure and simply falling back or to the side. This happens quite often in combat. I.33 places a tool in our hands for this situation: you should follow the one who flees. Liutger advised against going into a new guard and beginning the combat over again so to speak. He instead advises to maintain pressure and follow up—usually with a thrust—after the fleeing one.

If the opponent draws back his blade, simply thrust into an opening as he moves. If the opponent steps back then follow up with a thrust or blow, depending on your starting position. This denies the opponent a fresh beginning which would allow him to collect himself and again get into a good position.

Here Liutger gives clear instruction to fight forcefully, harry your opponent, and not allow any respite. This is very important. A fencer will refuse to bind and seek more distance if he feels he is no longer up to the situation and that is exactly the moment you should attack. You should not allow your opponent to begin the combat anew from a greater measure. Do not give your opponent any breathing space, especially not when he needs it most!

The fencers are in the bind.

Black flees the bind. He pulls his blade back into the Fifth Guard and takes a step back. As Black is moving, White immediately thrusts into his opening.

The fencers are in their guards.

White has fallen under sword and shield.

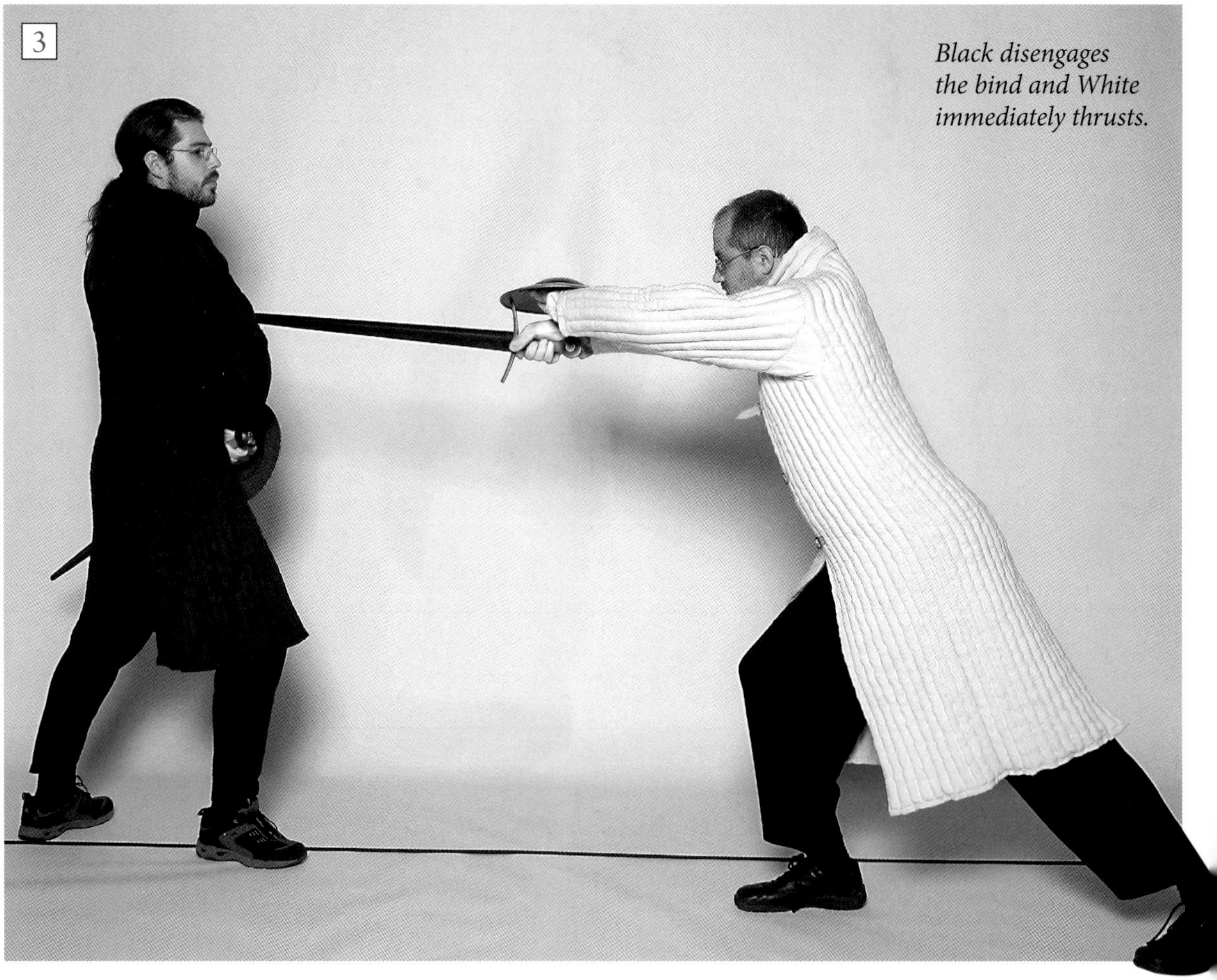

Black disengages the bind and White immediately thrusts.

The fencers are in the bind.

Black disengages the bind and pulls back. White follows up immediately and thrusts at the opening.

Tactics from I.33: Opportunities from the Bind

The system contained in I.33 seeks the bind—or crossing of the blades—and is based on working with the bind. Only someone who has mastered all of the possibilities from the bind can understand this system. In order to work from the bind properly, one must first be able to assess the situation. Three types of bind are used:

- bind in the forte
- bind in the middle of the blade
- bind in the foible

This only takes into consideration which part of one's own blade is touching the opponent's blade. This is often the basis for deciding which technique to use. One should also consider on which part of the opposing blade one's blade is touching. This is also often a decisive factor in selecting a technique.

If you engage in a bind—consciously crossing blades—then it is often advantageous to do this with a blow. The object is not to knock the opponent's blade out of the way; instead, it is to briefly cause the opponent to lose control of his blade. Instinctively he will try to regain control of his blade and you use this brief interval for your attack. In many situations in the bind—for example Crutch against Crutch—this blow irritates the opponent long enough for you to carry out a technique in relative safety.

The situation, the type of bind, the opponent's posture, the direction of pressure of the blades, and the position of the arms and buckler produce a series of possibilities for overcoming the opponent and exploiting the bind to your advantage.

6.1 The Over-Bind and Under-Bind

"Over-Bind" is understood to mean that you push on the right or left side of the opponent's blade with your blade in such a way that your blade comes to rest on the blade of your opponent. This usually happens when the opponent attempts to bind your blade to gain control. This is especially clear in the First Play (see section 7.1). You can also arrive in this situation when you yourself seek to bind.

Over-binding of the opponent's blade only works if you have bound with the middle of your blade or the forte. Ideally your blade rests on the opponent's foible, or at least on the middle of his blade. This enables you to exploit the leverage effect and over-bind the opposing blade. You are able to exert more force if you bind with the edge on the opponent's sword and not with the flat.

THE OVER-BIND

In a normal bind one blade is to the left of the other. You now push the opponent's blade downward. You assume control, as your blade is on top, and you exert force on the opponent's blade. Pay special attention to you buckler as you do this. The buckler hand should always come to rest under the sword hand. If you hold the buckler hand over the sword hand you block yourself and can only strike a blow with great difficulty. This mistake occurs frequently in the very beginning. Naturally this almost only happens if one over-binds on one's own left side. A shield strike or thrust strike is usually carried out from the Over-Bind. It is also possible to attack the arms, however.

THE OVER-BIND

The fencers are standing in their guards.

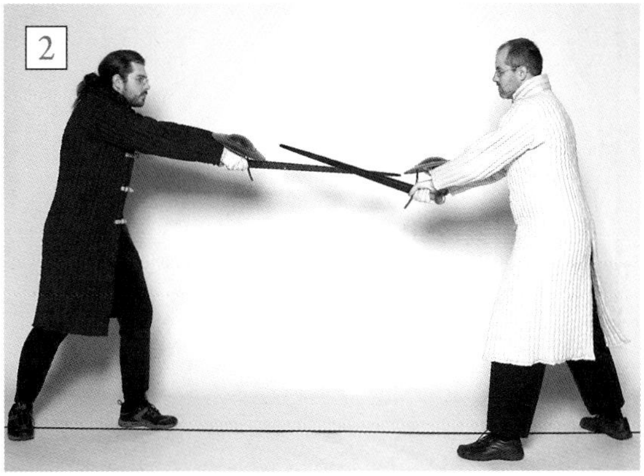

White has over-bound Black's Long-Point. He controls Black's blade with his own blade.

White takes control with his buckler …

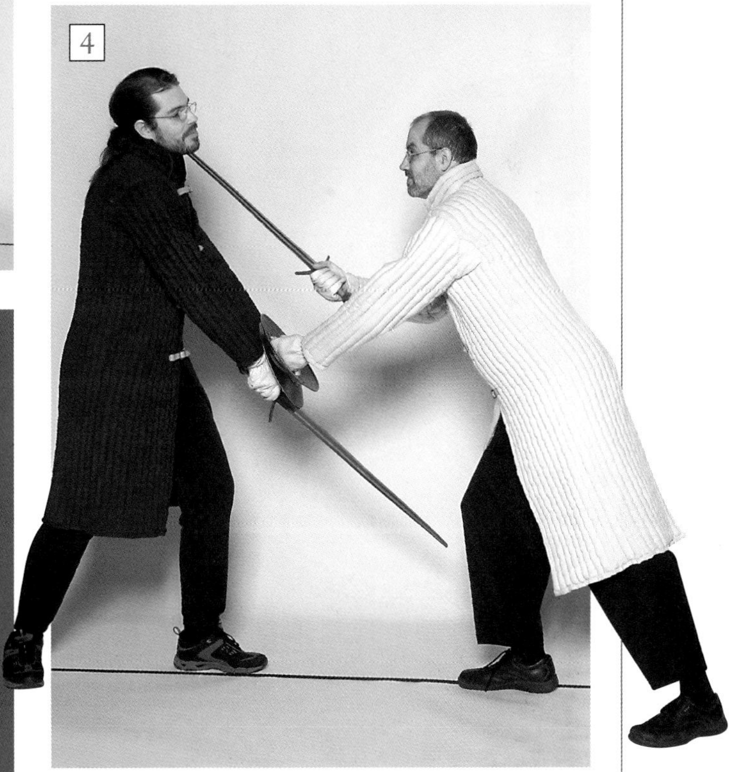

… and with his now free blade strikes Black's head.

EXAMPLE:
You are in a binding position, the opponent's blade is on your forte or at least in the middle of the blade.

Step 1

ARMS: Push the opponent's sword down to the left or right, so that your sword ends up on the opponent's blade.

BODY: Bleiben Sie aufrecht, und arbeiten Sie aus der Hüfte heraus. Sie bekommen die nötige Energie für den Schildschlag durch eine Hüftdrehung.

LEGS: If possible, you should now be able to take a step to the open side. If you have over-bound to the right then you should be able to step your left leg forward to deliver, for example, a shield strike.

THE UNDER-BIND

One can also often intentionally under-bind, even though that is the poorer position in the bind. Nevertheless, there are a few situations in which it is an advantage to under-bind. Following the correct procedure with an under-bind is also important for the following reason: if the opponent over-binds your blade, then that inevitably means that you are in the under-bind position. You should therefore also be able to cope with the under-bind. The Under-Bind is also the starting position for the Change of the Sword (see section 6.6).

THE UNDER-BIND

The fencers are standing in their guards.

White under-binds Black's Long-Point …

… takes control with his buckler and strikes at the head.

EXAMPLE:
Your opponent holds his blade in front of him, for example in a Long-Point.

Step 1

ARMS:	You place your blade under the opponent's blade from the left or right.
BODY:	This depends on the technique to follow. It is usually correct to remain upright, to be able to generate the required power.
LEGS:	Footwork also depends on the following technique. If possible, you should be able to step to the side of your sword.

6.2 Taking the Arms

"Take the Arms" is a term that does not come from I.33. I have introduced this term to give a name to the action it describes. Its purpose is simply to initiate grappling or wrestling. Essentially, one only grasps at the opponent's arms if bound at the forte, otherwise the measure is too great.

There are two variations: in one variation you look the opponent in the face. Here you usually clasp the opponent's arms with your sword arm. In the second variation, you turn your back to the opponent. Here you can use both the shield arm and the sword arm to grasp the opponent, though the sword arm is used most often. Both variations are cited in I.33.

When taking the arms, it is important to grasp as far back as you can so you possibly catch the opponent's elbows. Ideally you grab him just above the elbows. This gives you much better leverage and you are easily able to unbalance the opponent. You also have control of the opponent's blade because you are in a binding position. You do not disengage this bind until you have grasped the opponent's arms. If you are standing in the binding position then step left or right, maintaining the bind. You thus tilt your sword around the point of contact and retain control of the opponent's blade.

Grasp the opponent's arms while you turn your back to him, then use this rotation for a throw: when grasping the arms, try to bring your hip as close to the opponent as possible. Place your hip against the opponent. As soon as you have grasped the opponent's arms, turn so that he is levered over your hip. In addition, you also exert pressure over the opponent's elbows.

TAKE THE ARMS (1)

EXAMPLE 1:
You are standing in Half-Shield, your opponent in the First Guard. He falls under sword and shield. You over-bind. As you do so, you step left and forward, strike the opponent in the face with your buckler, grasp his arms and throw him over your hip.

Step 1

ARMS: You over-bind, then strike the opponent in the face with the edge of your buckler and reach down, behind his elbows. You push his arms together and pull them to your right hip. The pressure on the elbows, the blow in the face, and the rotation around your hip and over your legs should make the opponent fall. If he does not because he is somewhat bigger or heavier, then strike him in the face with your pommel. Throughout the entire movement you control the opponent's sword with your blade. You grasp his arms with your buckler hand.

BODY: The rotational movement generates sufficient force to throw the opponent off balance.

LEGS: With the blow to the face, you step your left leg forward so that your hip is against the opponent. Your left leg blocks the opponent's legs, causing him to fall over your leg.

The fencers at the beginning of the set-play.

White falls under sword and shield. Intending to thrust, White lands in the bind with the middle of the blade.

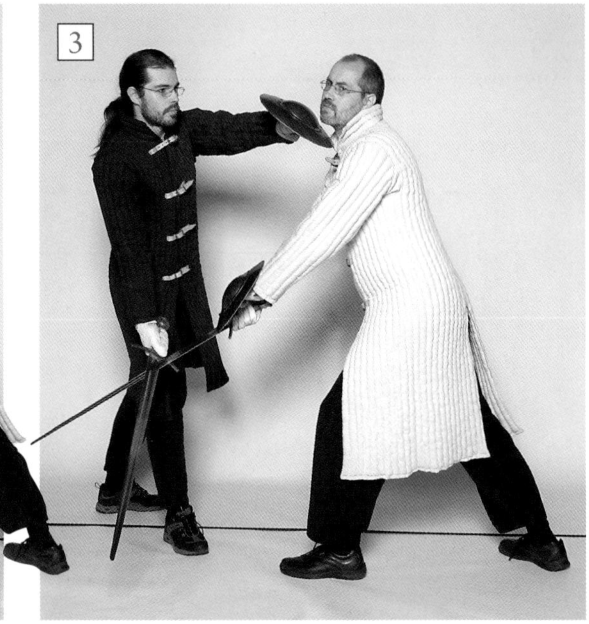

Black over-binds, steps forward, and strikes White in the face with his buckler.

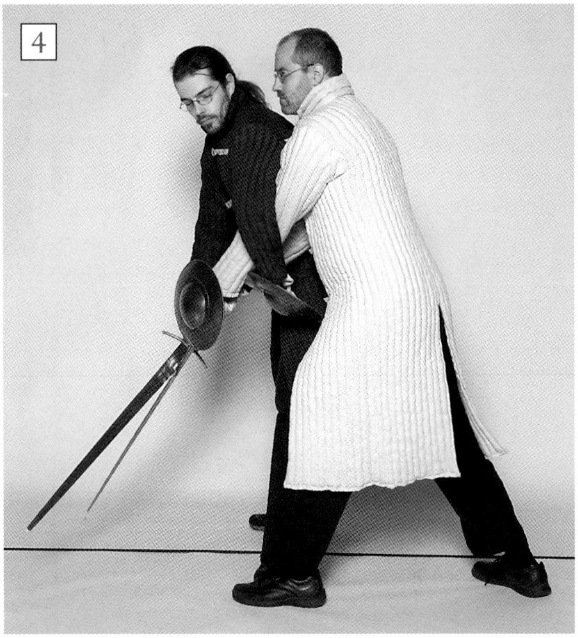

In a fluid movement Black grasps at White's arms …

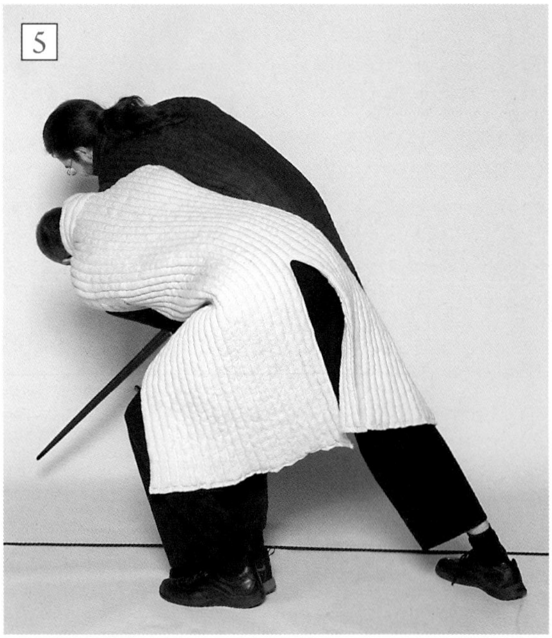

… and throws him with a rotating movement.

DIE ARME NEHMEN (2)

White in the First Guard, Black in the Half-Shield.

EXAMPLE 2:
You are standing in the First Guard and your opponent is in the Half-Shield. You fall under sword and shield and your opponent over-binds. You now step forward, take the opponent's arms, and throw him forward over your hip.

Step 1

ARMS:	You remain in the bind, but raise your hilt and right elbow until you can reach over your opponent's arms with your sword arm. During the grasping movement you strike the opponent in the face with the pommel, then reach under and grip behind the opponent's elbow and throw him over your hip and legs. Should the opponent be too large or heavy to throw then strike him in the face with the edge of your buckler.
BODY:	Do not lean too far forward; instead, remain upright. Here too, the necessary force is created from the rotation. Be sure to bring your hip against the body of your opponent.
LEGS:	After falling under the opponent's sword and shield step right and forward so that you are close enough. If possible, you should block the opponent's legs with your right leg.

White falls under sword and shield, intending to thrust immediately. As a result, White lands in the bind with his forte. Black parries the attack outward.

White raises his hands, remaining in the bind.

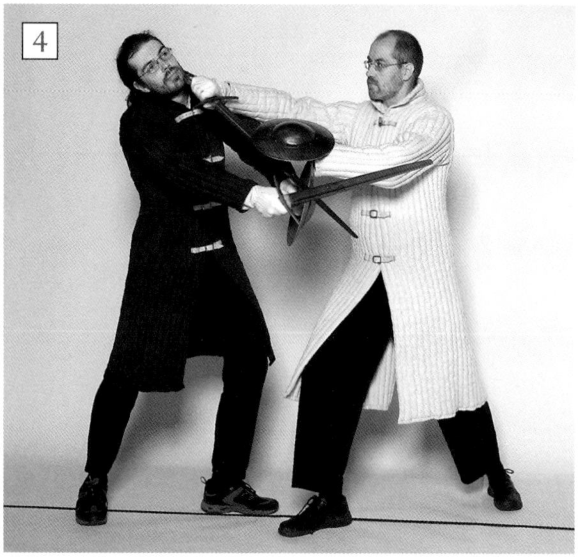

As he reaches over his opponent's arms, White strikes Black in the face with the pommel.

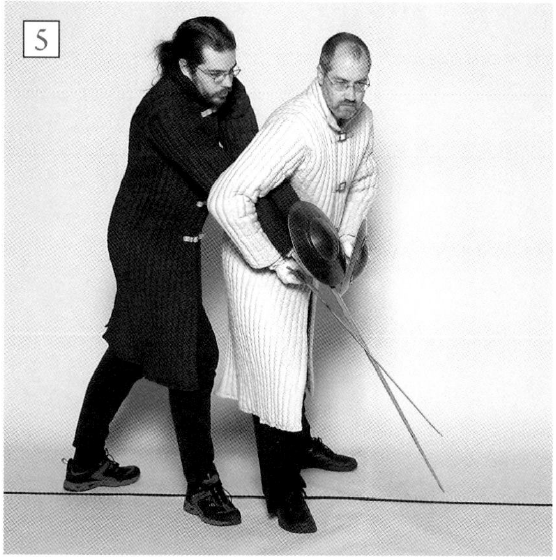

White has grabbed Black's arms and can now grapple. He is not in contact with White's hip.

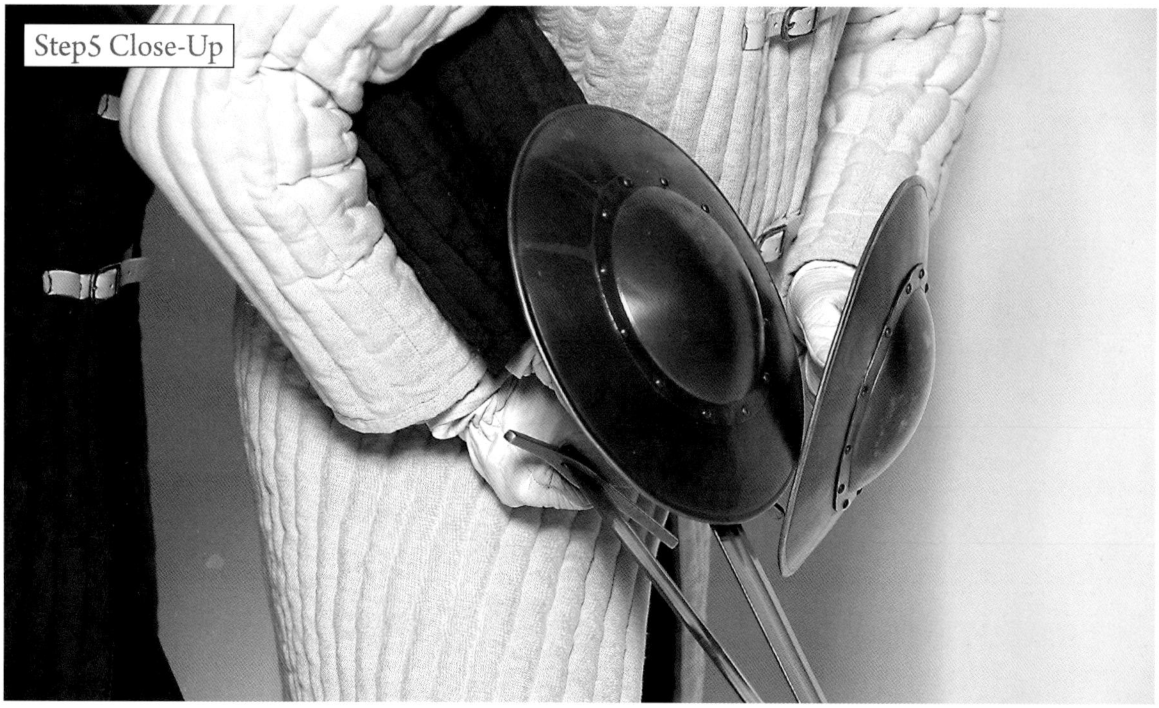

Raise the arms as high as possible while retaining control of the opponent's hands.

Other possibilities present themselves in addition to or instead of a throw. For example, if you and your opponent are directly facing each other and you have grasped his arms then employ your sword. You can render the opponent unable to fight with a powerful pommel blow. You can also slice through the opponent's face or neck. If you have grasped with your sword hand use your buckler and strike at the opponent's face with the edge of the shield.

As mentioned, taking the arms can be accomplished with either the shield hand or sword hand. No matter how the arms are taken the break is always the same: if your opponent has taken your arms let your sword and buckler drop, pull the arms through and back, and grasp the opponent by the shoulders and cause him to fall by kicking his knee or back. The break to this break is to simply turn around and thrust.

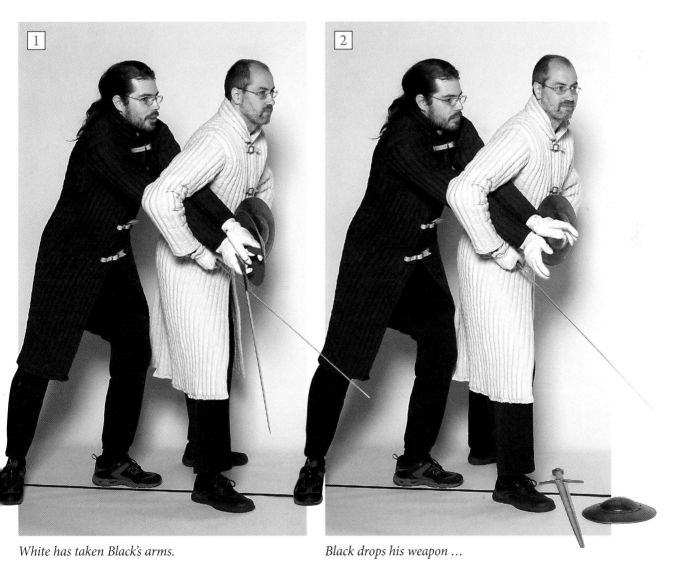

White has taken Black's arms.

Black drops his weapon …

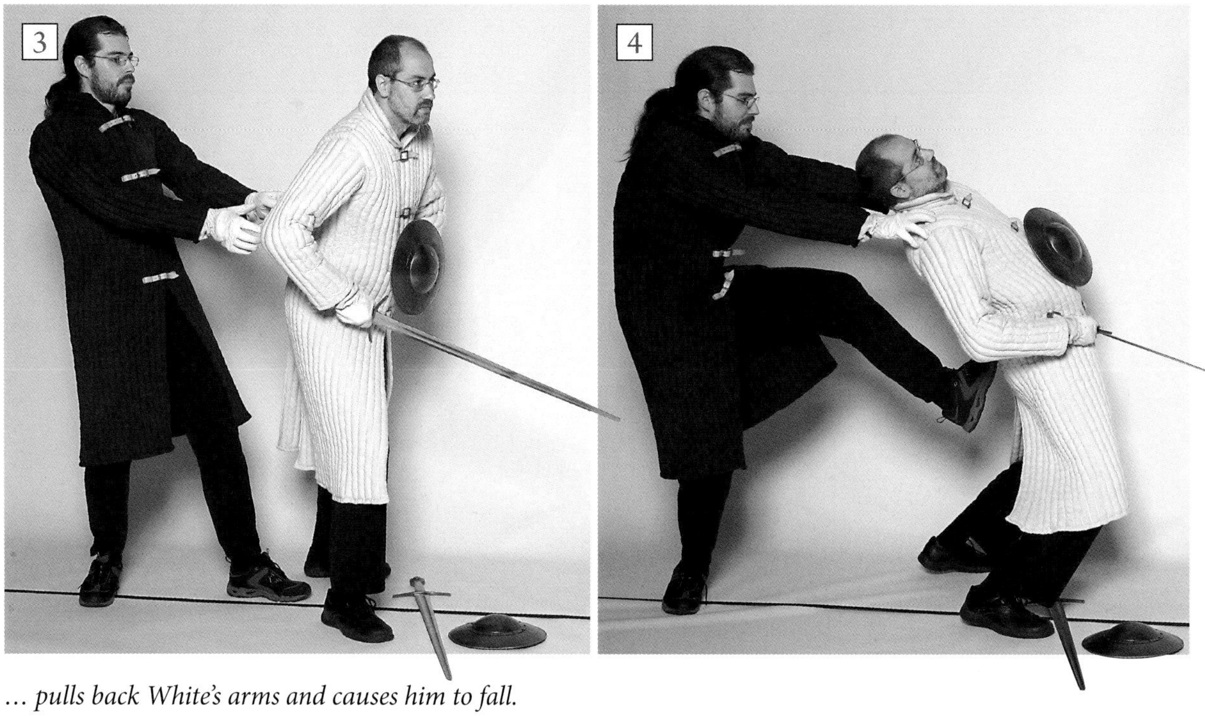

... pulls back White's arms and causes him to fall.

BREAKING THE BREAK

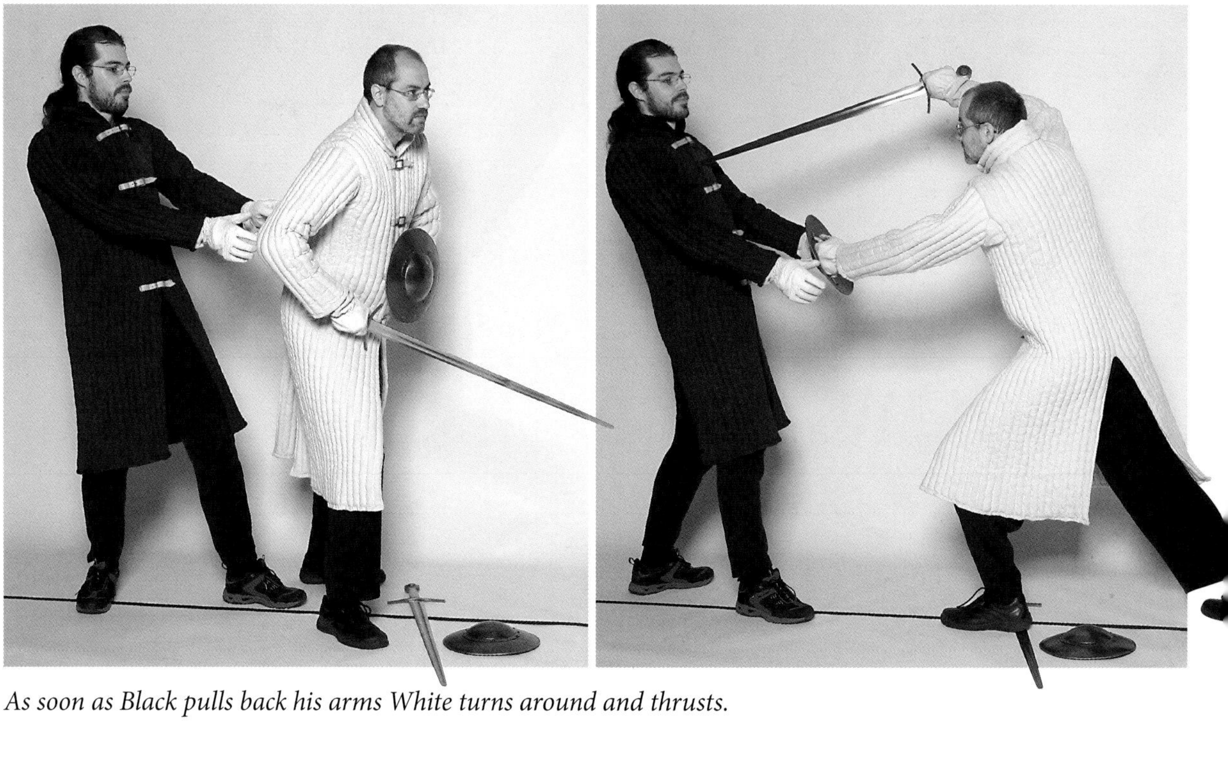

As soon as Black pulls back his arms White turns around and thrusts.

6.3 Thrust from the Bind

When you have under- or over-bound you almost always have the opportunity to thrust from the bind or strike the opponent's arms. You can do this from the Crutch to Crutch bind, from an under-bind to an over-bind, or when you are over-bound from the Half-Shield. As soon as you are over-bound, with your blade under the opponent's blade step slightly to the side, away from the opponent's blade, and strike his arms from below with your short edge. Depending on the measure you can also make an immediate thrust from this position. This technique is only possible if you are bound in your foible, or at most in the middle of the blade.

Should your opponent try to strike at your head as soon as you disengage the bind then simply raise your sword and buckler and execute a shield strike or thrust strike.

THRUST FROM THE BIND

Step 1

ARMS: From below, strike directly at your opponent's arms with the short edge. Immediately after the blow try to land a thrust. You can also try to combine strike and thrust. Be sure to keep your movements as short and quick as possible.

BODY: You may possibly have to lean forward slightly to reach the necessary measure.

LEGS: Step to the side opposite the opponent's sword. If, for example, the opposing blade is left of your blade then you step to the right.

White was over-bound.

White steps to the side and from below strikes at Black's arms with the short edge.

White then immediately thrusts at the lower opening. One can also omit the strike on the hands and immediately strike at the opening from the bind, depending on which seems easier.

6.4 Nod from the Bind (*Aus dem Band nucken*)

Nodding can often be used, such as after a Change of Sword or from an over-bind. The Nod is a very quick attack that cannot usually be broken. If you do it correctly, then after the Nod you are standing behind your blade and you have closed the opponent's line of attack.

The Nod simply means to strike upward from the bind with your short edge at the opponent's head. You must control the opponent's weapon with your buckler as you do so. This means you can only Nod if you are close enough to your opponent.

NOD FROM THE BIND

Black attempts a thrust from the Fifth Guard ...

... and is over-bound by White. From the bind ...

Step 1

ARMS: From the over-bind, after a Change of Sword or from some other high bind you simply strike directly at the opponent's head with your short edge. You control both the opponent's sword and buckler with your own buckler. The Nod works especially well if your weapon is held somewhat low.

BODY: You can possibly use your body to close the distance by leaning forward, for example. During the Nod be sure that your body is behind your blade and thus covered.

LEGS: You take no more steps during the Nod itself. You are already within your blade's range, as you must bind with the buckler.

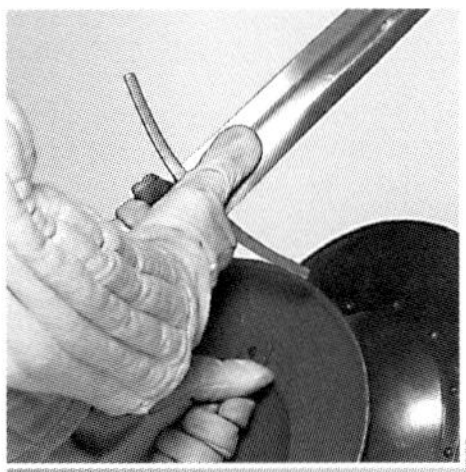

Close-Up of the Nod: The thumb is on the flat of the blade and the sword is held almost transversely in the hand. Control is maintained with the buckler.

... White takes control with his buckler and nods at the head. It is important here to cover Black's line of attack. White is protected by his blade. This is why White is holding the hilt so low.

6.5 From the Bind Directly at the Head

Striking directly at the head from the bind is essentially the same as the Nod only the long edge is used. Another difference is that it is not always covered by the buckler. There are situations where you strike at the opponent's head from an under-bind without having control with your buckler. Of course, instead of striking a blow you can also thrust if the measure makes that seem more appropriate.

If you dispense with covering with the buckler then your posture, direction of movement, and the push from the opponent must be directed away from you at the moment you disengage the bind. You can only dispense with the cover provided by your buckler when it takes your opponent longer to redirect his direction of attack at you than it takes you to strike his head.

6.6 Change of Sword (*Schwertwechsel*)

The purpose of the Change of Sword is to move from an under-bind—which is rather negative—to an over-bind. This involves changing the side on which one is in the bind from being under the opponent's blade to over it.

From the bind ...

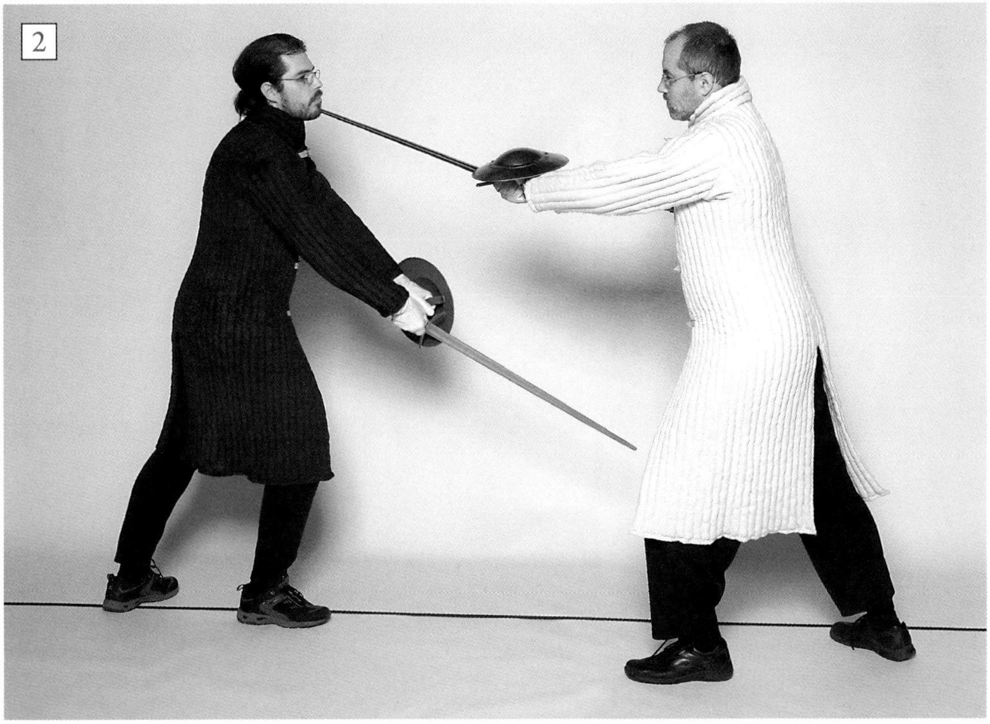

… White steps to the side and strikes directly at his opponent's head. This is only possible if Black's direction of pressure is downward. Otherwise the danger to White would be too great.

From the bind …

… it is also possible to make a direct thrust. Here, too, pay attention to the direction of pressure.

The Change of Sword (mutation Gladii) is explained twice in I.33 (3v/6 and 8r/15). Both times the protagonist is in an under-bind and covers his left with his buckler. In the Change of Sword he then changes from an under-bind to an over-bind and also changes the side on which the buckler is held. At the end, the protagonist's sword is on the opponent's sword and his buckler covers right. This is a very important point: this buckler position is a precautionary measure against a strike at the arms from below. The Change of Sword can only be carried out if you are bound in the foible of your sword; otherwise, the measure is too close.

Please ensure when executing the Change of Sword you not only make a strike against the opposing blade but also sweep back and down the opponent's blade. This brings the opponent's blade down and outside the danger zone so that it is very difficult for him to make a thrust.

After the Change of Sword it is possible to Nod, but you can also make a descending cut at the head from the left. In doing so, you should consciously cover left toward the opponent's blade with your buckler.

When you Nod, take a big step to the right to the opponent's side; only then have you also closed his line of attack so that any attack is automatically intercepted by your blade. The same applies to the Change of Sword itself. If your opponent senses how you are going to disengage the bind he can also attack. You can parry this attack by moving your blade in a circular fashion. In practice, the entire Change of Sword is often executed more quickly and concisely than shown here. The correct movement is important and then the shortening of the technique takes place almost automatically.

CHANGE OF SWORD

The fencers are in their guards.

Step 1

ARMS: You are over-bound. This means that the opponent pushes your sword downward in order to execute a technique, probably a shield strike. When you feel that your opponent is beginning his over-bind disengage the bind. Place your sword hand over your buckler hand, move your point around the opponent's blade in the smallest possible arc, and strike his blade from above. This blow is very important, as it briefly deprives the opponent of control. Your blade is now on the opponent's blade, your buckler hand is beneath your sword hand, and your buckler covers right. You can now simply Nod, for example, as that is the simplest and quickest solution.

BODY: Your body is bent slightly forward during the entire Change of Sword.

LEGS: During the Change of Sword you step slightly forward and out of line to the right.

White falls under sword and shield and binds with the foible, provoking a reaction from Black.

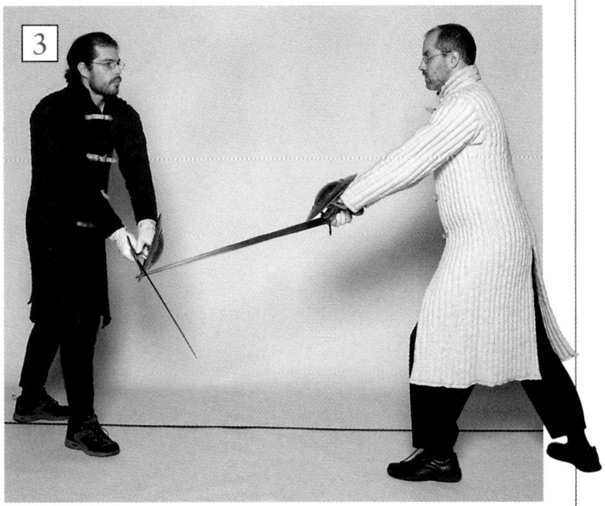

Black over-binds …

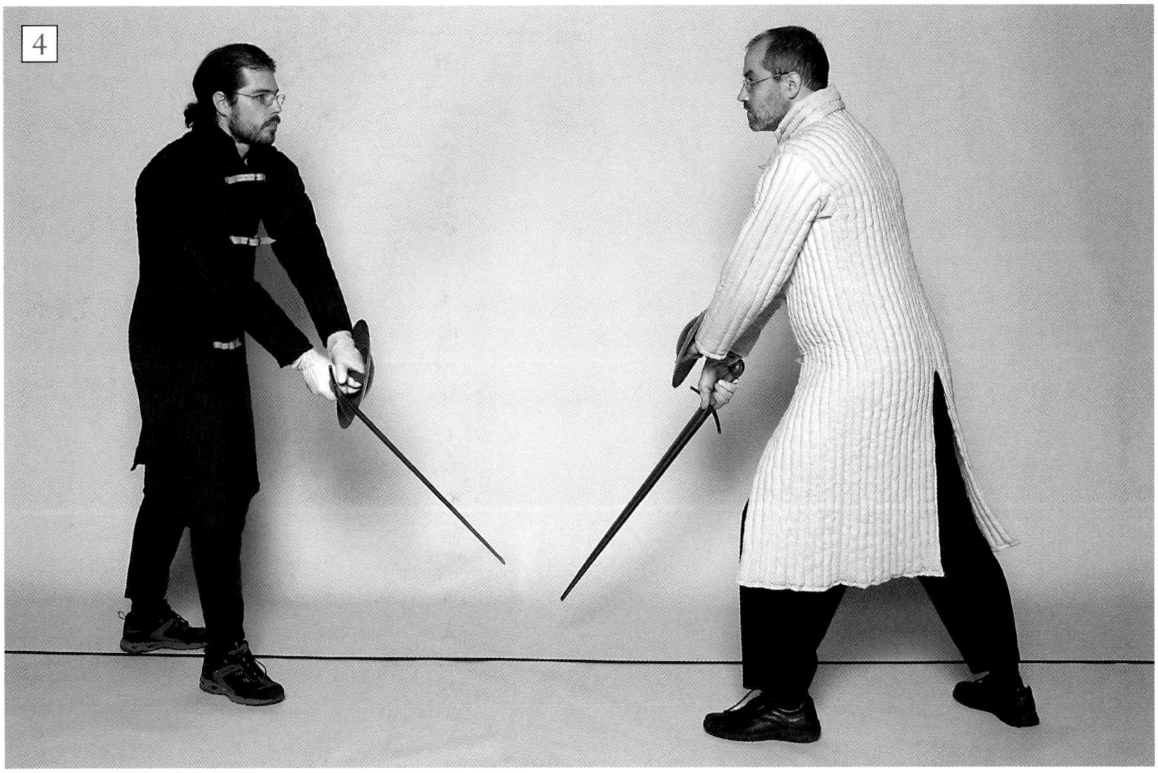

… and White continues the movement in a circular fashion …

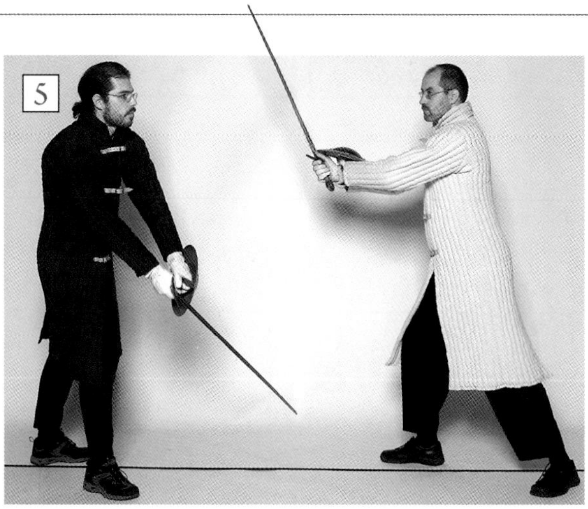

… and strikes Black's blade from above with his long edge.

It is important here to give the opposing blade impetus, so that the opponent cannot react immediately.

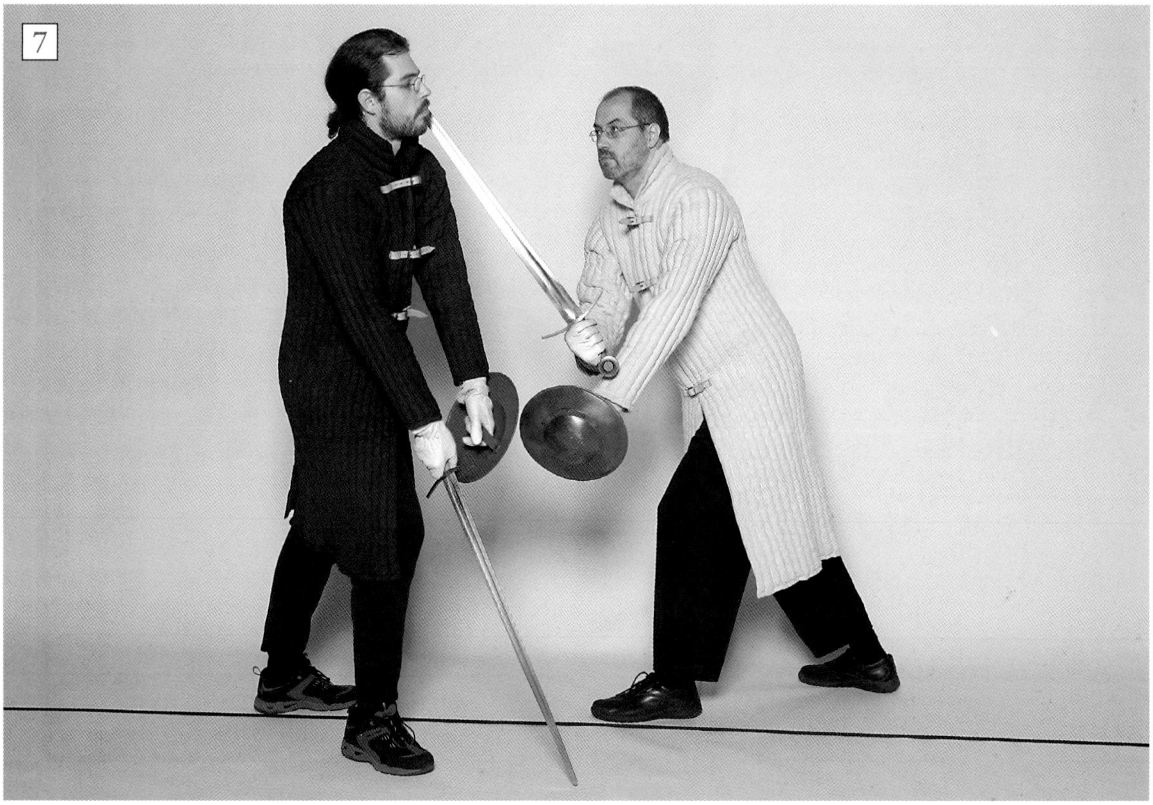

From the bind White nods at the head, covering with his buckler.

White has fallen under sword and shield.

Black over-binds ...

... and while White makes the Change of Sword, Black tries to attack with a strike.

However, White catches Black's attack during the Change of Sword movement ...

… and deflects it.

5

6

White nods at the head from the bind.

CHAPTER 7

Complex Combat Sequences: The Individual Plays

In I.33, the techniques are combined in sequences or "plays" similar to the "devices" in later systems. They usually begin in a guard. The opponent subsequently goes into a protection or a counter-guard. One of the two now reacts to the situation and begins the Play, whereupon the other reacts to the new situation and so on. One can organize the plays if one orients oneself on the guard that the first fencer assumes at the start. The play revolves around this guard. (In this book I generally use the term "Guards" instead of "Custodias" and "Counter-Guard" instead of "Obsesseos.")

7.1 The First Guard and its Plays

Two counters for the First Guard are mentioned in I.33: the the Half-Shield and the Long-Point. Later the Crutch and the Walpurgis are also identified as counters.

THE FIRST GUARD VERSUS HALF-SHIELD

The opening situation: one fencer goes into the First Guard, whereupon his opponent assumes the Half-Shield counter-guard (usually with the right leg forward). The Half-Shield creates a threat, seeks the advantage, and offers the opponent a target. If the fencer in the First Guard hesitates then the opponent will attack him immediately and directly (11v/22).

Without hesitation, the fencer in the First Guard falls under the sword and shield of the fencer in the Half-Shield. He engages in a bind with the intention of reaching a thrusting position. He can also feel what the opponent does and react immediately. He will try to make a thrust from the bind if the opponent fails to react. The man in the Half-Shield will probably react to this threat by over-binding. If he strikes directly at the head his opponent should break this with a thrust strike.

Should the one in the Half-Shield now strike at the head of the attacker, the latter will simply raise his hands, deflect the opponent's blade to the right (from his vantage point) with his own, and execute a thrust strike. If the fencer in the Half-Shield over-binds the attacker's blade down and to the right then the First Play bifurcates. Each fencer now has a selection of possibilities. The formula in the box below is intended to make the whole thing more clear.

POSSIBLE TECHNIQUES	THE ONE STANDING IN THE HALF-SHIELD	THE HAT FROM THE FIRST COMING
Take the arms	If the opponent has engaged a bind in his forte	If the fencer has bound with his forte and over-binds the opponent
Over-bind and shield strike	If the opponent has engaged in a bind with the middle of the blade or foible	
Step through		If the fencer has bound with the middle of his blade and over-binds the opponent
Change of Sword		If the fencer has bound with his foible and over-binds the opponent

THE FIRST PLAY: FIRST GUARD VS. HALF-SHIELD

The First Guard (assumed by White) is countered with Half-Shield.

White falls under sword and shield, he engages in a bind with the short edge.

Step 1

ARMS: With your short edge strike the opponent's forte, roughly at the height of his shoulders. Your buckler shields up and to the right and your sword hand is under your shield hand. If possible the point is aimed at the opponent. From this position you can thrust immediately or slice through his face with a pushing cut.

LEGS: Step forward and left out of line to reach the desired measure and necessary angle to thrust behind the opponent's weapon.

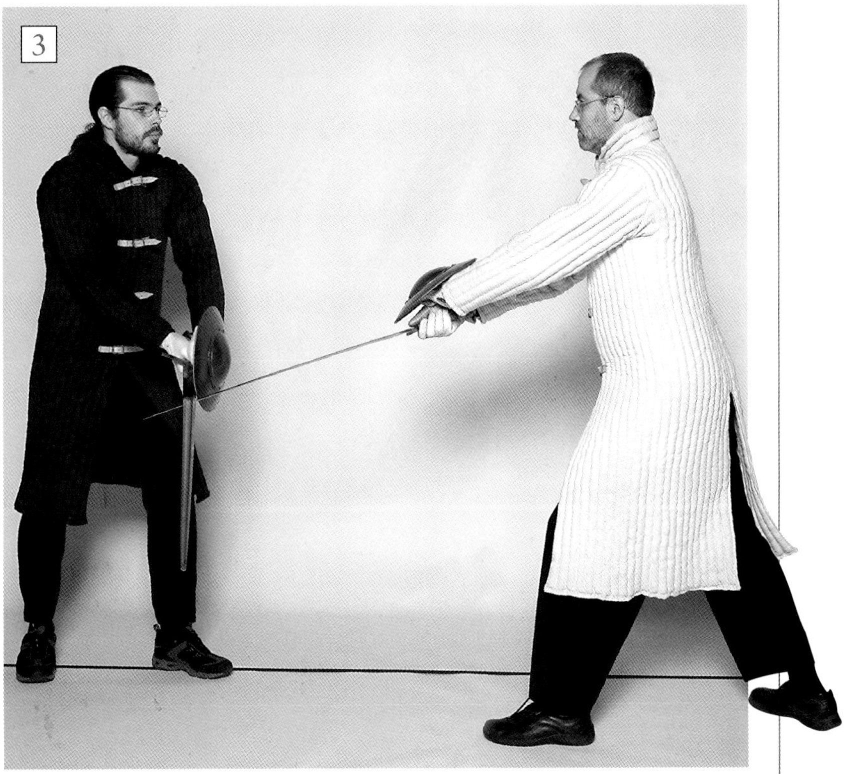

To escape White's thrust Black over-binds.

Let us first concern ourselves with the two possibilities you have if you are in the Half-Shield: over-binding and shield strike or taking the arms.

1) Over-Bind and Shield Strike

Your attacker has fallen under sword and shield and stepped left out of line. He has made his attack in such a way that the foible (the middle of his blade) is against your forte. You over-bind to the right and downward. As a result, you now have control over the opponent's sword. You then step forward and left or make a shield strike from above against the opponent's buckler. This blow allows you to take control with your buckler. Your sword is now free and you strike at the opponent's head with your long edge. If you strike at your opponent's head without the shield strike he will probably respond to your attack with a thrust strike.

OVER-BIND AND SHIELD STRIKE

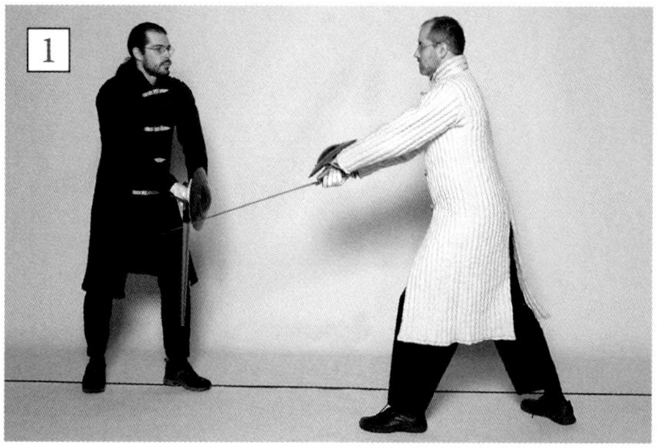

Black has over-bound.

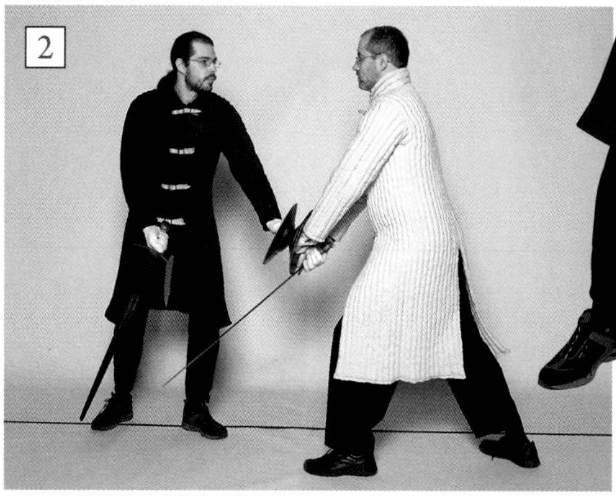

Black takes control with his buckler, striking White's buckler from above.

As soon as control is established with the buckler Black strikes at White's head. If possible Black's buckler should engage in the bind from above.

The same action with reversed roles. The fencers are standing in the Half-Shield (now White) and the First Guard.

Black falls under White's sword and shield.

Step 1

ARMS: Move your blade down and to the right, taking the opponent's blade with you. You have the opponent's blade under control with your forte. At the same time you have made a counter-movement and are now in an optimal position for a strike.

BODY: Move your left shoulder and left hip forward. This rotation movement is important for Step 2 – the shield strike.

LEGS: At this point no step is taken.

Step 2

ARMS: You have the blade under control. With the rotation of your body you make a shield strike against the opponent's buckler and sword and take control of his weapon with your buckler. As a result your sword is free, and immediately after the buckler strike you strike with your sword over your shield hand at the opponent's head.

BODY: The rotation movement begun in Step 1 creates the necessary energy for the strike with the buckler. If the buckler lands your entire body is in a counter-movement. Now bring your right shoulder forward with the blow.

LEGS: Depending on the measure you step forward with the left shield strike. The strike at the opening is also carried out from this posture.

All of this is carried out smoothly in one motion.

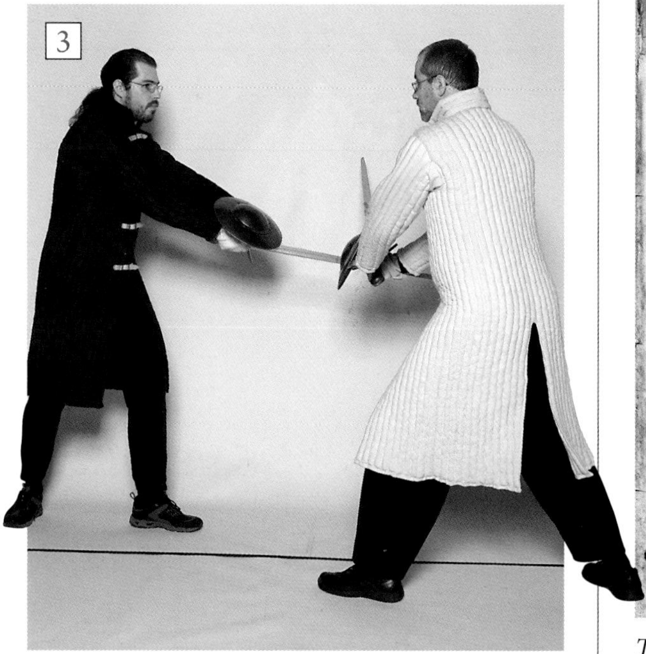

White over-binds Black's blade …

The technique is in I.33, page 2r/3. Here is the execution of falling under sword and shield …

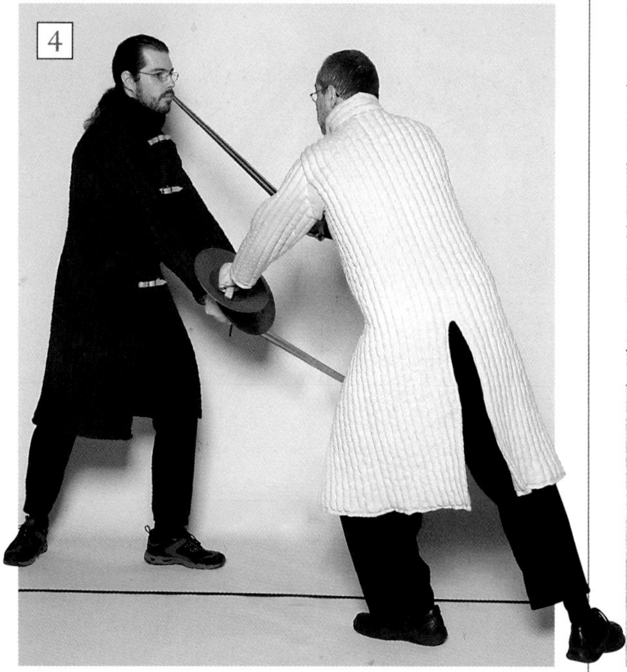

… and executes a shield strike.

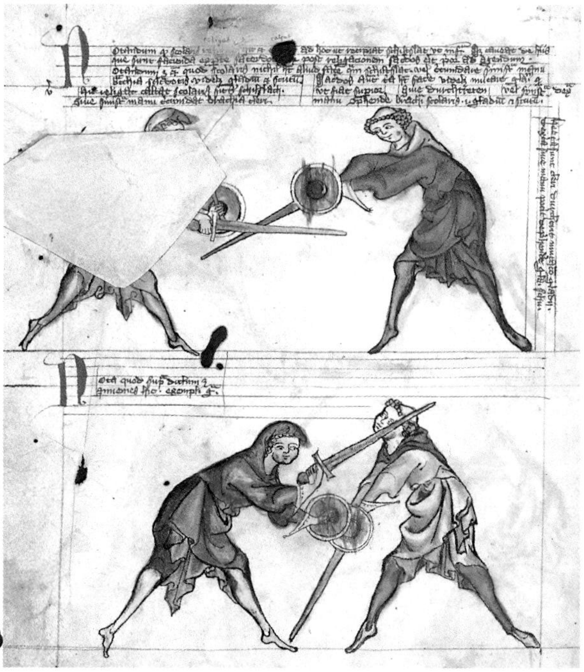

… followed by an over-bind and the shield strike (Page 2v/4).

2) TAKE THE ARMS

The attacker has fallen under sword and shield and stepped left out of line. He has made his attack in such a way that the forte of his blade is against your forte. As your opponent is thrusting directly at you, you respond with an over-bind and do not wait for the bind. You over-bind to the right and downward. This gives you control over the opponent's sword. As you over-bind, step your left leg forward and strike the opponent in the face with your buckler. Reach down around his arms behind his elbows and push them together. By continuing this rotating movement you throw the opponent to the ground in front of you. Should your opponent not fall voluntarily then strike him in the face with the pommel.

TAKE THE ARMS

Step 1

ARMS:	Over-bind the opponent's blade by pushing your blade out to the right. Be sure not to over-bind too low, otherwise you will not be able to grip the arms as well. Be absolutely certain you maintain contact and control. At the same time strike the opponent's face with the edge of your buckler.
BODY:	Remain as upright as possible, otherwise you will later be in a poor position for the throw.
LEGS:	Take a step straight forward with your left leg.

Step 2

ARMS:	In the same movement as the strike with the edge of the buckler reach over the opponent's arms with your left arm. Be sure to grip the arms behind the elbows if possible. Press the arms together. Your right still controls the opponent's sword.
BODY:	Here you rotate right, so that in the end you are standing with your back to the opponent. Be sure to place your hip right against the opponent, as this is the only way you can develop the lever effect.
LEGS:	You can step back with your right leg to strengthen the lever effect produced by your body rotation.

The fencers again begin in the Half-Shield Guard (Black) and the First Guard.

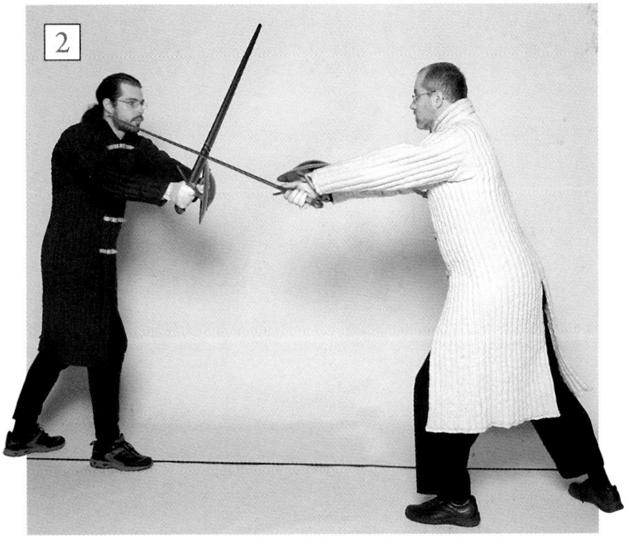

White falls under Black's sword and shield. As White wants to thrust immediately, he engages in a bind in the middle of the blade. Black comes toward him in the bind.

Black over-binds, steps forward, and strikes at White's face with his buckler.

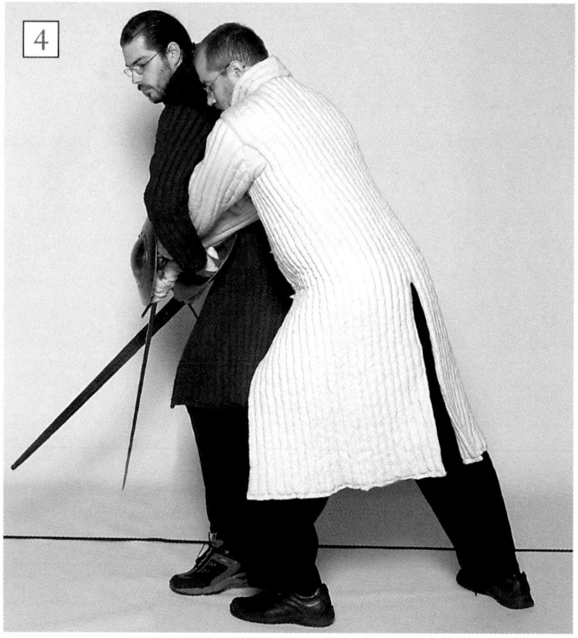

Black continues the movement and reaches over White's arms. The position of the hip is important here. It should touch the opponent's body, forming a fulcrum for the subsequent throw.

By continuing the rotation movement the buckler throws White off balance.

If you leave the First Guard then you are offered three possibilities: Change of Sword, Step Through, or Take the Arms.

1) CHANGE OF SWORD

You have fallen under the sword and shield of your opponent who is standing in the Half-Shield. You have engaged in a bind with your foible against the opponent's forte. Your opponent over-binds. As soon as you sense his over-bind, accept the over-bind and absorb the momentum. Raise your hilt, move the blade in a circular motion from below left to above left, and strike the opponent's blade, moving the sword hand over the buckler hand.

You have now executed a Change of Sword. Your buckler, which faced right in the beginning, is now facing left in preparation for a shield strike. Simultaneous with the Change of Sword, step your right leg forward or to the side. As soon as you have struck the opponent's blade Nod at his head. Stand so that the opponent's line of attack is covered by your blade. The Change of Sword is carried out quickly. Avoid large movements.

CHANGE OF SWORD

Step 1

ARMS:	You have fallen under your opponent's sword and shield in such a way that you have engaged in a bind in his foible. If you now sense that your opponent is about to over-bind begin a counterclockwise circular motion. Your buckler still shields to the right.
LEGS:	This technique usually requires you take a small step to the right.

Step 2

ARMS:	Move your sword around the opponent's blade in as small a circle as possible and make a descending strike at the opponent's blade with your long edge. As you do so try to knock his blade downward. This movement with your blade is made over the buckler hand, so that in the end your sword hand is over the buckler hand. You subsequently execute a shield strike.

Step 3

ARMS:	From the strike on the opponent's blade immediately strike at his head in such a way that you land with the short edge and have the sword diagonally in front of you. Your thumb can be on the flat of the blade. Your hilt is quite low, thus covering the opponent's line of attack.
LEGS:	You should be standing almost at right angles to your opponent here to be able to act stably and surely. You must correct the position of your legs depending on the measure and posture.

1

The starting position of the First Play.

2

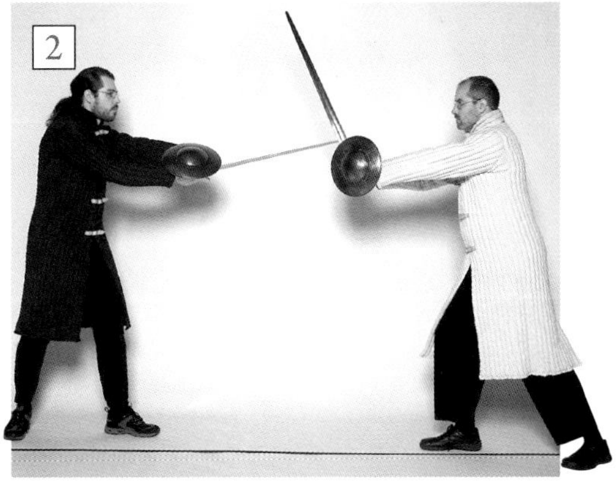

Black falls under White's sword and shield. Black engages in a bind in his foible and provokes a reaction from White.

White reacts promptly and over-binds.

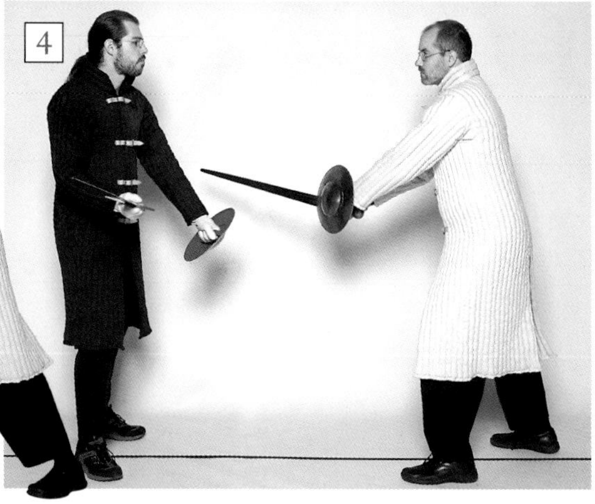

Black subsequently disengages the bind, steps to the right, and rotates his blade counterclockwise to the outside.

The movement of Black's blade should be as minimal as possible, but sweeping enough to intercept potential attacks by White and permit a powerful blow against White's blade.

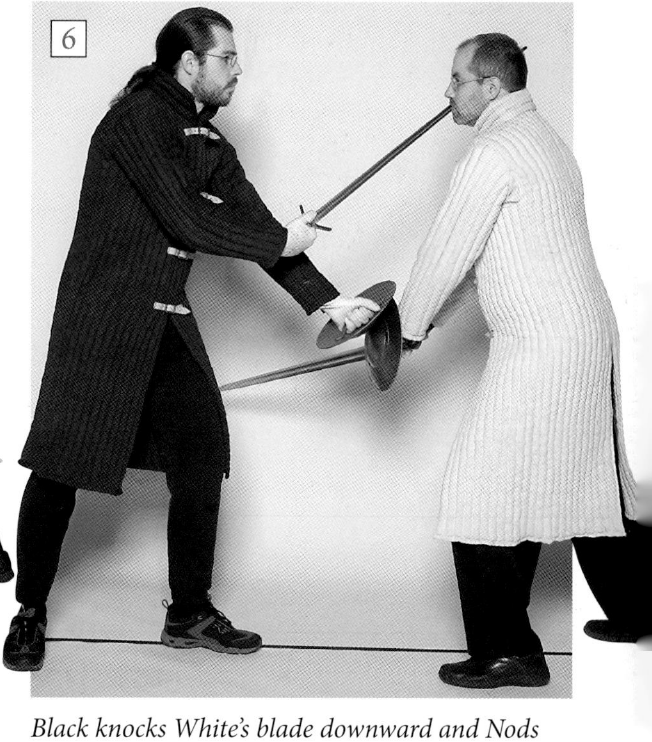

Black knocks White's blade downward and Nods at his head. Here Black Nods to his opponent's left side. One can also nod to the right side, however.

Additional technique:
Instead of the Change of Sword, one can of course also strike at the opponent's head while shielding to the left with the buckler. This works if the measure or footwork places one close enough to the opponent. Alternately one can also simply make an ascending strike at his arms, thrust into his abdomen, or sometimes also strike at his legs while stepping forward.

If the distance is correct, from the over-bind one can …

… step forward, push the opponent's weapon aside with the buckler …

… and strike at the head.

2) STEP THROUGH

You have fallen under the sword and shield of your opponent, who is standing in the Half-Shield. You have engaged in a bind with the middle of your blade against the opponent's forte. As soon as you sense his over-bind raise your hilt and remain engaged in the bind. Your arm should form an arc beneath which you execute a strike with your buckler straight at the opponent's buckler. At the same time slice through your opponent's face or strike his head with your pommel. Alternately you can also strike at the opponent's head from your right.

STEP THROUGH

Step 1

ARMS: The middle of your blade or the foible is against the opponent's forte. As soon as you feel he is over-binding raise the hilt, forming an arc with your sword and arm.

Step 2

ARMS: Beneath this arc, thrust your buckler forward and execute a shield strike. As soon as you have control of the opponent's weapon with your buckler strike at his head with your sword.

LEGS: With the shield strike, take a step forward with your right leg.

The fencers begin in the First Guard and the Half-Shield.

White falls under sword and shield and binds in the middle of the blade.

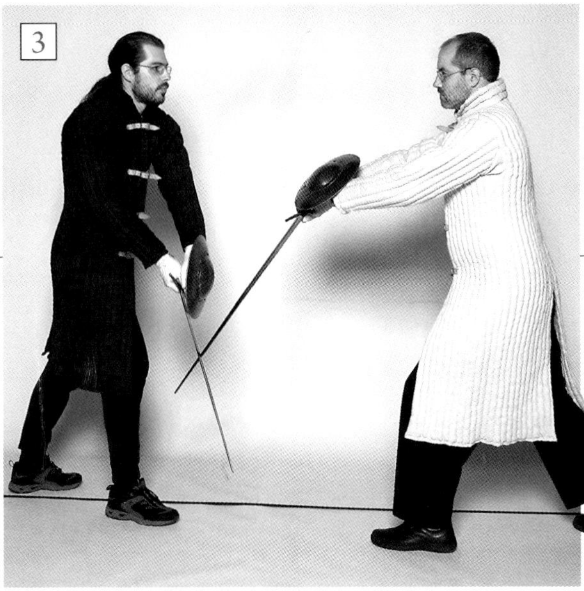

Black over-binds as usual …

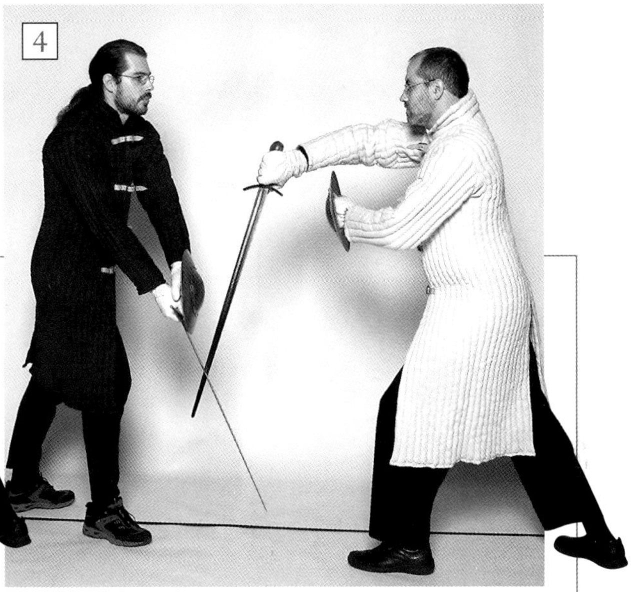

… whereupon White raises his hilt but remains engaged in the bind.

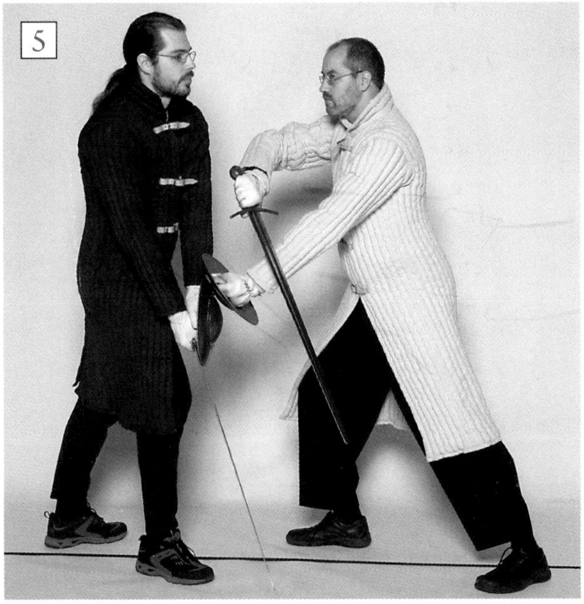

White steps forward to the right, makes a strike with the buckler under the sword hand, and thus takes control of Black's weapon. The bind is disengaged.

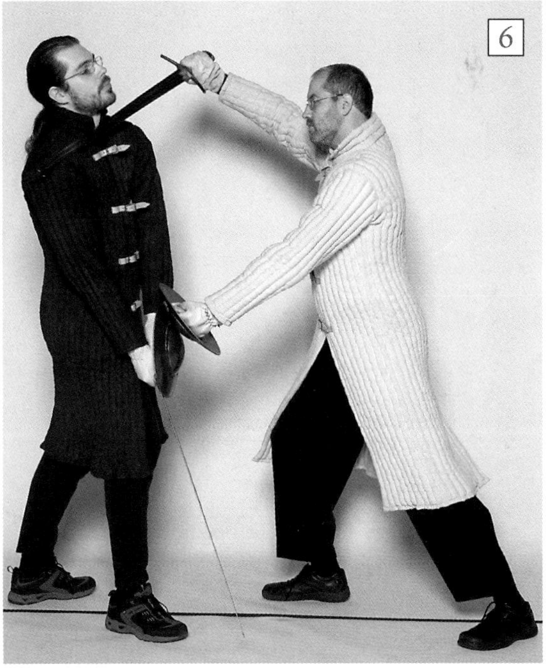

Now White can easily strike at Black's head.

3) TAKE THE ARMS

You have fallen under the sword and shield of your opponent, who is standing in the Half-Shield. You have engaged in a bind with your foible against the opponent's forte. Your opponent over-binds. As soon as you sense his over-bind remain in the bind, raise your hilt without disengaging the bind, and with your sword hand reach over the opponent's arms. Try to get behind the opponent's elbows, as this will make the throw easier. While raising your hilt, step forward with your right leg and strike your opponent's face with your pommel. As soon as you have grasped the opponent's arms continue turning and throw him to the ground in front of you. Should your opponent not fall voluntarily then strike him in the face with your buckler. This technique is primarily used if you immediately try to deliver a thrust as you fall under sword and shield, then you bind in your forte and try to reach the opponent with your point. When taking the arms I always advise a blow in the face, though this is not in I.33.

TAKE THE ARMS

The fencers begin as usual.

Step 1

ARMS: You fall under sword and shield. Based on your assessment you immediately try to strike the opponent, as a result of which you bind in your forte.

LEGS: Here you either step out of line to the left—not as far as usual—or subsequently step or spring all the more to the right.

Step 2

ARMS: You feel that your opponent is displacing your sword and your attack fails. You raise the hilt but definitely remain in the bind. Now reach your sword hand over the opponent's arms and grasp them behind the elbows. As you grasp him strike the opponent in the face with your pommel.

BODY: Here you once again turn as you make the grasping movement. At the end you are standing with your back to the opponent. Be sure to have your hip against the opponent. This will enable you to produce the lever effect for the throw.

LEGS: With the grasping of the arms, the pommel strike, and the body rotation, step your right leg forward and finish the entire sequence with a step back with your left leg. The circular step with the left leg will give you the necessary rotation for the throw.

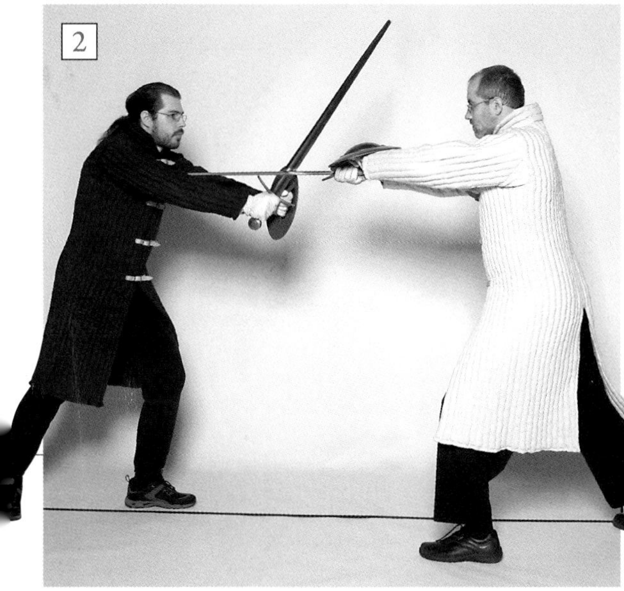

White falls under sword and shield and immediately makes a thrust.

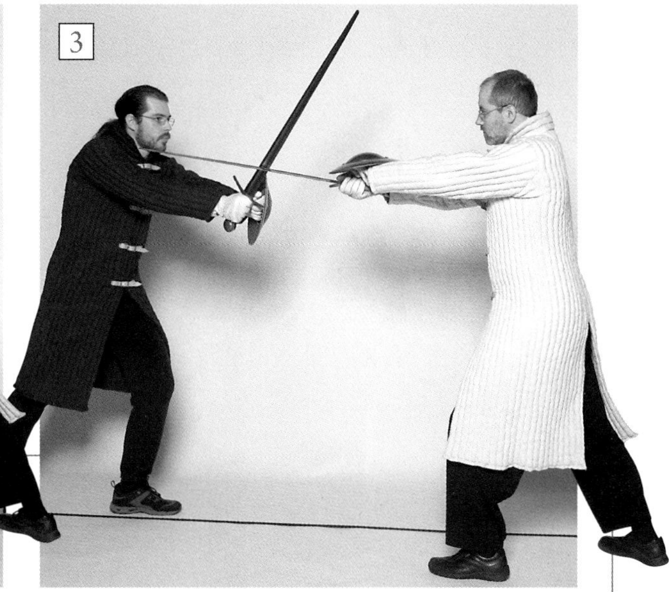

Black prevents this by displacing the thrust outward.

White steps forward to the right and strikes at Black's face with his pommel while covering the line of attack with his buckler. The bind remains engaged. This enables White to feel what Black is doing with his blade without having to look.

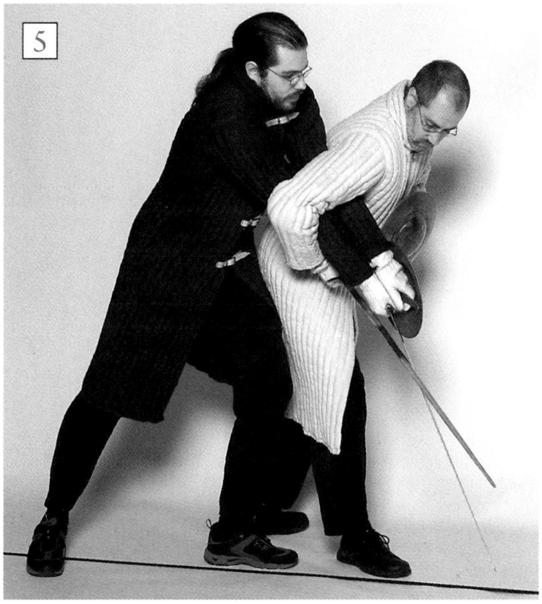

In a smooth motion White reaches over Black's arms. Here it is again important to grasp the arms on or behind the elbows and bring the hip as close to the opponent as possible.

THE FIRST GUARD VERSUS THE CRUTCH

The beginning situation: one fencer assumes the First Guard. His opponent responds with the Crutch counter. Liutger advises you thrust immediately if the one in the First Guard hesitates. The Crutch gives you a distance advantage. If you are in the First Guard and your opponent assumes the Crutch position you are bound immediately. There are two possible responses: first you can over-bind normally. It is important that the bind takes place from your right side, as this restricts the fencer in the Crutch's ability to move. Second, one can best counter the Crutch with another Crutch. In this case you bind on the left side, otherwise your own ability to move will be restricted.

The fencers are standing in their guards.

White hesitates in the First Guard. Black immediately thrusts at him. Depending on the measure, Black only needs to twist his wrist or take a lunge step forward. It is important not to take a long step, as this would take too long. Instead take a broad half step to close the distance.

OVER-BINDING THE CRUTCH:

You have over-bound normally from the First Guard. Step forward and, from your right side, strike the opponent's head while executing a shield strike. You can only execute this smoothly if the Crutch was held high enough.

OVER-BINDING THE CRUTCH

The fencers are standing in their guards.

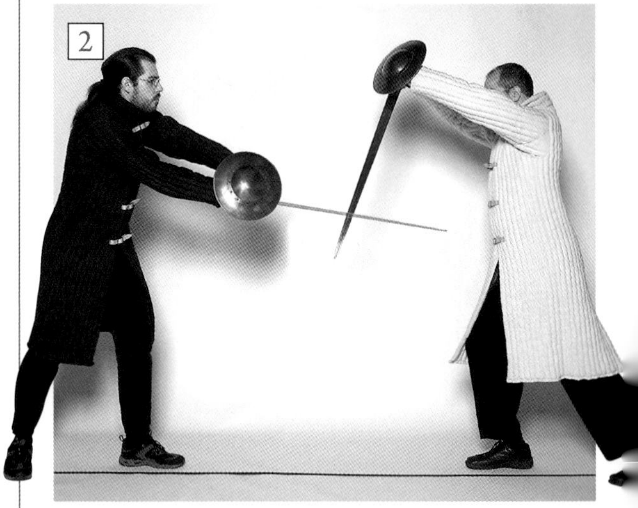

Black over-binds White's Crutch. White's ability to move is seriously limited by the over-binding on the right side.

Step 1

ARMS: You over-bind the Crutch on the—from your point of view—right side. This gives you control and you can feel every action by your opponent. In this bind you may calmly exert some force.

LEGS: Depending on the measure, take a step forward.

Step 2

ARMS: You make a shield strike on the opponent's buckler. Simultaneously with the shield strike, strike or thrust at the opponent's head.

LEGS: Depending on the measure you may have to step forward slightly to execute the shield strike with power.

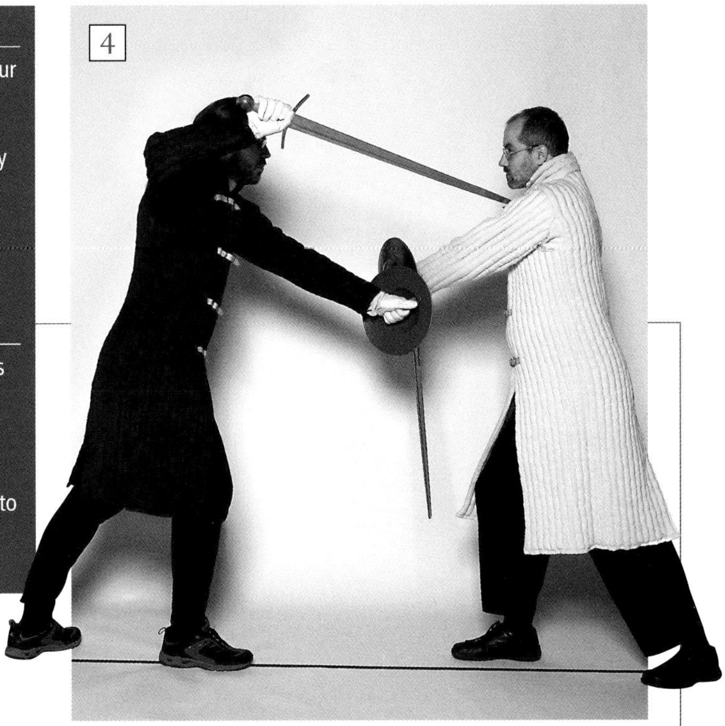

... and thrusts at the upper or lower opening.

Immediately after over-binding Black delivers a shield strike ...

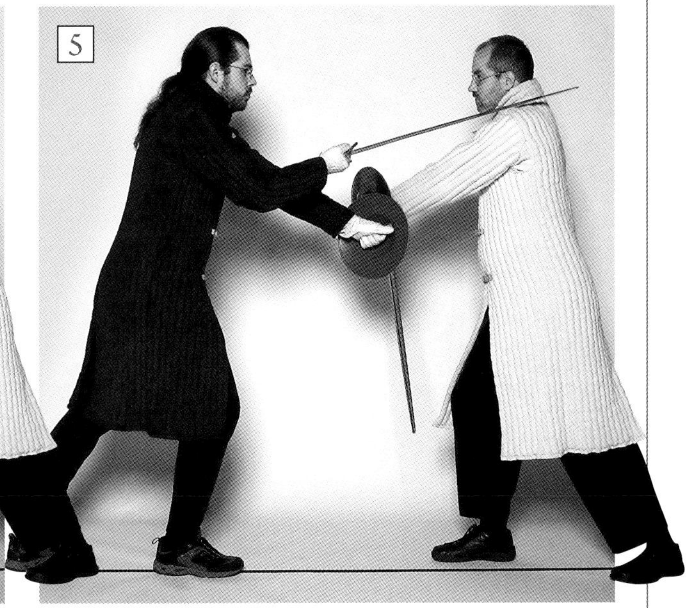

In addition to the thrust, Black can also strike at the head.

CRUTCH AGAINST CRUTCH:
If from the First Guard you have bound with a Crutch against Crutch then both fencers can exploit the same opportunities because they are in the same guard. What matters here is who is quicker and is first to employ his technique. The following techniques therefore apply to both fencers.

1) From the Crutch bind, thrust at the opponent while maintaining the bind. You take a small step to the side to achieve a strong bind. I recommend you roll the buckler over the sword hand for added protection against the opponent's weapon. Liutger expressly declared one should watch out for one's head when using this technique because it leaves the opponent a clear path to strike. For this reason I find it important to shield to the right with the buckler to if necessary block his hands and his attack.

THRUST FROM THE BIND

Step 1

ARMS: You are in the bind, Crutch against Crutch. You have engaged the bind on the left side, as seen from your point of view. Now twist your sword with the hilt somewhat down, remain in the bind, and thrust at the opponent's lower opening. As mentioned, you can control the opponent's weapon with your buckler or hold the buckler beside the sword hand on the left.

LEGS: For the thrust step slightly out of line to the left. This places you at a better angle and makes it more difficult for the opponent to attack your head.

The fencers have bound, Crutch against Crutch.

White strikes from the Crutch while maintaining the bind.

2) From the Crutch bind you can strike directly at the opponent's head. This blow is struck from the left side. The sword hand lies over the shield hand and the buckler shields against the opponent's weapon to the right.

STRIKE AT THE HEAD FROM THE BIND

Step 1

ARMS: From the bind of the Crutches, instead of a thrust you can strike at the opponent's head. To do so you simply shield to the right on the opponent's hands with your buckler and strike or thrust at his head from the left.

LEGS: Depending on the measure you may have to take a step. I recommend you take a slight step out of line to the left here.

From the bind Crutch on Crutch ...

... White strikes at the opponent's head, pushing Black's hands down with his buckler.

SHIELD STRIKE AGAINST CRUTCH

If you are standing in the Crutch and are over-bound you can execute a shield strike and strike the opponent's head. It is a common mistake of beginners to have the buckler hand over the sword hand instead of the reverse. In this case you should not hesitate, instead immediately striking or thrusting at the opening from the left. This is a good possibility if the measure is shortened sufficiently. Ideally you place the buckler hand over the sword hand, take control with the buckler, and strike at the opening. I.33 does not contain the shield strike from the Crutch in this form, but it works very well.

SHIELD STRIKE AGAINST CRUTCH

Step 1

ARMS:	With your buckler you knock the opponent's arms or weapon down and forward. Depending on the measure, try to wedge the opponent's weapon or hands between your buckler and the opponent's body.
LEGS:	Step forward to acquire the necessary force and close the distance.

Step 2

ARMS:	Now strike at the head. Should your sword hand be under your shield hand then thrust or strike at the head from the left. To do so you must work from the outside over the opponent's arms.

White was over-bound in the Crutch.

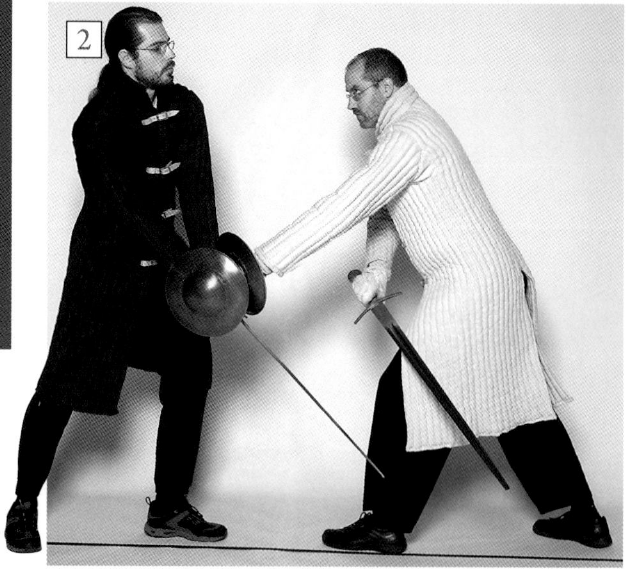

He strikes Black's hands with his buckler, forcing them downwards.

White's sword hand is under his shield hand. White therefore thrusts from the outside at Black's upper opening.

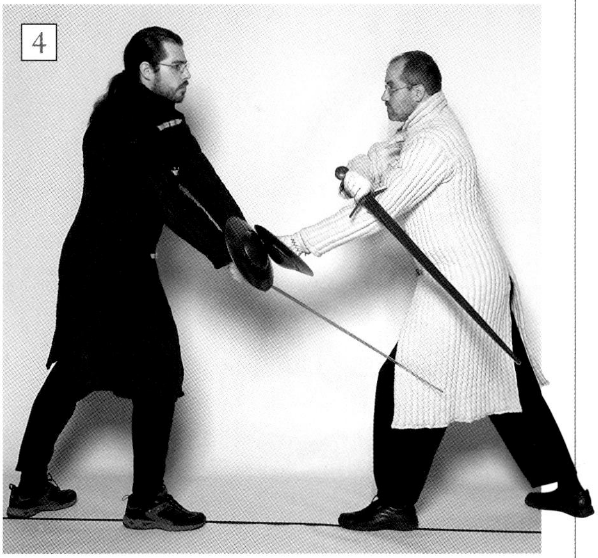

Ideally the sword hand is held high while delivering the blow

… can easily strike at the opening.

TAKE THE ARMS FROM THE CRUTCH

If you were over-bound in the Crutch, then you can also take the arms of the opponent. To do this, you reach over the opponent's arms with your buckler hand, if possible behind the elbows. Liutger shows the sword simply hanging down. From this position you can slice through the opponent's face or neck or you can employ the pommel. You can also slice through the lower openings from below.

The break of this technique looks like this: your opponent can escape your reaching for his arms by placing his sword on his breast in a position similar to that of the Sixth Guard. If you continue attacking then at most you will catch his blade, and your opponent then stands in a good thrusting position. In I.33, however, Taking the Arms takes place with the shield hand (4v/8). Both variations work.

TAKE THE ARMS FROM THE CRUTCH

Step 1

ARMS: You are standing in the Crutch and your opponent has bound you on the outside. Remain engaged in the bind and with your buckler hand reach around the opponent's arms. Reach over the sword hand with the buckler hand, then slice through the lower opening. Reach through under the sword hand, then slice the opponent through the face or strike him with the pommel.

LEGS: Here you must take a small step forward.

Step 2

ARMS: If your opponent tries to take your arms pull your sword back with the pommel to your chest. Your opponent thus attacks your blade. In addition, if the measure is close strike at his face with your buckler; otherwise make a thrust.

LEGS: If there is sufficient time then step back, which may enable you to deliver another thrust.

Black is standing in the Crutch ...

... and is over-bound by White.

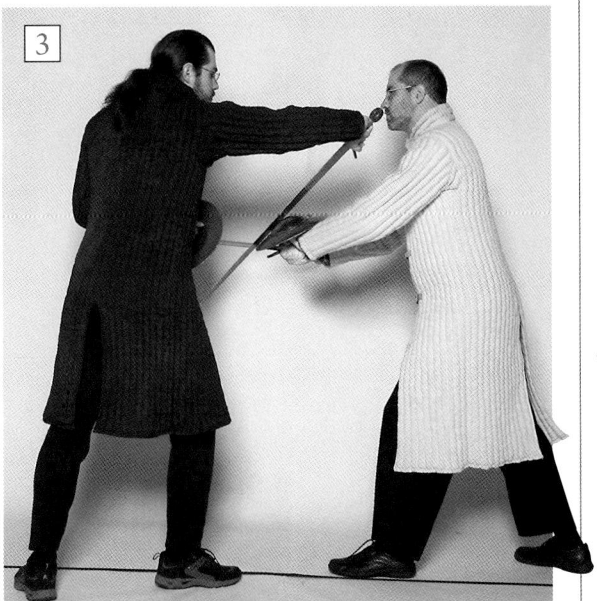

Black steps forward, strikes at White's head with his pommel ...

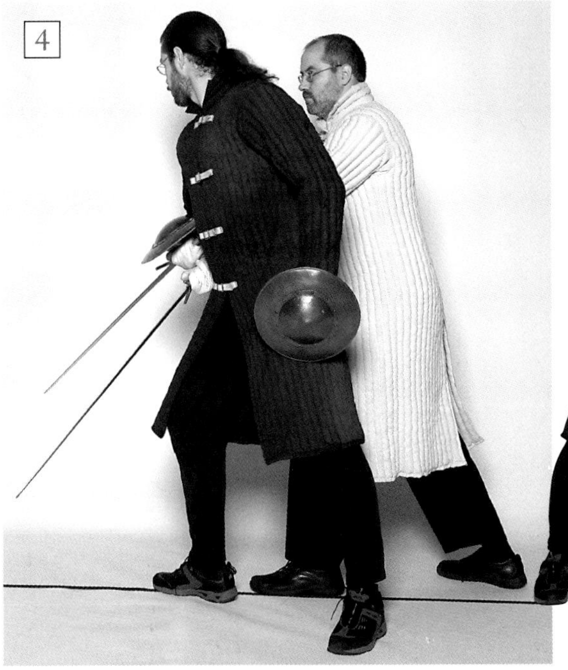

... and takes the arms as usual.

THE BREAK TO TAKING THE ARMS

White is standing in the Crutch ...

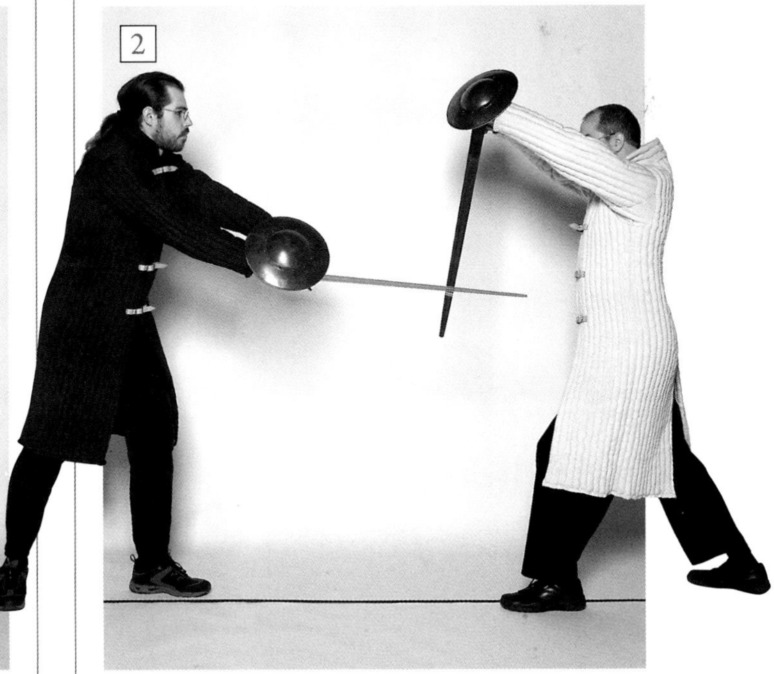

... and is over-bound by Black.

White tries to take Black's arms …

… but Black pulls his sword back and is thus in a thrusting position.

Liutger points out that in the First Guard play against the Crutch, the one who is bound can try to flee. In this case attempt to follow him. This is of particular importance with the Crutch.

The fencers are again in the Crutch and the First Guard.

White overbinds Black's Crutch.

Black disengages the bind and steps back.

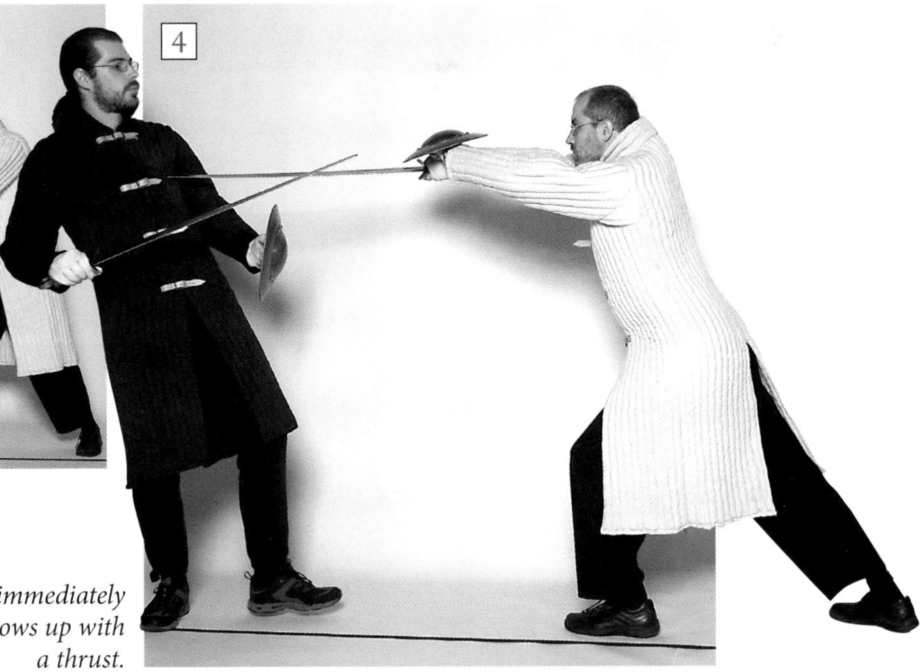

White immediately follows up with a thrust.

THE FIRST GUARD VERSUS LONG-POINT

The Long-Point counter against the First Guard combines two extremes. The Long-Point is a guard that optically keeps the opponent at a distance. The fencer stretches his sword forward, presents himself threateningly, and sets up a barrier. The opponent finds himself confronted by the point and cannot make a direct attack. The First Guard, on the other hand, is the complete opposite. It keeps its distance and is completely defensive. The opponent is lured closer; he is invited to begin a direct attack.

This combination is also very interesting in a tactical aspect. Liutger explains that the Long-Point is a frequently-used counter. The response to it is the possibility of binding, either over or under. It is important to state again that an over-bind is better than an under-bind.

The beginning situation: you are standing in the First Guard and your opponent moves into the Long-Point. The two possible binds follow:

1) Over-Bind

You over-bind and push the opponent's blade downward. This results in a bind in which your blade comes to rest on the right side of the opponent's blade as seen from your perspective. Your buckler covers to the left. From this position you make a shield strike and strike at the opponent's head.

OVER-BIND AND SHIELD STRIKE

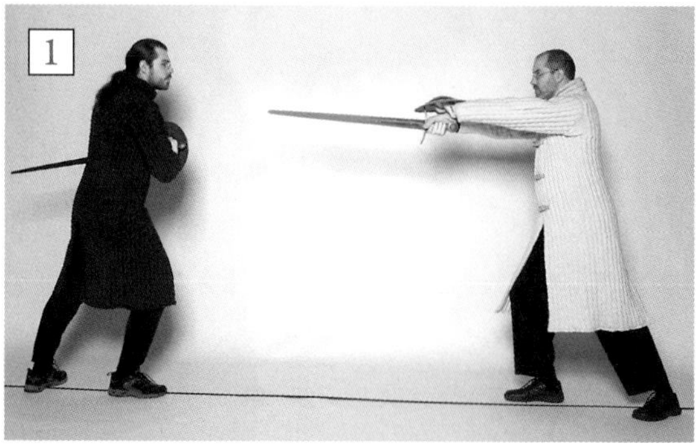

White is standing in Long-Point, Black in the First Guard.

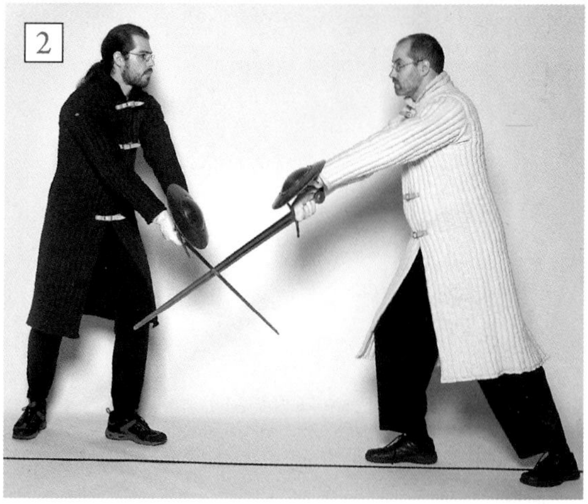

Black steps forward and over-binds White's Long-Point, pushing the opposing blade downward.

Step 1

ARMS: From the First Guard over-bind the opponent's blade and push it down and to the right or outward. You thus control the opponent's blade with your sword.

Step 2

ARMS: Now deliver a shield strike by striking with your buckler at the precise spot where buckler and sword intersect. You are now in control of both weapons with your buckler. Now simply strike a blow at the opponent's head with your long edge.

LEGS: Step your left leg forward during the shield strike.

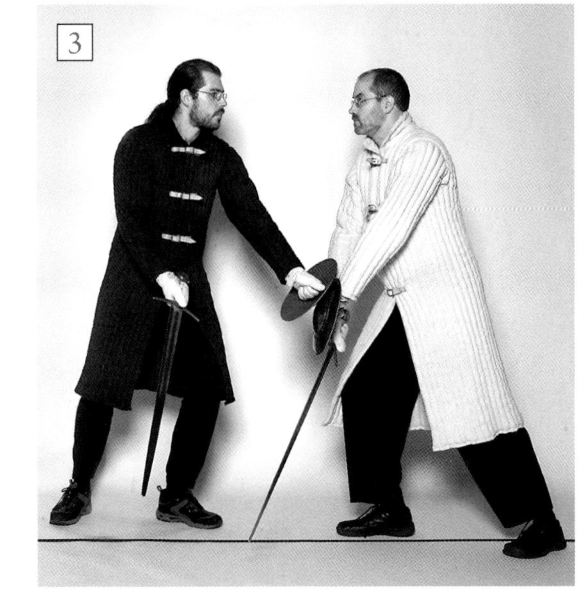

Black regains control with his buckler …

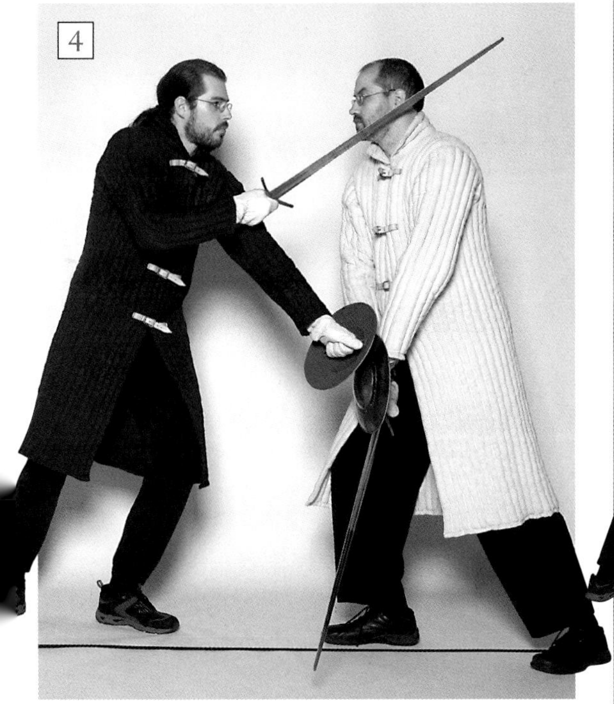

… and strikes at White's opening with the free blade.

2) Under-Bind and Change of Sword / Nod

You under-bind on the right side of the opponent's blade as seen from your perspective. As you are now in the poorer position, you execute a Change of Sword by striking the opponent's blade from above with

OVER-BIND AND CHANGE OF SWORD / NOD

Step 1	
ARMS:	You have under-bound on the right. As soon as you feel pressure from the opposing blade move your blade in a clockwise circular motion around the opponent's blade and strike his blade with the long edge of your sword. Then Nod at his head.
LEGS:	Step out of line to the right with the Change of Sword and the Nod.

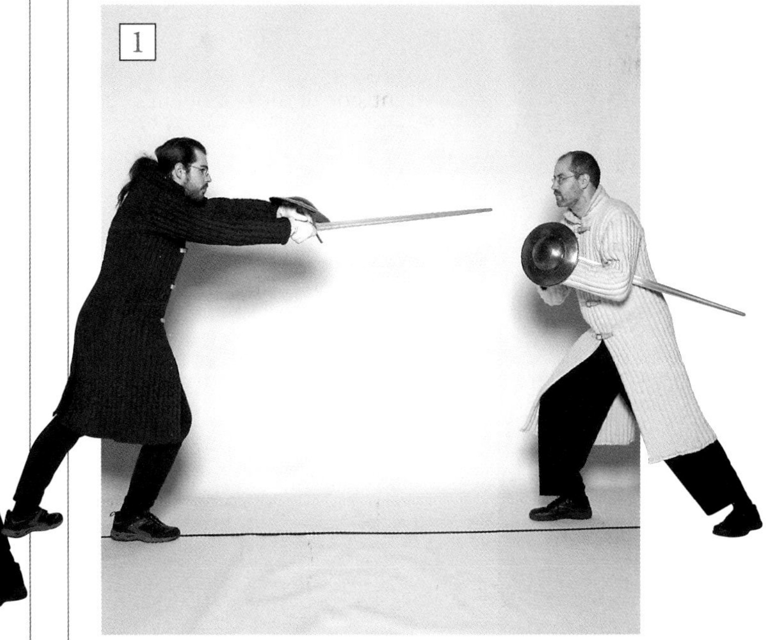

The fencers are facing each other.

your blade. Be sure to place your sword hand over your buckler hand as you strike. From this position you can again Nod. Your under-bind merely gives the opponent the incentive to act and with the Change of Sword you can "trap" him, so to speak. This works very well, especially when there is some distance between the fencers.

White under-binds Black's Long-Point, displacing his blade outward.

White makes a Change of Sword while Black attempts an attack.

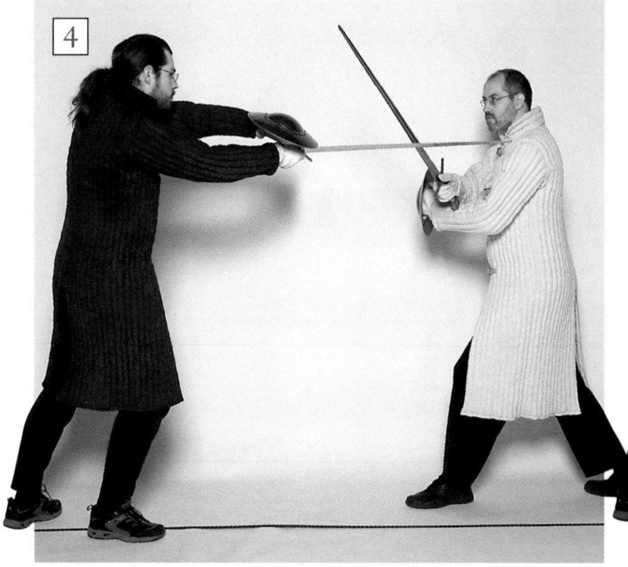

White's Change of Sword captures Black's attack. Be sure to move the sword hand over the shield hand at this moment.

White has executed the Change of Sword, over-bound, and strikes Black's blade from below.

White immediately takes control through a strike with his buckler …

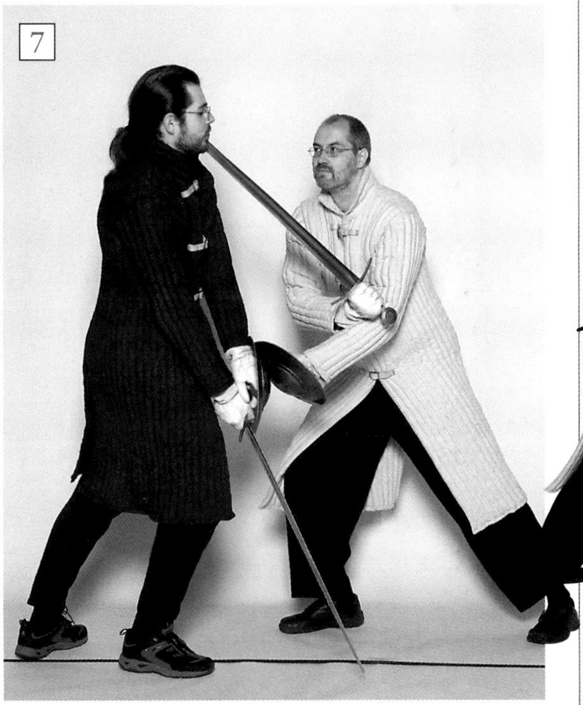

… and Nods at Black's head.

ADDITIONAL TECHNIQUE: STEPPING THROUGH

If you engage in the bind from below right then you create other possibilities. You can step through very well from the low bind. To do so, you engage in the bind as described and push the opponent's blade up and to the left while with your right arm you form a sort of arch and hold your hilt high. Move straight forward with your buckler and step through beneath the arch. As soon as you are the proper distance deliver a shield strike and, as soon as the bind disengages, make a descending strike with your blade from the left at your opponent's head or slice through his face. As you are beginning from the First Guard you have the correct hand positioning and this technique can be executed very quickly. It is entirely in the sense of I.33 and is equivalent to the stepping through movement from the First Play.

The fencers are standing in the Long-Point and First Guard.

White underbinds Black's Long-Point …

… knocks Black's hands to the side with his buckler and strikes at his head. It is important to work with the buckler hand under the sword hand.

Liutger offers a third possibility in response to the statically outstretched blade of the Long-Point. This somewhat unorthodox method can often be used effectively in free fighting: your opponent stands in front of you in the Long-Point and you are standing in the First Guard. Now, with your left hand, grasp your sword by the blade—roughly at the midpoint—so that your right hand is free. With it grab the opponent's point, hindering him. Here Liutger also states that the fencer in the Long-Point cannot free his sword unless he strikes a blow with his buckler. The simplest thing is to now thrust with the sword or—if you reach a close measure—strike with the buckler.

The break to this is quite simple: the fencer standing in the Long-Point thrusts the edge of his buckler forward along his blade while pulling his sword back. As a result, he ends up in a thrusting position. In practice this break is very difficult, especially if, after grasping your blade, your opponent immediately pushes on your right side, steps forward with his left leg, and makes a descending thrust. This attack with the sword is the logical thing to do, but it does not appear in I.33.

GRASP THE BLADE AND THRUST

Step 1

ARMS: You are standing in the First Guard. Now move your sword forward along the inner side of your buckler hand and grasp your sword at the midpoint of the blade. To the opponent this looks like a normal attack with the sword.

Step 2

ARMS: Grasp your blade with your left hand, let go of the grip with your right hand, and grasp the opponent's point. Push the point down and to the right and deliver a descending strike at the opponent's face with the buckler/sword combination.

LEGS: When you reach for the point step your left leg forward and slightly out of line to the left. The whole thing must take place smoothly and quickly.

The Break to the Grip on the Long-Point

ARMS: If your opponent reaches for your point, then you can only break this grip by moving your buckler forward along the blade and striking the opponent's fingers with the edge of your buckler while drawing back your sword.

The fencers are standing in their guards. White in the First Guard can very easily attack the blade of the sword in the buckler hand without Black noticing it.

White steps forward and grasps Black's point.

White pushes Black's blade to the side, steps further forward, and thrusts at the opening from above.

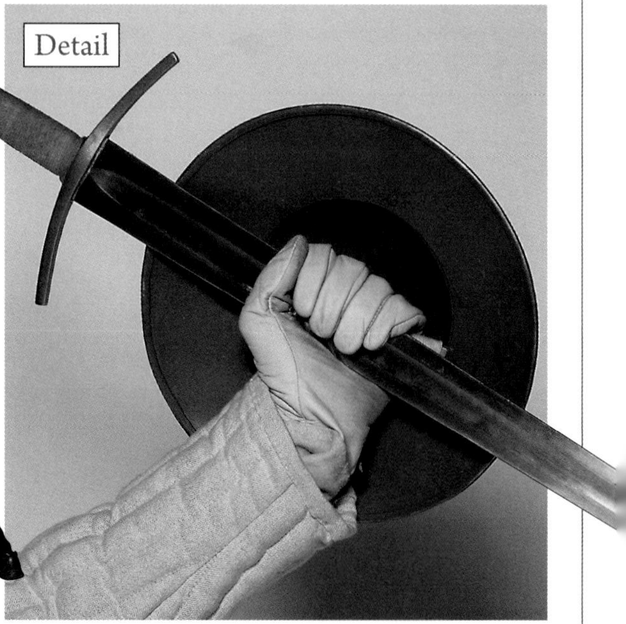

The left hand from the other side.

With some practice you can grasp the blade with the buckler hand very well. If you know your sword then you also know where you should grasp the blade to deliver a surprising and easy-to-handle sword-buckler combination.

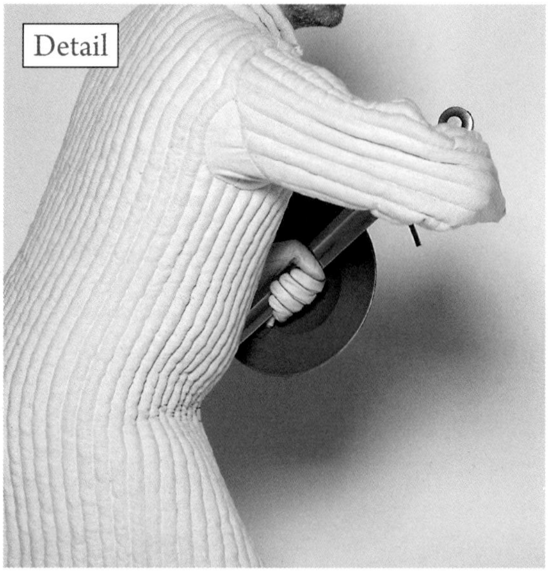

Another illustration of gripping the blade. It is most convincing if you grip the blade as you are moving forward. In this way your opponent cannot anticipate the grasping of the blade.

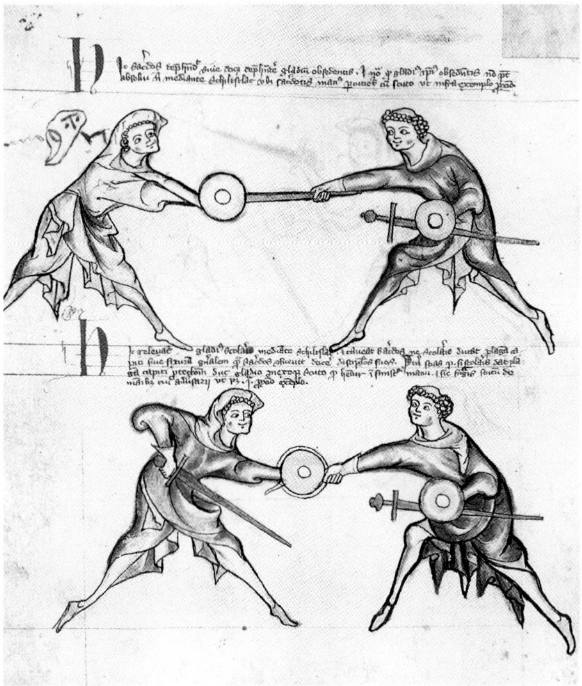

Page 16v/32 from I.33: grasping the blade in Long-Point and the associated break.

FIRST GUARD VERSUS THE FOURTH GUARD

Here the Fourth Guard is met with the First. Actually, the Fourth Guard is the first to be assumed and the First Guard is executed as a counter to it. The fencer in the Fourth Guard finds himself facing the First Guard and immediately shifts into the Half-Shield. The possibilities explained previously arise from this combination of First Guard against Half-Shield.

Black in the Fourth Guard can do little against the First Guard.

For this reason Black changes into the Half-Shield, placing him in a very good position. The First Guard play against the Half-Shield can begin.

7.2 The Second Guard and its Plays

The Second Guard is one of the most natural of the seven guards. With the sword over the shoulder, it is the starting point for particularly powerful attacks. The most probable attack from the Second Guard is an over-cut. Interestingly, Liutger only offers the Upper Displacement and the Half-Shield as a response or counter to the Second Guard. This is a clue to how important and effective the displacement is.

The Second Guard versus the Upper Displacement
The play begins with one fencer in the Second Guard, whereupon his opponent changes into the upper displacement. Any direct attack by the fencer in the Second Guard would now practically be suicide, as this attack could be met at any time by a shield strike or thrust strike. There is just one possibility left to the fencer in the Second Guard: he must bind to gain control of the opposing blade. He binds in a posture similar to the upper displacement with the long edge of his sword.

The Second Guard and the upper protection.
In the lower illustration the protection is bound (Page 9r/17 in I.33).

From this position both fencers have the same opportunities. Again, it depends on who moves first. Liutger mentions here that the fencer in the counter-guard has the advantage. The situation discharges itself explosively at the moment of binding. How to thrust from the displacement is shown on 10v/20 in I.33. Regardless of which position you find yourself in, there are now three possibilities open to you:

Black is standing in the Second Guard, White is in the upper protection.

Black has bound the upper protection.

1) Step Through: step to the left beside the opponent's hands. As you move sideways strike at the opponent's head with your long edge while you control his weapon from the left side with your buckler. This technique is similar to Doubling with the long sword and is not only very fast, but also difficult to break. Like Doubling, it works best if the opponent is strong in the bind.

STEPPING THROUGH

Step 1

ARMS:	From the bind, twist your blade and strike at the opponent's head with the long edge. With your buckler you shield the opponent's weapon from the left so that his weapon is now between your buckler and your sword.
BODY:	Be sure that when you deliver the strike you are standing to the left of and beside the opponent's hands. If necessary lean outward slightly.
LEGS:	As you step through step left beside the opponent's hands.

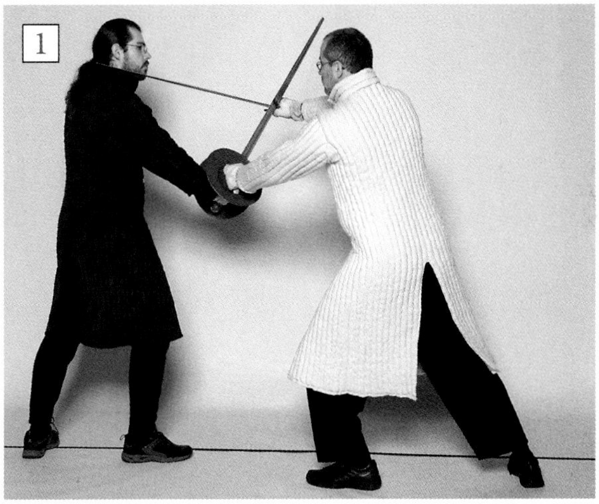

White steps to the left out of line, shields the opponent's weapon with his buckler, and gently pushes it downward. At the same time White strikes at Black's head behind his blade. Black's blade is against White's cross guard.

Stepping Through from the other side: here White has bound Black's upper protection.

Black steps out of line …

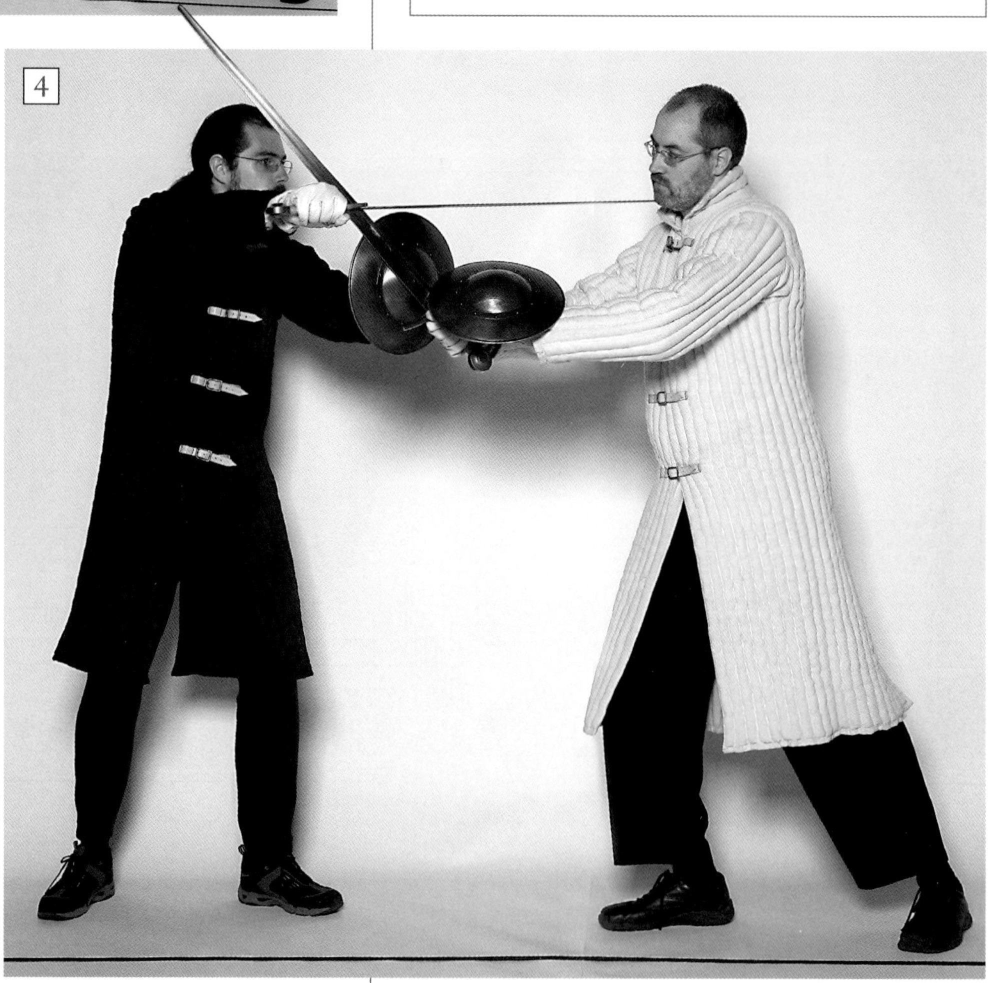

… and strikes at White's head behind his blade. With his buckler he controls White's hands and thus his weapon.

ALTERNATIVE TO STEPPING THROUGH

There is an alternative method of stepping through: you are standing in the upper protection and your opponent has bound. At the moment your opponent binds you, push his blade down and to the left with your short edge, strike his hands with your buckler, and simultaneously make a descending strike against his arms or head. With this action you lean slightly to the right or take a small step to the right with your front leg.

2) You can strike at the opponent's head from your left side. At the same time as your strike you simply make a small shield strike against the opponent's hands. He is thus controlled for a short time and you can strike at his head. At the same time step to the right or lean forward to the right to protect your head.

STRIKE AT THE HEAD FROM THE LEFT

Black has stepped out of line and has engaged a bind against the upper protection.

Step 1

ARMS:	From the bind you deliver a short shield strike against the opponent's weapon. This short strike with the buckler is made essentially from the wrist. At that moment you have taken control with the buckler and can now strike at the opponent's head with your sword.
BODY:	Step slightly out of line to the right to get a good angle and dodge somewhat around the opponent's weapon

The fencers are again standing in their guards.

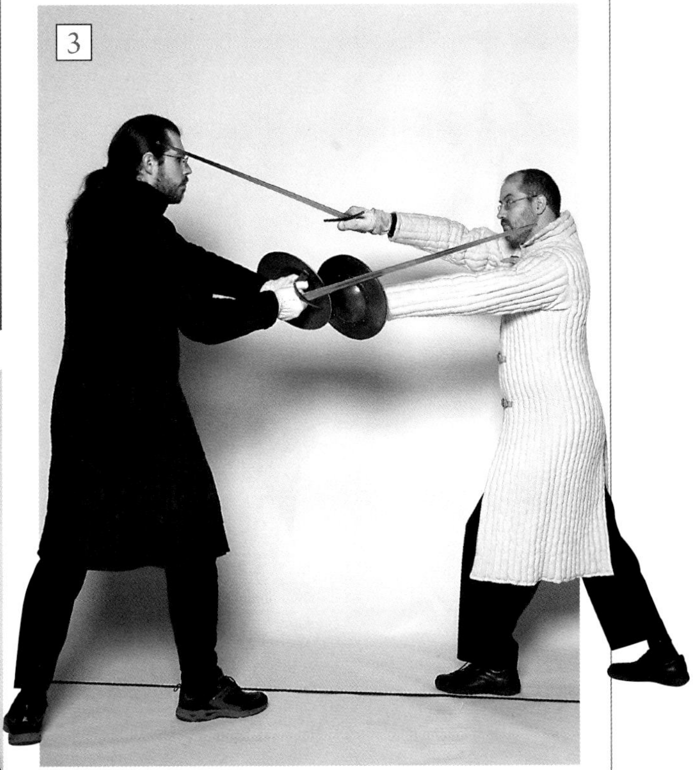

White pushes Black's hands to the side and strikes at the left side of his head. White has stepped out of line to get a better angle.

3) Just as with the blow from the left side you can also strike from the right side. Once again, you deliver a shield strike and strike directly at the opponent's head, this time from the other side.

STRIKE TO THE HEAD FROM THE RIGHT

Step 1

ARMS:	As in the strike from the left, here too a short shield strike is made from the wrist, followed by a strike at the head from the right. Alternately you could also thrust at the face simply by allowing the point to drop. The backs of your hands face left. Sword and buckler are moved while close together, rather than as a unit. This enables you to strike simultaneously with sword and buckler.
BODY & LEGS:	Lean somewhat to the right or step slightly out of line to the right.

From the bind against the upper protection ...

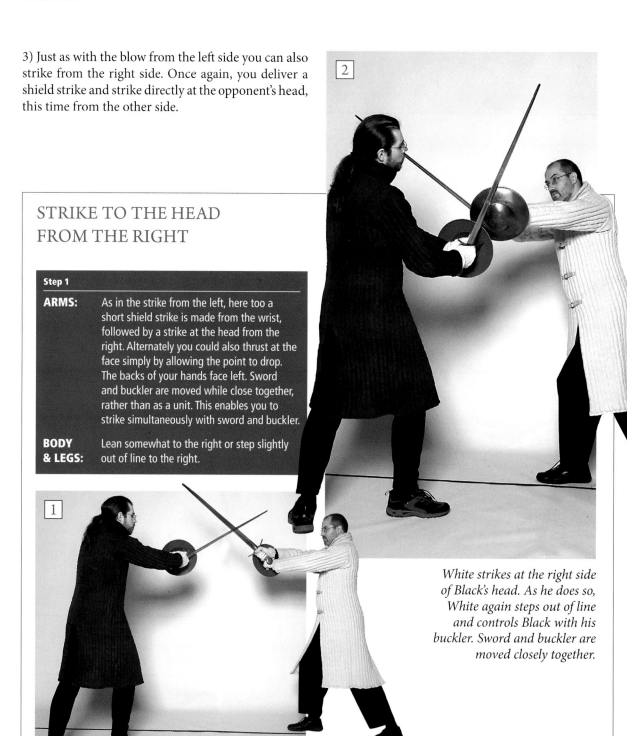

White strikes at the right side of Black's head. As he does so, White again steps out of line and controls Black with his buckler. Sword and buckler are moved closely together.

The Break for these Techniques

The break against the techniques from the upper displacement largely depends on when you initiate the break. If you begin the break early—almost immediately after the opponent binds—then you can simply over-bind to the left, push the opponent's sword down, and strike at his head. This is easiest to execute if your opponent's blade is in motion.

THE BREAK AGAINST THE STEP THROUGH

The fencers are again standing in the Second Guard and the upper protection.

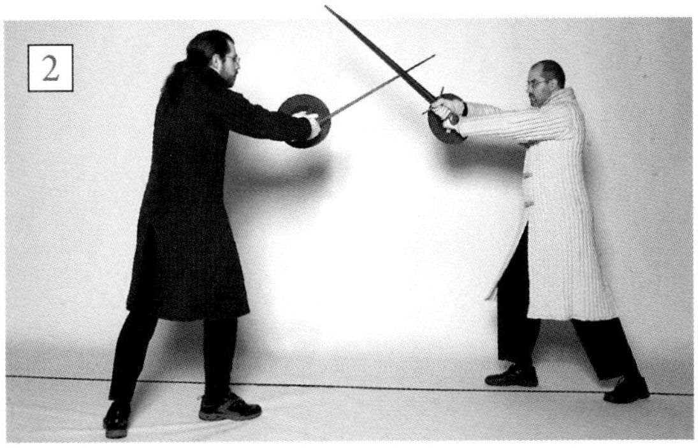

Black again steps out of line and engages the bind.

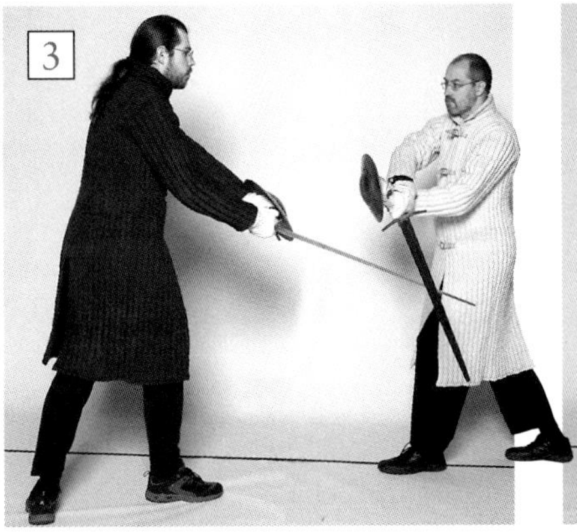

White over-binds to the left. Be sure to move the buckler under the sword hand. As he over-binds, White steps forward.

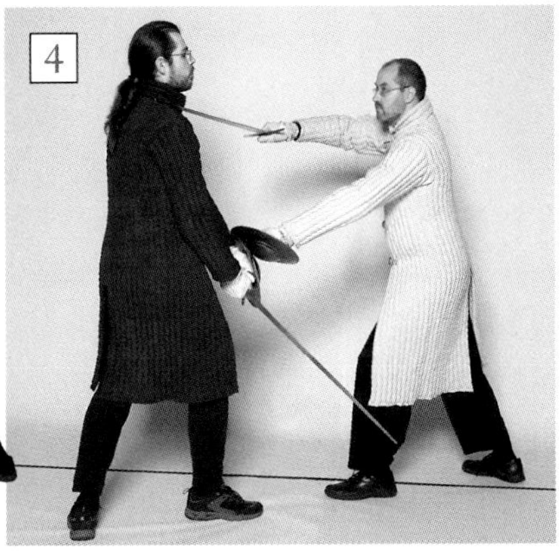

White immediately takes control with the buckler and strikes at Black's head.

Step 1

ARMS: Your opponent binds against your protection and also takes the initiative. He is therefore the first to begin an attack from the bind. Move your blade down to the left, thus over-binding. This is quite easy if you begin soon enough, as the opponent's blade is in motion.

Step 2

ARMS: Deliver a shield strike beneath your sword hand and strike at the opponent's head.

LEGS: You may have to take a step forward here.

On the other hand, if you begin your break rather later then you can take the opponent's arms. To do this you simply reach over the opponent's arms with your sword arm and turn so that your right shoulder rests against the left shoulder of the opponent. Continue this rotation movement and throw your opponent. You should gain a light grip on the opponent's arm behind or on the elbows. While you take the arms, in the same movement you can also strike the opponent in the face with the pommel.

THE BREAK FOR THE BREAK:
Breaking the over-bind is very simple: you simply continue the movement in a circular motion and from your left side thrust upward at the opponent's head while making a shield strike to the right. This is one of the few situations that your shield hand lies over your sword hand.

THE BREAK TO THE BREAK

Step 1	
ARMS:	If you are over-bound then simply continue moving clockwise under your buckler hand and thrust at the opponent's head from the other side. Meanwhile, shield right with your buckler and push the opponent's hands outward.

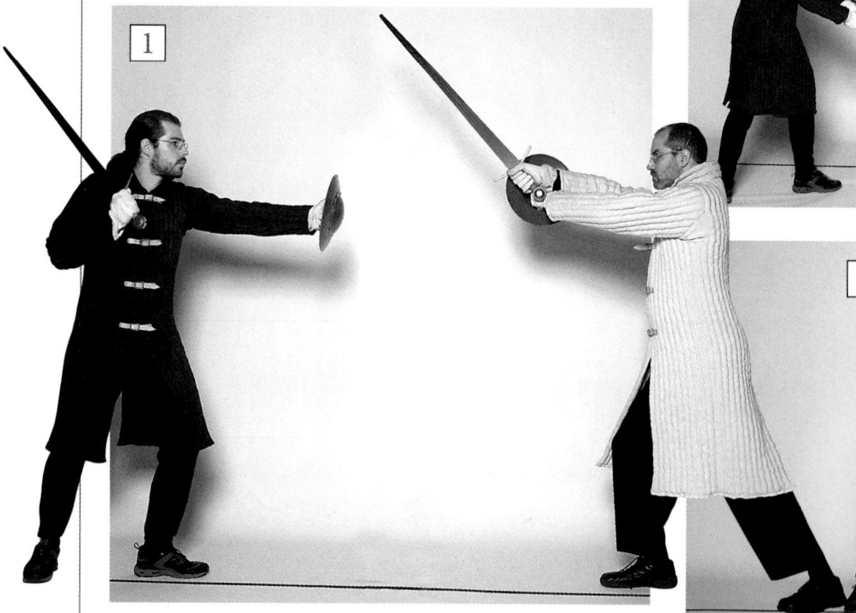

The fencers in the familiar starting position.

Black has again engaged the bind.

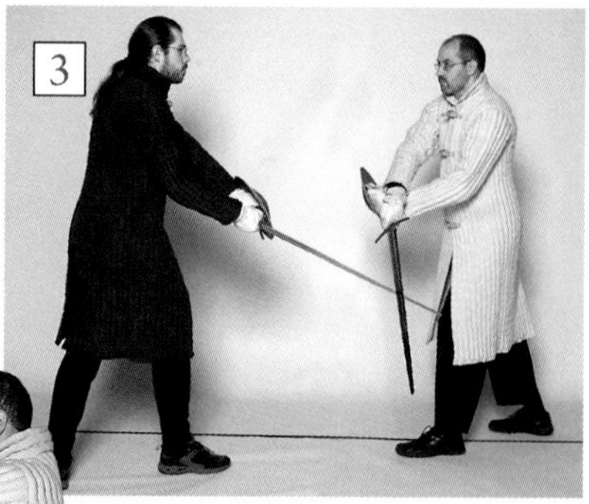

White over-binds, …

… whereupon Black immediately interrupts White's bind with his buckler, …

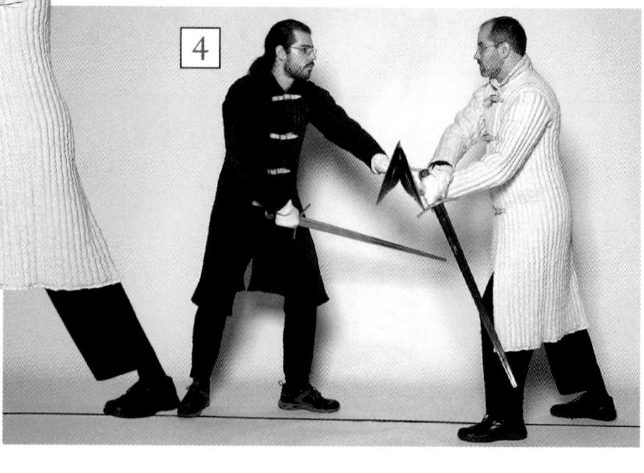

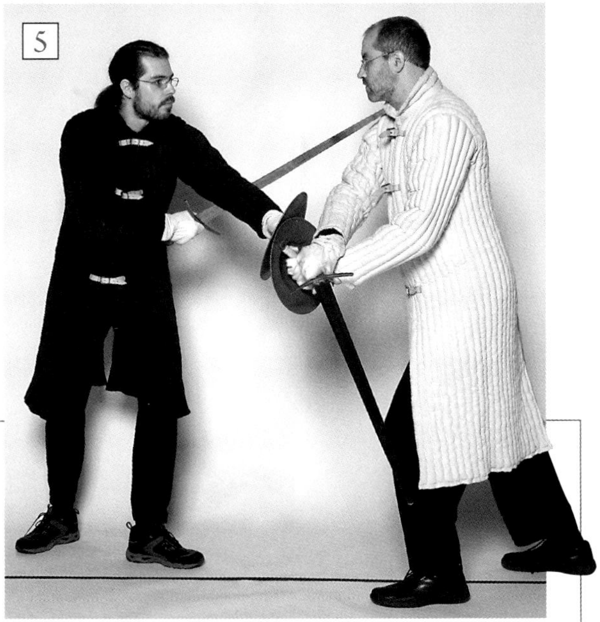

... continues moving his blade clockwise, and thrusts at the head from the left outside. This is one of the few situations in which it makes sense to work with the sword arm under the shield arm.

The thrust from the outside seen from the other side.

TAKE THE ARMS

The fencers are standing in the Second Guard and the upper protection.

Black engages the bind.

Step 1

ARMS:	Push the opponent's blade to the left and with your sword arm reach over the opponent's arms, if possible behind the elbows. Place your right leg behind the opponent's legs. You can then throw him backward by his neck. But pay attention to his weapons as you do so and protect yourself with the buckler. Alternately: Push the opponent's blade to the outside as usual, and with your buckler hand reach over his arms. Then strike him in the face with the pommel.
LEGS:	Depending on the measure, take a step here.

White strikes Black's weapon with his buckler and thus is in control for a sufficient time. Simultaneously White steps forward and strikes at Black's chin with the pommel.

While White maintains control with the buckler he grasps over Black's arms.

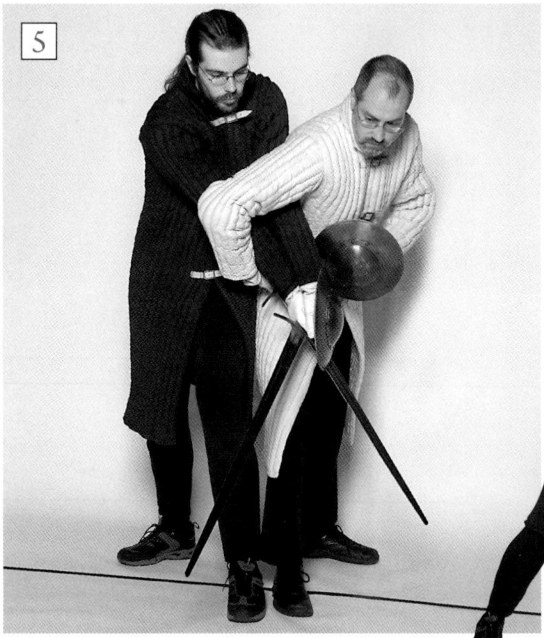

Here is the grasping of the arms from the front. Control with the buckler can be plainly seen.

THE SECOND GUARD VERSUS HALF-SHIELD

Like almost every guard, the Second Guard can be answered with the Half-Shield. Liutger states here that ordinary fencers would try to separate sword and shield with a powerful descending blow or strike between sword and shield. This technique is obvious, and it also works against fencers who either react too slowly or are not prepared for it.

SEPARATE SWORD AND SHIELD

Step 1

ARMS:	In the Half-Shield, turn so that your buckler intercepts the opponent's strike and simultaneously thrust or strike at the opponent's opening.
BODY:	Lean slightly to the side here to get out of the danger zone.
LEGS:	A step to the side—to the left or right, depending on the attack—not only puts you in a safe position, it also presents you with a better attack angle.

Black in the Half-Shield, White in the Second Guard.

The correct reaction is the thrust strike. One strikes the opponent's blade with the buckler while making an attack. For an attack to your right side in particular it is important to place the sword hand over the shield hand.

White makes a powerful descending strike along Black's blade. As a result, White can strike between Black's sword and buckler and reach his hands.

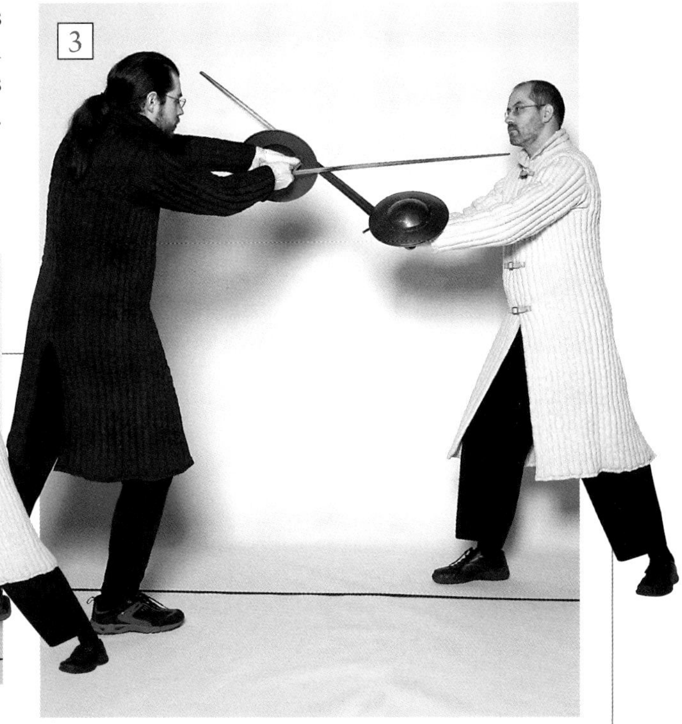

Black can simply take the blow with his buckler by turning the shield upward …

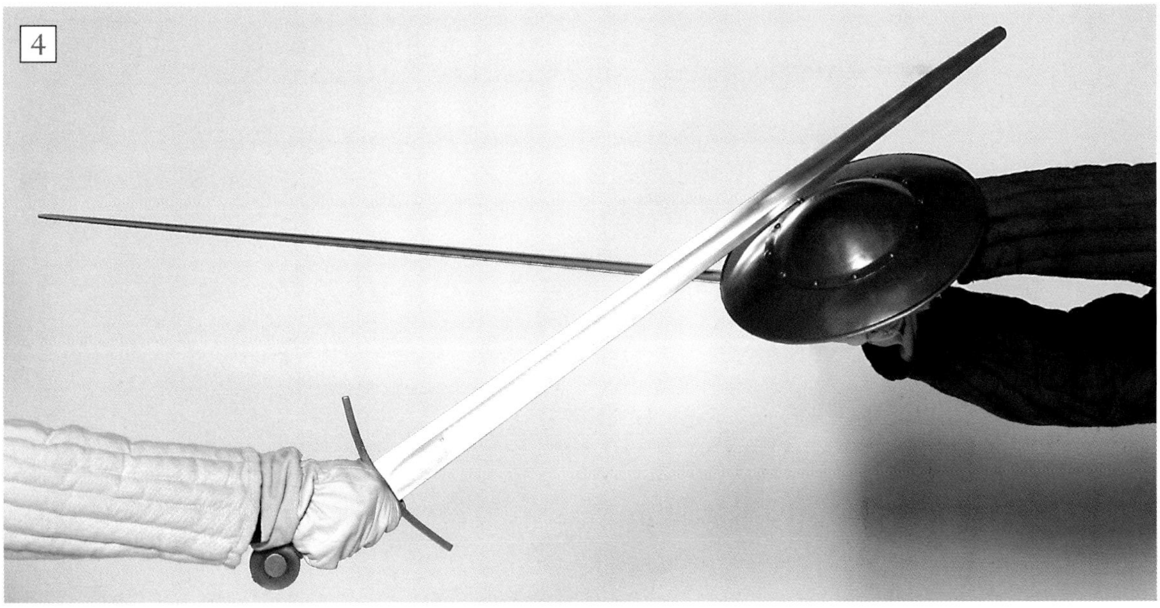

… and simultaneously thrusting or striking forward.

7.3 The Third Guard and its Plays

The Third Guard resembles the Second. The sword lies over the left shoulder; therefore, a left over-cut is the most likely attack. The three upper guards—the Second, Third, and the Fourth—are all very similar. They are the three guards from which over-cuts are most often struck.

The Third Guard versus Displacements

If the Third Guard is countered with the middle displacement then one should over-bind from the Third Guard immediately and without hesitation. The cover provided by the buckler is important. Should you do something else, then you have no control over the opponent's weapon. Every direct attack will probably be answered with a thrust strike or shield strike. From the bind you can execute a shield strike in combination with a strike at the head.

The Third Guard and the upper protection are depicted at the top of the page while the bind is shown at the bottom (Page 12r/23 in I.33).

SHIELD STRIKE FROM THE BIND

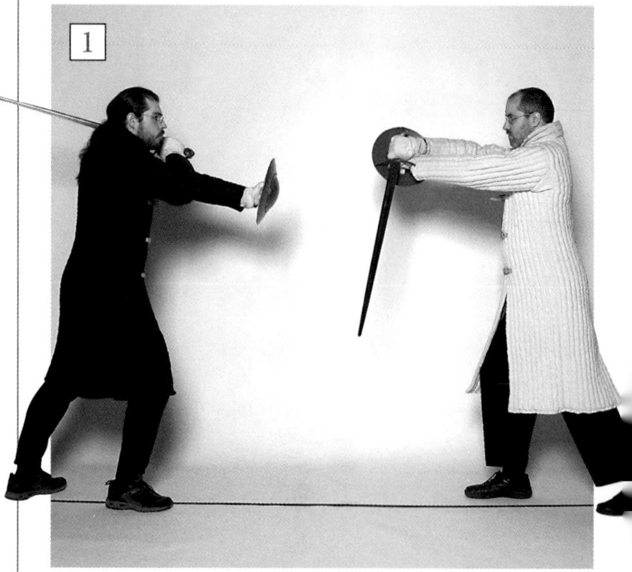

The fencers are in the Third Guard and the middle protection.

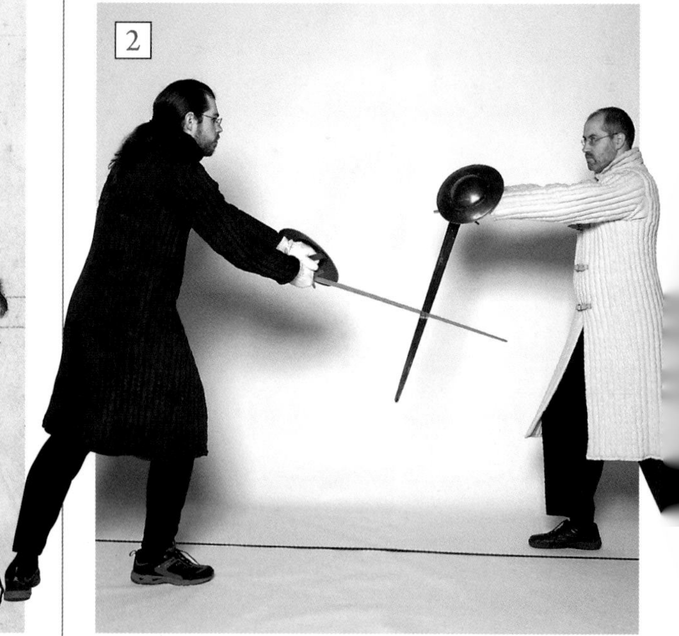

Black binds White's middle protection and White moves his buckler to the left.

3

Black delivers a shield strike …

4

… and strikes at White's head.

Step 1

ARMS: Engage the bind on top of the opponent's blade. Be careful not to bind too much in the foible, as this will leave you in a position that is too low. Ideally you bind in the middle of the blade.

LEGS: You may possibly make a forward gliding or adjustment step to close the distance somewhat.

Step 2

ARMS: Deliver a shield strike and strike at the opponent's head.

LEGS: You may possibly have to shorten the measure here.

The break for this is Taking the Arms. If your opponent has over-bound your middle displacement then you take his arms. In I.33 this is carried out with the shield hand, which is also why you move the buckler to the left if your opponent binds. But you can also take the opponent's arms with your sword hand. This places you somewhat out of the danger zone.

If you take the arms with your shield hand then raise your sword slightly and with your buckler attack

TAKE THE ARMS WITH THE BUCKLER HAND

Step 1

ARMS:	Maintain the bind, reach through beneath the sword hand with the buckler hand, and clasp the opponent's arms. As soon as you have a sure grip on his arms slice through his face or strike with the pommel.
LEGS:	As you grasp the arms, step forward with your left leg to close the distance.

The fencers again in the Third Guard and the middle protection.

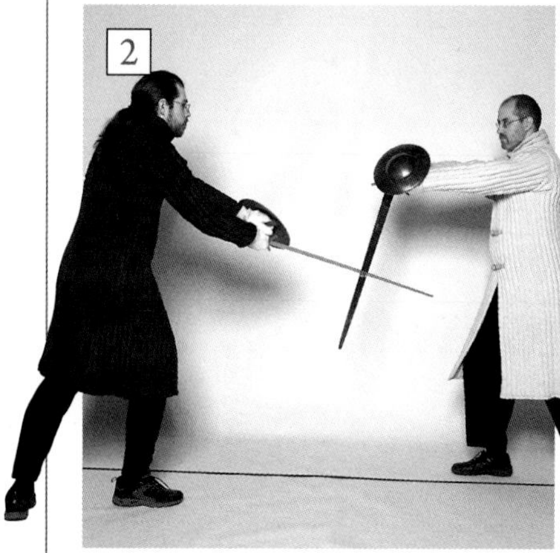

Black binds the middle protection.

White reaches over Black's arms with his buckler, taking a step forward with his left leg.

White reaches over Black's arms with his buckler, taking a step forward with his left leg.

straight forward beneath the sword hand at the opponent's arms. This places your sword hand over your shield hand, enabling you to slice through the opponent's face.

If you take the arms with your sword hand then you again turn your right shoulder toward the opponent, reach over his arms, and continue the rotation movement.

TAKE THE ARMS WITH THE SWORD HAND

Step 1

ARMS: Maintain the bind and turn your right shoulder to the left so that you are standing with your back to the opponent. As you are turning, reach over the opponent's arms with your sword hand. Be sure to get as close to the opponent as possible. If possible, grasp behind the elbows.

LEGS: You must get as close to the opponent as possible.

Black has again engaged the bind.

White reaches over Black's arms with his sword hand. White maintains the bind so that he can feel what Black is doing at all times. The buckler is likewise shielding downward.

White seizes Black's arms and begins grappling.

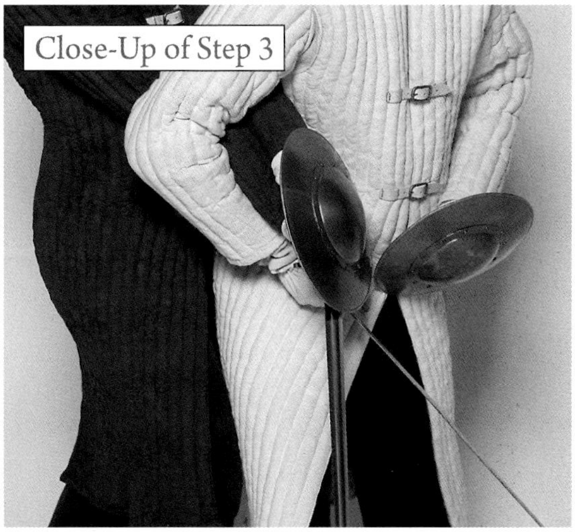

Close-up of taking the arms.

If you are standing in the middle displacement against the Third Guard and your opponent hesitates you should try to begin an attack. Here this attack is a thrust during which your buckler protects the top of your sword hand.

THE THRUST FROM THE MIDDLE PROTECTION

Step 1

ARMS: Thrust at the upper opening. This must take place explosively.

LEGS: You should close the distance as quickly as possible. Spring into the thrust, but be sure to have good balance and leg positioning after the thrust. Should your opponent parry the thrust you must be able to react immediately.

The fencers are standing in their guards.

Black hesitates, whereupon White immediately thrusts from the middle protection.

The Third Guard versus Half-Shield

If your opponent counters your Third Guard with the Half-Shield then you have the same opportunities as before in the First Guard. If the opponent assumes the Half-Shield you should fall under sword and shield. All subsequent positions then develop from this position (as in section 7.1: The First Guard and its Plays).

From the Third Guard you can fall under sword and shield with the short or long edge. If you fall under sword and shield with the long edge it makes sense to over-bind and then slide downward, forcing the opponent's blade to the side. This places you in a better thrusting position.

The fencers in the Half-Shield and the Third Guard.

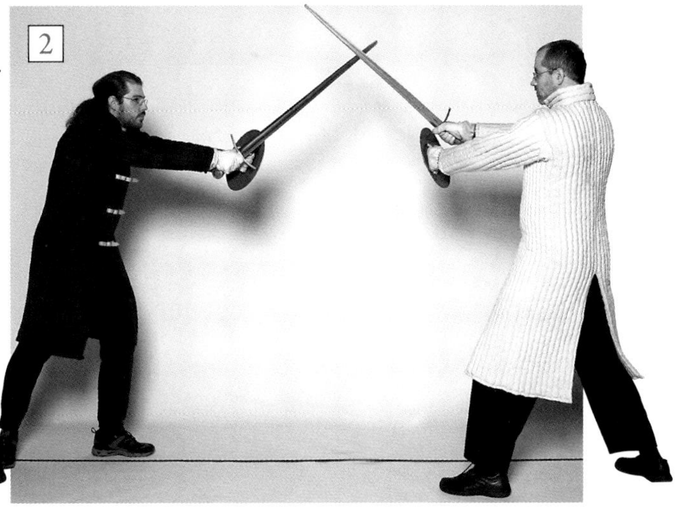

White binds with the long edge in Black's foible, ...

... pushes Black's blade aside, while he slides under ...

... and then immediately thrusts at the opening.

As the Third Guard against the Half-Shield offers the same possibilities as the First Guard (see section 7.1), here they are only summarized. If you fall under sword and shield from the Third Guard, depending on the bind you have the following possibilities:

- Thrust if your opponent does nothing.
- Your opponent over-binds and you have bound in your foible: Change of Sword.
- Your opponent over-binds and you have bound in the middle of the blade: Step Through.
- Your opponent over-binds and you have bound in your forte: take the arms.

The fencers in the Half-Shield and the Third Guard. Here Black is shielding to the right with his buckler, as the attacks are expected from that side.

White binds with the foible.

Black over-binds, ...

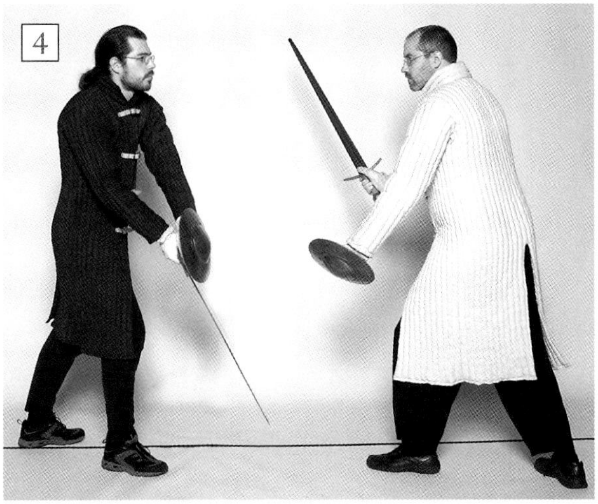

... whereupon White executes a Change of Sword.

This is followed by a strike on the opponent's sword.

The Play is concluded with the Nod.

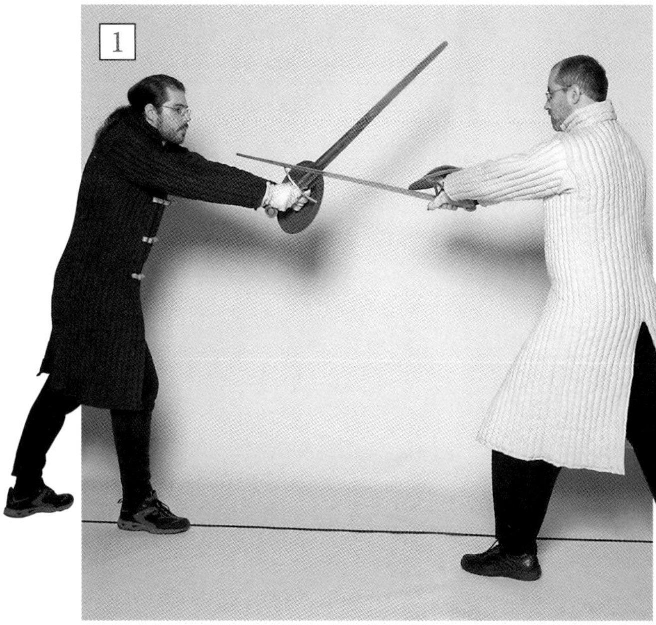

White has fallen under sword and shield.

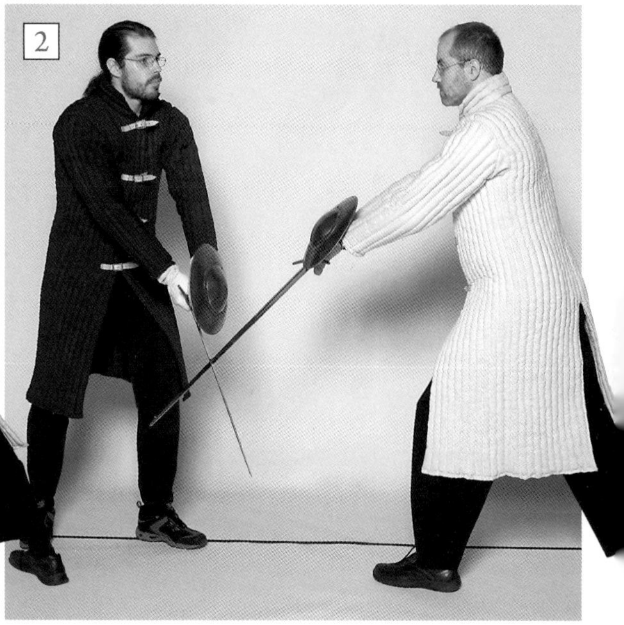

Black subsequently over-binds.

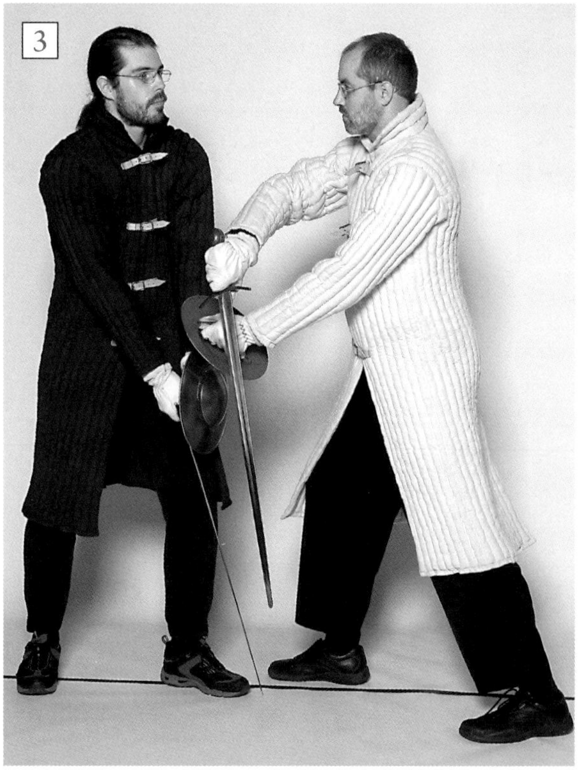

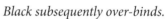

White steps through …

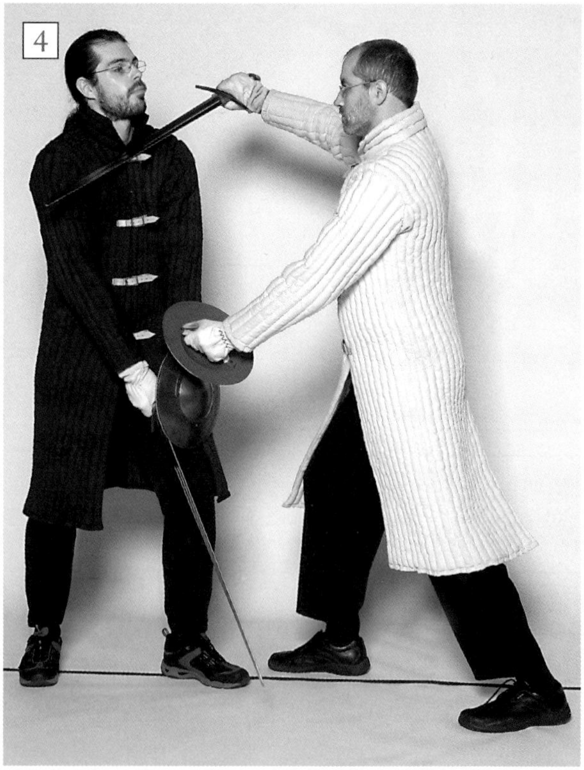

… and strikes at Black's neck.

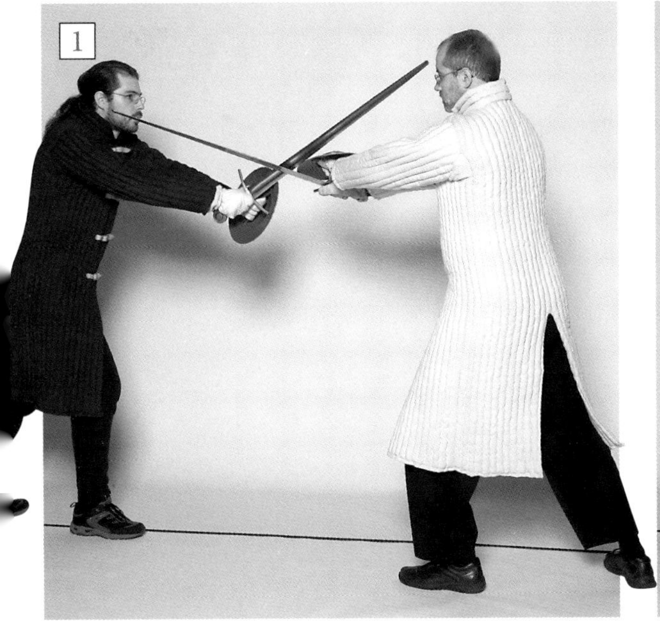

White has fallen under sword and shield with his forte.

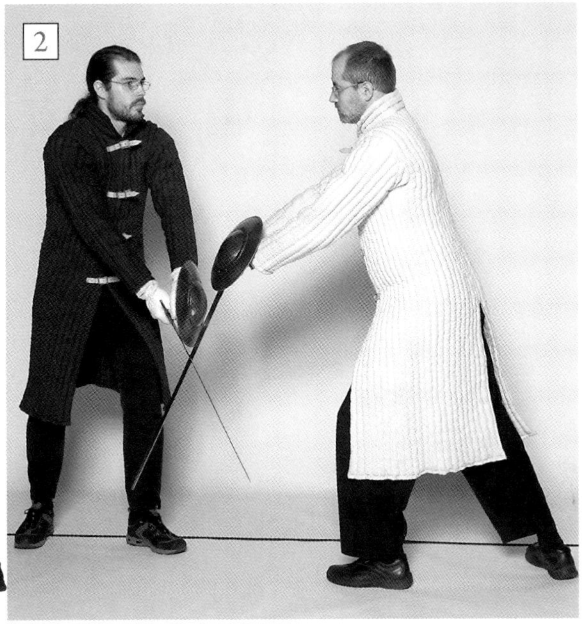

Black over-binds.

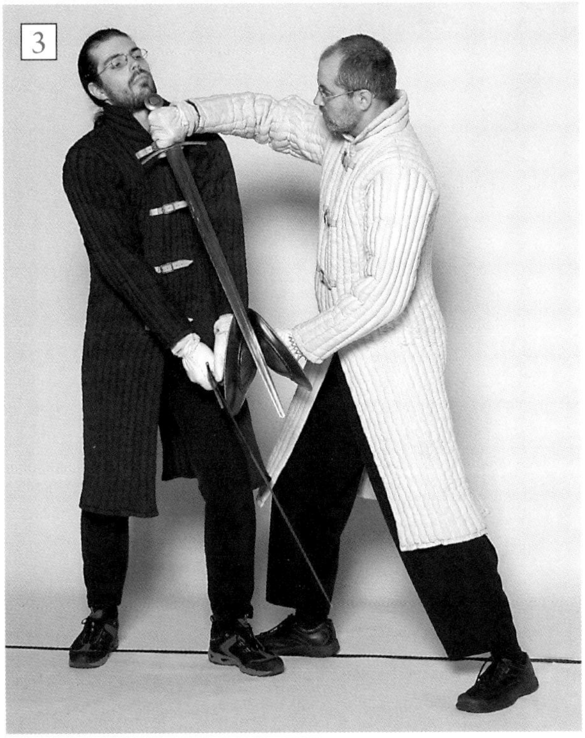

White delivers a shield strike, steps forward, and drives his pommel into Black's face.

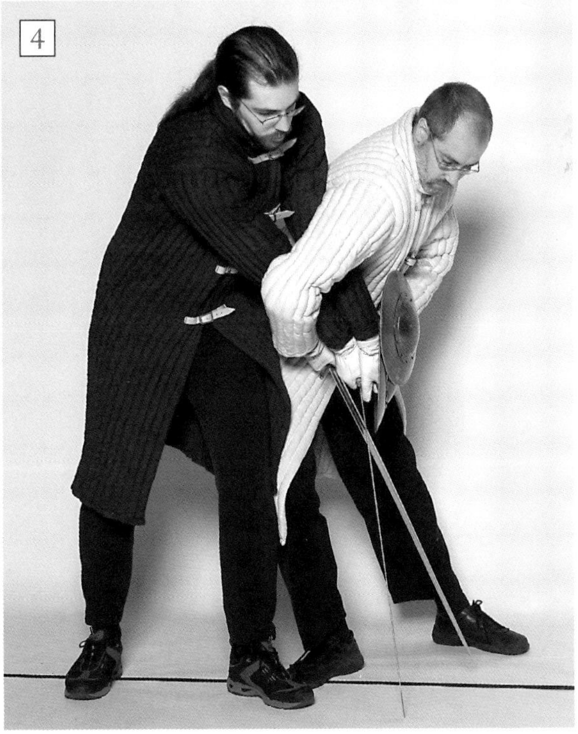

White subsequently takes Black's arms.

Conversely, if you are in the Half-Shield and your opponent falls under sword and shield two opportunities present themselves. You can over-bind and:

- If your opponent has bound in his foible or middle of the blade carry out a shield strike and strike at the head.
- Take the opponent's arms, especially if the opponent has bound in his forte.

The Third Guard versus Long-Point
You counter the Long-Point with a right or left over-bind or under-bind. The over-bind is recommended from the Third Guard. Nevertheless, an under-bind is possible. The conclusion is then a shield strike.

In principle, one has the same opportunities here as in the First Guard versus the Long-Point (section 7.1).

The fencers in the Long-Point and the Third Guard.

White over-binds from the left ...

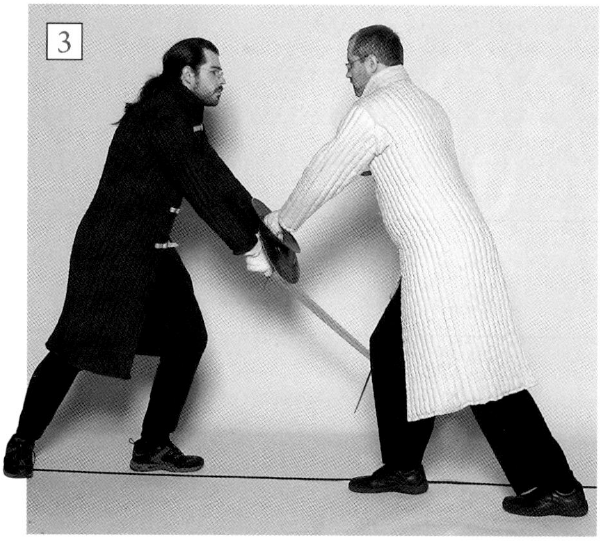

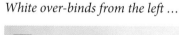

... takes control with his buckler ...

... and strikes at the opponent's head.

White under-binds the Long-Point.

The Play is concluded with a shield strike and a strike at the head. Basically this is also a stepping-through.

The Third Guard versus the Priest's Hat
If the Third Guard is countered with the Priest's Hat, I.33 advises not to remain in the Third Guard, as the opponent will most likely make a thrust from the Priest's Hat.

This thrust happens similarly to the thrust from the middle displacement. When making this thrust, it is important to cover the opponent's line of attack.
Stand in the Third Guard, then:

- Attack immediately, covering to the right with your buckler, with the shield hand over the sword hand.
- Immediately engage a bind should your opponent go into a displacement. If your opponent holds his displacement so low you cannot engage a bind then I recommend a straight over-cut with the buckler covering downward.

ATTACK FROM THE THIRD GUARD

Step 1

ARMS: You could attack with any over-cut; in principle little changes as a result. It is important for you to cover your right side with the buckler and move the buckler hand under the sword hand.

LEGS: Depending on the posture and direction of attack take a step or spring into the attack.

Binding into the Protection

ARMS: If your opponent goes from the Priest's Hat into the lower protection then bind immediately. You can engage the bind from the left or right. Do not bind too low, otherwise your body position will be poor on account of the forward lean. Deliver a shield strike from the bind.

The fencers in their guards.

Black immediately strikes from the Third Guard. Be sure to shield downward with your buckler.

Black in the Third Guard, White in the Priest's Hat.

White moves into the lower protection, whereupon Black engages the bind, ...

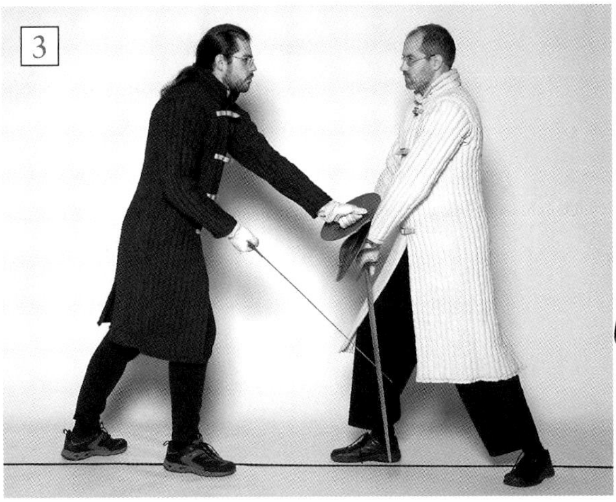

... delivers a shield strike ...

... and strikes at White's head.

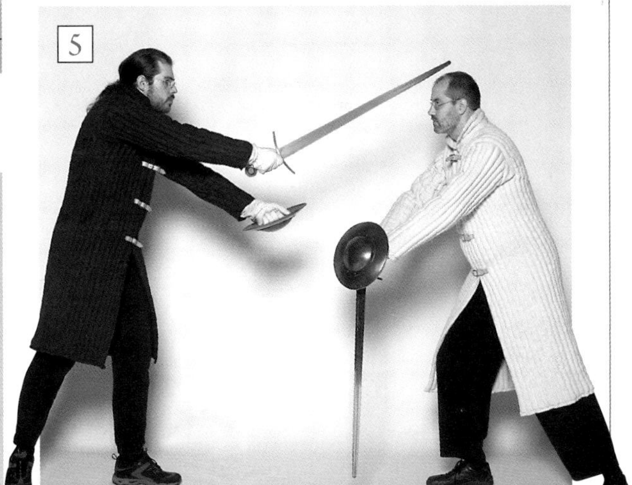

If White executes his protection very low then Black changes his plan and does not bind, instead striking directly at White's head. Black shields downward with his buckler.

If you are standing in the Priest's Hat, then:

- Thrust immediately should your opponent hesitate.
- Go into a lower displacement should your opponent attack. From the displacement you can quickly and smoothly meet the attack. Timing is important. If you go into the displacement at the exact moment of the attack then you will quickly stall your opponent. If you have time strike at his sword or shield hand from below or thrust at his chest.
- If the opponent falls on your sword and engages a bind when you are standing in a lower displacement execute a shield strike from the bind. With the shield strike you can strike at his arms from below or even better, thrust at his lower opening.

The fencers in the Third Guard and the Priest's Hat.

White thrusts directly at Black's head from the Priest's Hat.

PROTECTION AND ATTACK FROM THE PRIEST'S HAT

Step 1

ARMS:	From the lower protection, deliver an under-cut at the opponent's arms. Even if you only hit his buckler you are in a very good thrusting position, which you should exploit.
LEGS:	Take a step forward with your left leg as you deliver the under-cut.

The fencers are again in the Third Guard and the Priest's Hat.

Black begins the attack, White moves into the lower protection.

White steps out of line and attacks Black's arms with an under-cut.

4

5

From the protection White can also easily …

By turning his wrist, White then covers Black's hands with his buckler and thrusts at the opening.

6

… step out of line and strike at Black's head with his short edge while shielding up and right with his buckler. Whether to strike at the head or arms depends on the measure.

THE THRUST FROM THE BIND

Step 1

ARMS: You are standing in the protection and your opponent has engaged the bind. Deliver a shield strike if possible, otherwise cover your opponent's line of movement with your buckler and make an ascending cut at his arms with the short edge. Usually it is simpler to thrust at the abdomen.

LEGS: With the strike step forward to the right out of line to get a better angle and closer measure.

The fencers are in the Priest's Hat and the Third Guard.

Black moves in to the lower protection, …

… whereupon White engages the bind.

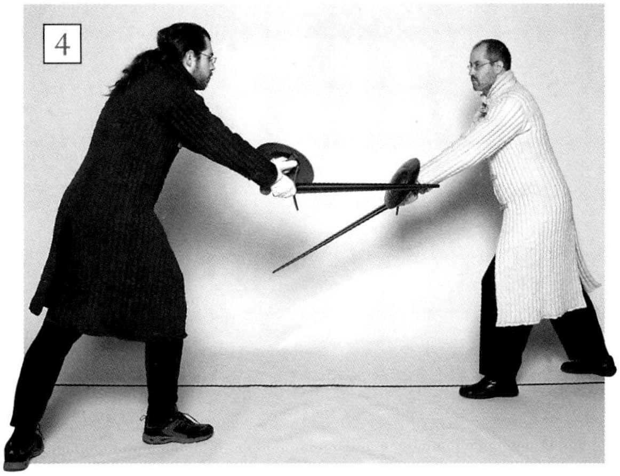

Black steps to the side and makes an ascending cut at White's arms with the short edge.

Immediately after the strike Black thrusts at the lower opening. This can also take place directly from the bind.

7.4 The Fourth Guard and its Plays

The Fourth Guard is held over the head and is very similar to the Second and Third Guards. The variations of the Fourth Guard can also be executed from the Second and Third Guards. Thus, the variations of the Fourth Guard and its Plays round off the possibilities from the Second and Third Guards to some extent.

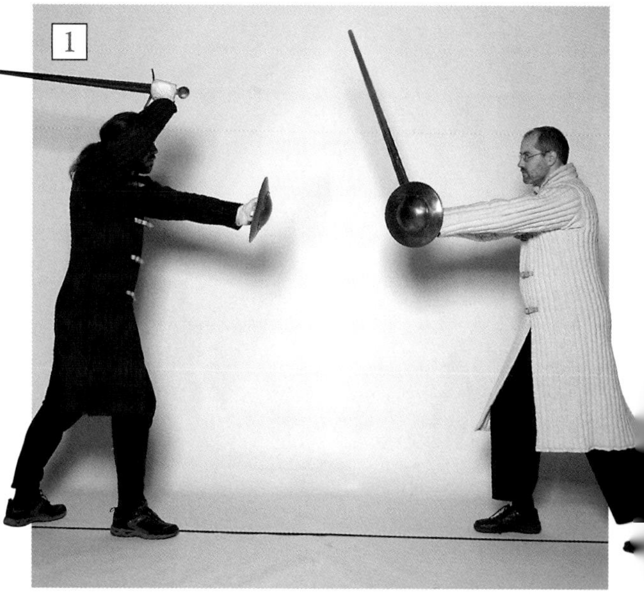

The fencers in the Fourth Guard and the Half-Shield.

The Fourth Guard versus Half-Shield

The following is again true in the Fourth Guard against the Half-Shield (as always against the Half-Shield): fall under sword and shield. The possibilities previously addressed in the First Guard's plays again arise from this.

If you fall under sword and shield, after binding you have the following possibilities:

- Thrust if your opponent does nothing.
- Your opponent over-binds and you have bound in your foible: Change of Sword.
- Your opponent over-binds and you have bound in the middle of the blade: Step Through.
- Your opponent over-binds and you have bound in your forte: take the arms.

Correspondingly, if you are standing in the Half-Shield and your opponent falls under sword and shield two opportunities present themselves:

- Execute a shield strike and strike at the head, especially if the opponent has bound in his foible or middle of the blade.
- Take the opponent's arms, especially if the opponent has bound in his forte.

From the Fourth Guard Black falls under sword and shield. The usual techniques can be carried out from this situation.

The Fourth Guard versus the First Guard

You are standing in the Fourth Guard and your opponent counters with the First Guard. As previously mentioned in the First Guard, you are well advised to change from the Fourth Guard to the Half-Shield. This puts you in the familiar First Guard versus Half-Shield position (see section 7.1).

Against the First Guard, from the Fourth Guard it is advisable to …

… immediately change into the Half-Shield.

The Fourth Guard against the Priest's Hat: this situation is less than optimal for both fencers.

For this reason the Half-Shield can be assumed from the Fourth Guard while the lower protection is advantageous from the Priest's Hat.

The Fourth Guard versus the Priest's Hat

If the Fourth Guard is countered with the Priest's Hat, the play is exactly the same as from the Third Guard against the Priest's Hat (section 7.3). I.33 advises not to remain in the Fourth Guard, otherwise the opponent can make a thrust from the Priest's Hat. The fundamental rule in this situation is: if you are in the Fourth Guard then go into the Half-Shield; if you are in the Priest's Hat go into a displacement.

If you are in the Fourth Guard attack immediately, covering to the right with your buckler, shield hand under the sword hand. Should your opponent go into a protection immediately engage in a bind. There is also another way to proceed: immediately change into a Half-Shield; then your opponent cannot attack with a thrust from the Priest's Hat.

If you are in the Priest's Hat go into a lower protection and thrust from the protection. If you are in a bind against the lower protection then you can execute a shield strike and strike or thrust at the opponent's head. This is possible for both fencers.

If you or your opponent has changed from the Fourth Guard into a Half-Shield against the Priest's Hat then all the possibilities from the First Guard against the Half-Shield are again open to you. In this respect the Priest's Hat and the First Guard are interchangeable, so you are again in a familiar position. The advantage of the Priest's Hat here is that your blade ends up further forward, enabling you to react or attack more quickly.

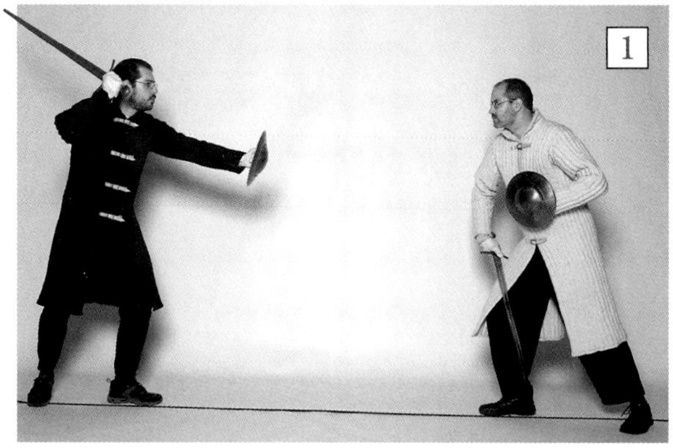

The fencers in the Fourth Guard and the Priest's Hat.

White hesitates, so Black steps out of line and attacks immediately. Note the position of the buckler.

Black in the Fourth Guard, White in the Priest's Hat.

White changes into the lower protection.

Black steps out of line and binds.

From the bind, Black delivers a shield strike and thrusts at the opening.

From the Priest's Hat, White changes ...

... into the lower protection ...

... and thrusts at the opening while stepping out of line.

From the bind against the lower protection ...

... White delivers a shield strike and thrusts at the upper opening.

7.5 The Fifth Guard and its Plays

Strangely, I.33 regards the Fifth Guard as preparation for a thrust, almost more than even the Sixth Guard, which would actually be predestined for it. Every other attack, apart from the right under-cut, has far too much distance to cover and is therefore very easy to break. That may be the reason why only the thrust from the Fifth Guard is mentioned. We also regard the thrust as the main attack from the Fifth Guard.

The Fifth Guard versus Priest's Hat

Your opponent is in the Fifth Guard and you assume the Priest's Hat. Go from the Priest's Hat into the lower protection, whereupon the only choice left to your opponent in the Fifth Guard is to bind. From this bind you go on working with a shield strike as usual.

From the Priest's Hat, the thrust from the Fifth Guard is best countered with the lower protection. This enables you to deflect the thrust to the left or right as required.

The Fifth Guard versus Special Priest's Hat (*Obsesseo rara*)

Here the Fifth Guard is countered with a slightly modified Priest's Hat. I call it "Special Priest's Hat" to give it a name. You assume a normal Priest's Hat and turn your left shoulder forward, holding the buckler in front of you. Your right leg is forward and your forte rests on your right thigh.

The Fifth Guard against the Priest's Hat.

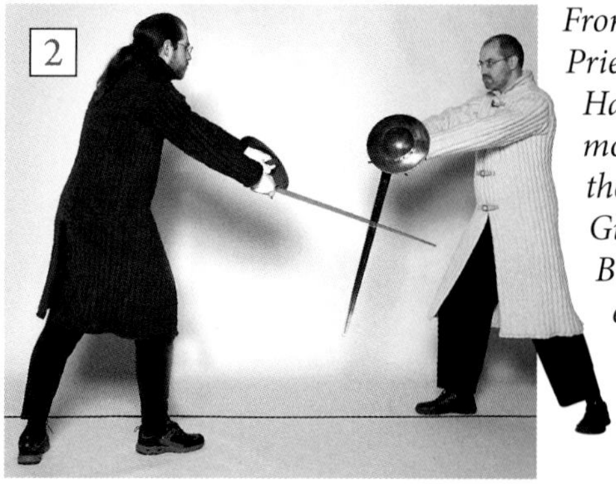

From the Priest's Hat, white moves into the Lower Guard. Black steps out of line and binds.

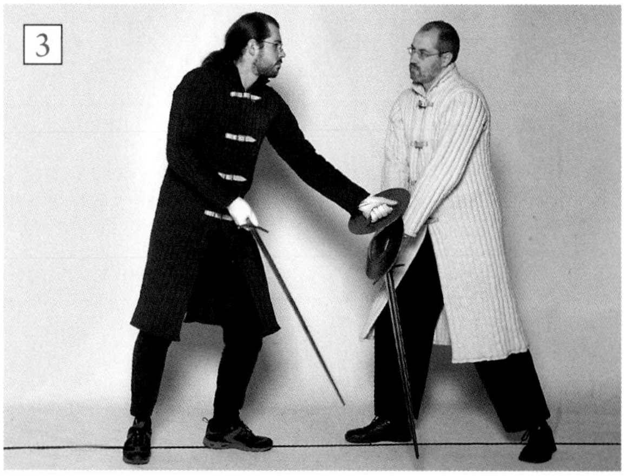

As usual, a shield strike follows ...

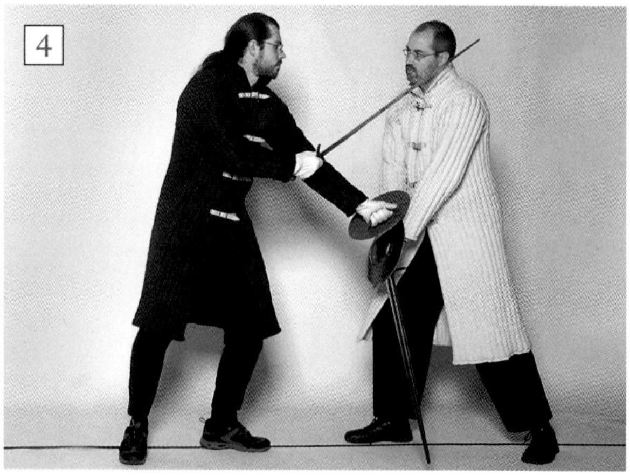

... and the thrust at the opening.

The Fifth Guard against the Priest's Hat.

From the Priest's Hat, White goes into the lower protection. Black steps out of line and parries Black's thrust.

It is important here to work with the buckler under the sword hand.

White delivers the shield strike …

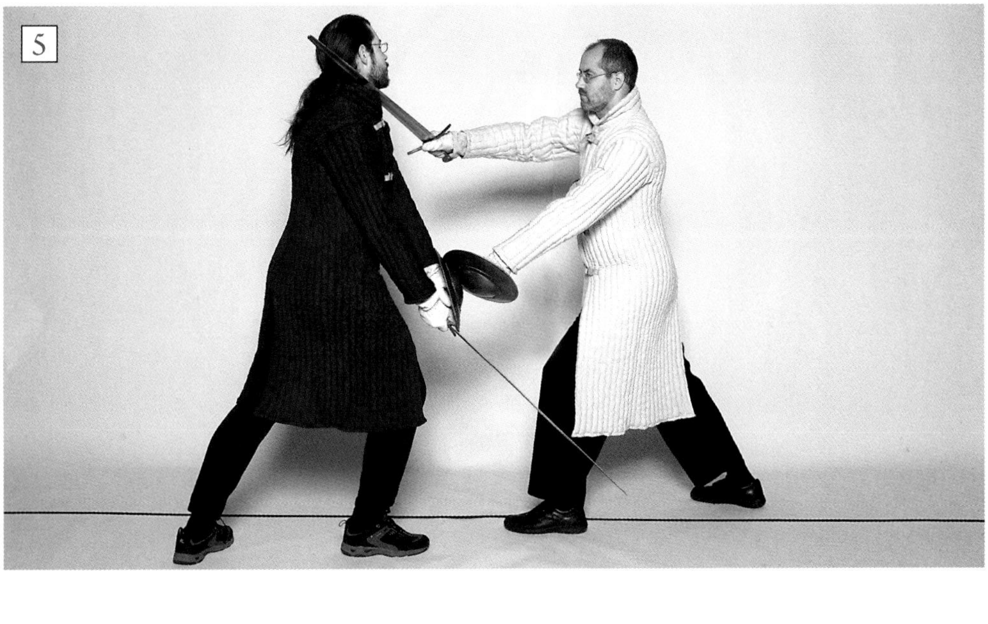

… and thrusts at the opening.

Liutger describes the situation of an attack with a thrust from the Fifth Guard. Against this thrust the fencer in the Special Priest's Hat steps his left leg forward or his right leg back. He thrusts at the opponent while taking this step. The thrust is very similar to the displacement with the long sword. One simultaneously closes the line of attack and thrusts. Incidentally, it is the only technique in I.33 in which the footwork is described.

The displacement works on both sides. It is important that the point is in a straight line from the Special Priest's Hat to the face or chest of the opponent. Depending on the situation, the hilt is drawn to the left or right to deflect the opposing blade. I recommend you always first set aside to the left (as seen from the Priest's Hat). If you sense the bind is not coming together, you can move the hilt out and to the right and set aside the thrust from the other side. In this sequence the window of opportunity is usually large enough.

If the fencer in the Fifth Guard does not make a thrust and instead goes into the Half-Shield, then immediately fall under sword and shield (best with a thrust) and return to the situation of the First Play (Half-Shield versus First Guard, section 7.1).

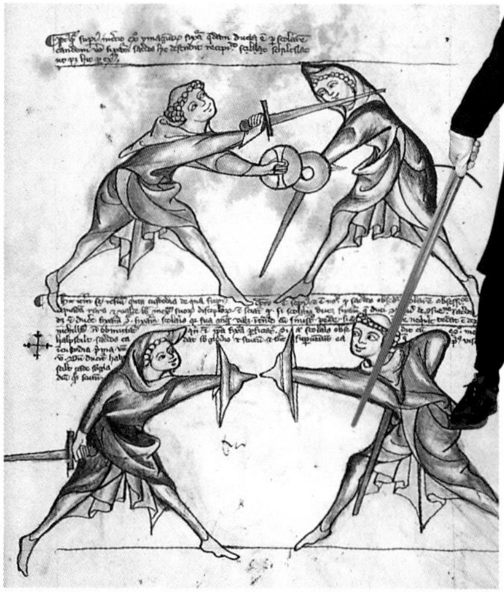

Page 29r/57 from I.33. The Fifth Guard against the Special Priest's Hat is explained at the bottom.

THRUST FROM THE SPECIAL PRIEST'S HAT

Step 1

ARMS:	You are standing in the Special Priest's Hat and your opponent is in the Fifth Guard. Thrust at the lower opening and during the thrust cover the opponent's line of attack. To do this hold your hilt outward. Your sword forms a wedge that deflects the opponent's blade.
LEGS:	Step forward here with your left leg. If you are forced to withdraw then step back with your right leg. Footwork is very important in this technique.

The fencers are standing in the Fifth Guard and the Special Priest's Hat.

The thrust from the Fifth Guard. The point is moved just past the leg and brought to the target in a straight line.

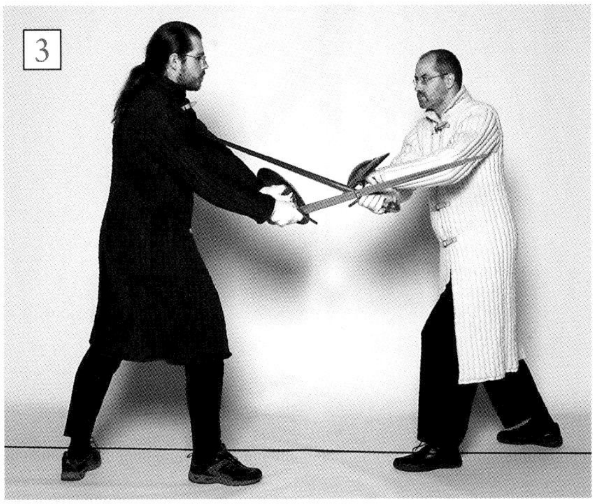

The thrust with the parry against the thrust from the Fifth Guard.

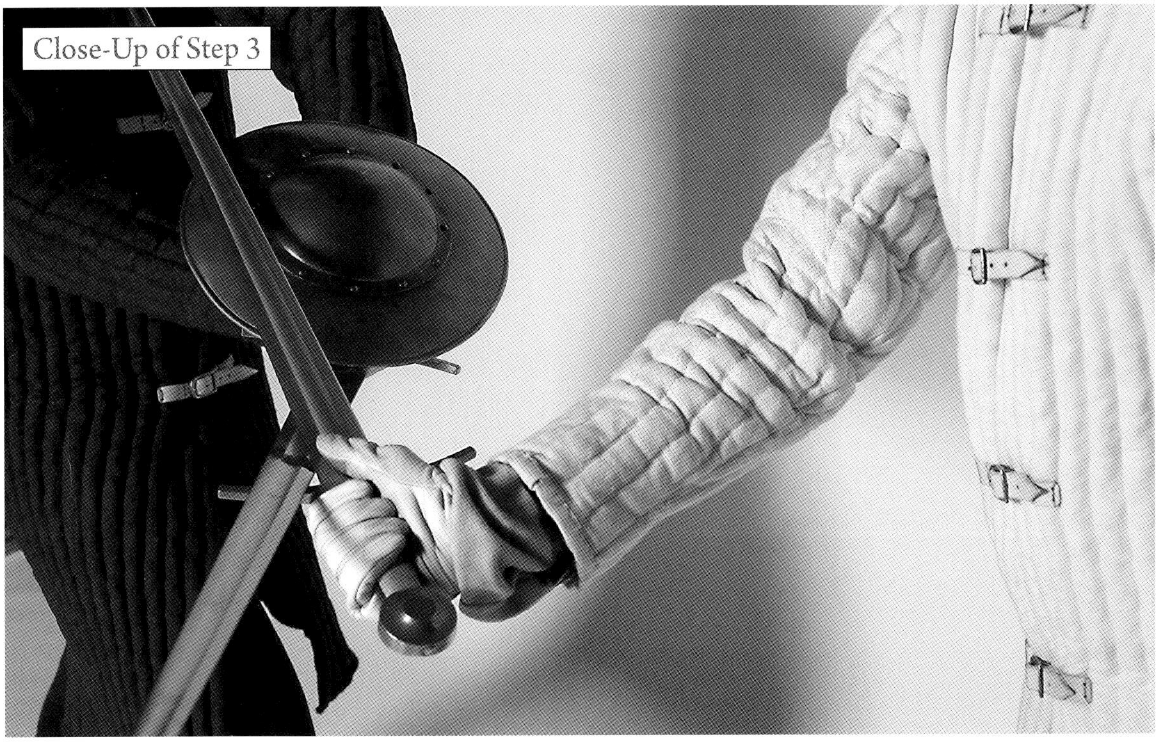

Parrying the thrust close-up. The buckler is left out here. One can clearly see that Black's blade is pushed aside by White's hilt and ends up safely in the Cross. This also works on the other side.

THE FIFTH GUARD VERSUS HALF-SHIELD

Like most guards, the Fifth Guard can also be displaced with the Half-Shield. In this situation, the one in the Fifth Guard is left with just two possibilities:

- He can make a thrust.
- He can try to separate the opponent's sword and shield with a powerful blow. I do not recommend you try this, however. One might be lucky, but there is a good chance that the attempt will be countered with a shield strike.

From the Fifth Guard against the Half-Shield …

… Black can execute a thrust if White is too slow in reacting. Here the thrust left of the blade.

The thrust can also be made to the right of the blade.

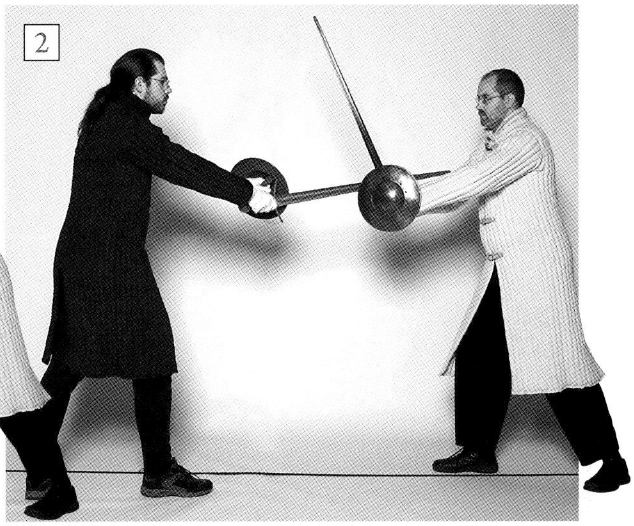

From the Fifth Guard, Black tries …

… to separate White's sword and buckler with a powerful descending blow.

In response, White turns his buckler to the blade, steps to the right, and strikes at Black's head.

The fencer in the Half-Shield should thrust immediately. That is the only way he can prevent the fencer in the guard from attacking. If the fencer thrusts from the Fifth Guard then from the Half-Shield you can deliver a shield strike or (if one is rather late in reacting) displace the thrust with a type of lower displacement.

SHIELD STRIKE AGAINST A THRUST FROM THE FIFTH GUARD

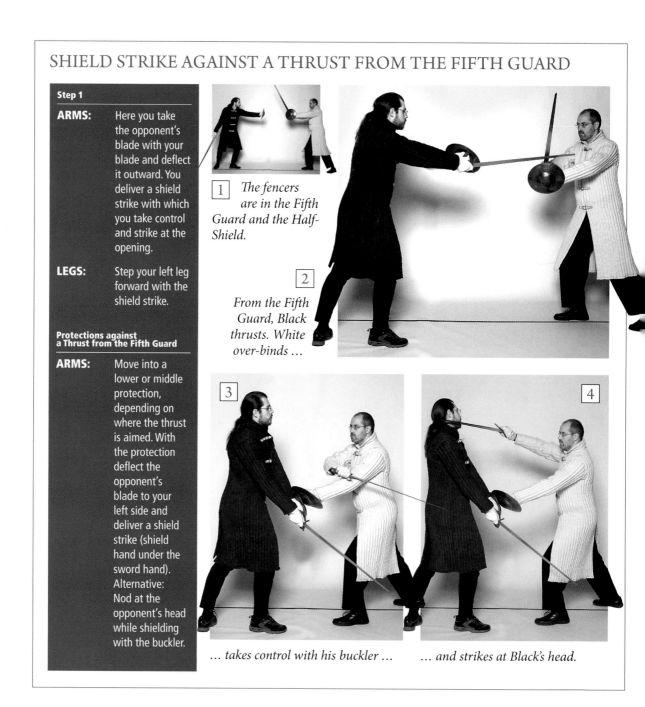

Step 1

ARMS: Here you take the opponent's blade with your blade and deflect it outward. You deliver a shield strike with which you take control and strike at the opening.

LEGS: Step your left leg forward with the shield strike.

Protections against a Thrust from the Fifth Guard

ARMS: Move into a lower or middle protection, depending on where the thrust is aimed. With the protection deflect the opponent's blade to your left side and deliver a shield strike (shield hand under the sword hand). Alternative: Nod at the opponent's head while shielding with the buckler.

1 *The fencers are in the Fifth Guard and the Half-Shield.*

2 *From the Fifth Guard, Black thrusts. White over-binds …*

3 *… takes control with his buckler …*

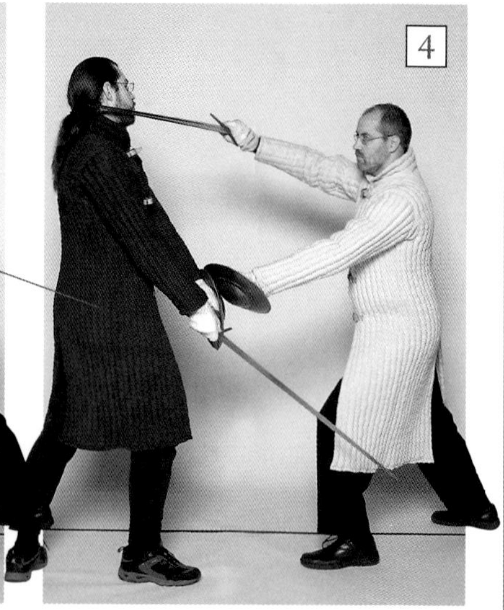

4 *… and strikes at Black's head.*

7.6 The Sixth Guard and its Plays

The posture of the Sixth Guard requires some explanation: at first glance the positioning of the hands as represented in I.33 appears all but impossible, or at least impractical. But if one turns the wrist not to the left but to the right in this position, then not only is it feasible, but with some practice even quite comfortable. If one also looks at the position of the elbow, it quickly becomes clear the sword is held with the long edge downward or perhaps outward. If one wants to execute the Sixth Guard conforming exactly to the sources then the right elbow must be pointed straight back.

The fencer thrusts from the Sixth Guard. Liutger explains that one executes the same thrust as from the Fifth Guard. This leaves us the possibility of thrusting left or right of the centerline. If our opponent is in the Half-Shield then we can thrust to the left or right of the Half-Shield.

Thrust left from the Half-Shield, then again fall under sword and shield—this time with the intention of thrusting—while at the same time taking a step to the left. Be sure that as you thrust you bring the short edge against the opponent's sword and cover the opponent's sword to the side with your buckler. It is basically the same as explained in the play of the First Guard (section 7.1).

The situation: you are standing in the Sixth Guard and your opponent attacks with an over-cut or comes toward you with the Half-Shield. The break for this is an over-bind followed by a shield strike and a blow to the head. This break can be used successfully against any thrust and with some practice in the I.33 system it turns out to be easy.

BREAK TO THE THRUST FROM THE SIXTH GUARD

Step 1

ARMS:	Your opponent thrusts at you from the Sixth Guard. Take the opponent's blade, deflect it to the right, and deliver a shield strike with a strike against the upper opening. This is the classic triple combination from I.33.
LEGS:	It is usually necessary to step forward somewhat when delivering the shield strike.

Black is standing in the Sixth Guard, White in the Half-Shield.

From the Sixth Guard, Black thrusts ...

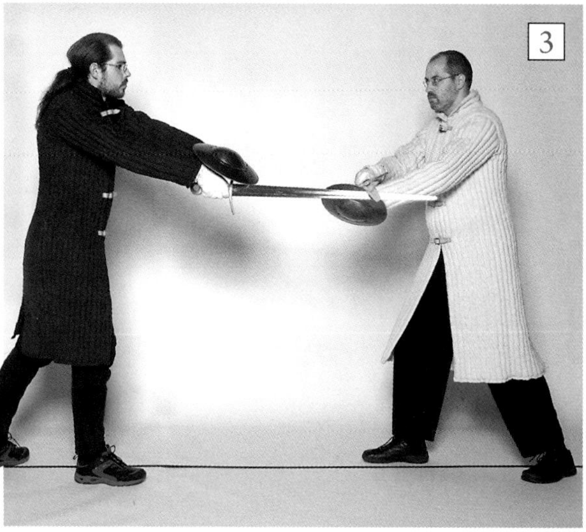

… is over-bound by White and …

… controlled with a shield strike.

The combat ends with a strike to the head.

Close-up of the Sixth Guard
(Page 17r/33 from I.33).

7.7 The Seventh Guard and its Plays

In many respects, the Seventh Guard occupies a special position among the guards. I will briefly describe the different aspects and resulting problems of the Seventh Guard. It is important to note that some of the inconsistencies have not yet been cleared up and may never be.

The Seventh Guard is unfortunately depicted quite differently in I.33. The Seventh Guard is executed with the sword pointing down and is also called the Long-Point. But now a guard is introduced that is called "Upper Long-Point" in which the sword points upward. Then there is another Long-Point in which the sword is pointed straight in front of the fencer. This "Middle Long-Point" is designated as a displacement, a counter, or obsesseo. Can one equate these Long-Point variants with the guard or not?

Once again, we have three types of Long-Point—the lower, the middle, and the upper.

- The Lower Long-Point is clearly referred to as the Seventh Guard and the Long-Point.
- The Middle Long-Point is referred to as the Long-Point and Obsesseo or counter-guard, but not as a guard.
- The Upper Long-Point is clearly referred to as the Long-Point and guard but not as the Seventh or last Guard.

So what is the Seventh Guard? If one is particular, one must say that only the Lower Long-Point meets all these criteria. Broadened somewhat more one must also include the Upper Long-Point, for it is referred to explicitly as a guard. But how do we then not count the Middle Long-Point as the Seventh Guard? After all, it represents an intermediate stage between the Lower and Upper Long-Point.

I personally see the Seventh Guard as the Lower Long-Point. The Middle Long-Point I regard as a counter-guard. I have therefore dealt with these variants with the corresponding guards, particularly the First Guard. The Upper Long-Point is a special case.

This decision is important with respect to a note from the first pages of I.33: "Note that the entire core of the fencing art exists in this last guard, which is called Long-Point. In addition, all actions of defense or of the sword are completed in it, which is to say that they end in it and not in others. Therefore consider this above-named guard first."

The Seventh Guard therefore represents the end point of the stroke. Another reference to the Seventh Guard as a Lower Long-Point is the fact that this verse appears at the beginning of I.33, where the Seventh Guard is only depicted as a lower Long-Point. All other variations of the Long-Point come later.

The Seventh Guard and the Bind

The Seventh Guard is the only one in I.33 that is not accompanied by a counter-guard. Instead, all the plays of the Seventh Guard begin directly in the bind. I assume that it did not seem important to Liutger from which position one reached the bind; it only mattered to him that one engaged the bind correctly. This leads me to the conclusion that this last guard was conceived not so much as a static guard as the completion of an attack to which one responds with a bind—at best before the movement is stopped. I.33 thus places in our hands a technique that is very advantageous in combat and in most cases places us in the stronger position. It means that in combat one does not wait until the opponent has completed his action; instead, one seeks the bind immediately after he acts if possible and works from there.

It often happens in combat that a bind is sought but for various reasons it ends up quite low. This is the right moment for the Seventh Guard plays. The techniques from the Seventh Guard bind can also be used if the opponent has strongly over-bound. Then we are often in a posture similar to the Seventh Guard.

The Seventh Guard is always answered with a bind. Liutger mentions often that there are four types of bind against the Long-Point: left upper and lower and right upper and lower. Three of these four binds are explained in I.33. The direction of the bind is always indicated from the view of the person initiating the bind.

1) Right Over-Bind

If you are standing in the Seventh Guard and your opponent over-binds then you can raise your hilt, thus shielding your head. Should your opponent try to make a shield strike then you take his arms with your sword arm.

Alternately, you could also disengage the bind and thrust directly at his head. The best time for this is the moment when you sense the opponent initiating the bind. That should be the signal to you to thrust immediately. You can also thrust directly from a bind in which you are on the bottom. If you do, it is advisable to step out of line and to thrust upwards directly with the short edge.

The priest is over-bound and thrusts from the bind directly at the head. This is one of the rare instances in which Liutger dispenses with taking control of the opposing weapons with the buckler (Page 20r/39 in I.33).

BREAK TO THE OVER-BINDING OF THE SEVENTH GUARD

Black has over-bound White in the Seventh Guard.

Step 1

ARMS:	You were over-bound. Now raise your hilt, forestalling a shield strike.

Step 2 – The Opponent's Shield Strike

ARMS:	Now simply reach your sword hand over the opponent's sword hand. Timing is decisive here, for you must practically work into the opponent's attack.
LEGS:	Depending on the measure and angle, step forward and slightly to the side.

Step 2: – Thrust to the Head Variation (No shield strike by the opponent)

ARMS:	Disengage the bind and thrust in a straight line at the opponent's head. Don't forget to close your opponent's line of attack with your buckler, which means shielding the lower left side.

Step 2: – Thrust or Strike at the Lower Opening (No shield strike by the opponent)

ARMS:	Disengage the bind and make an ascending cut at your opponent's arms with the short edge. Ideally you can also thrust at his abdomen.
LEGS:	Step slightly out of line to the right, giving you a better attack angle.

White raises his hilt and steps forward …

… takes the opponent's arms and begins grappling.

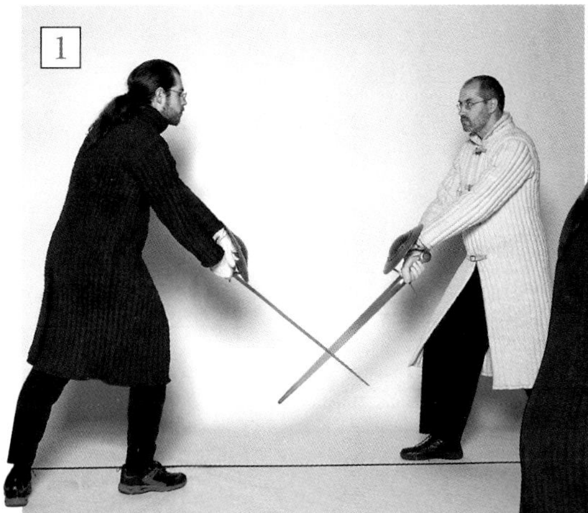

From the Seventh Guard bind …

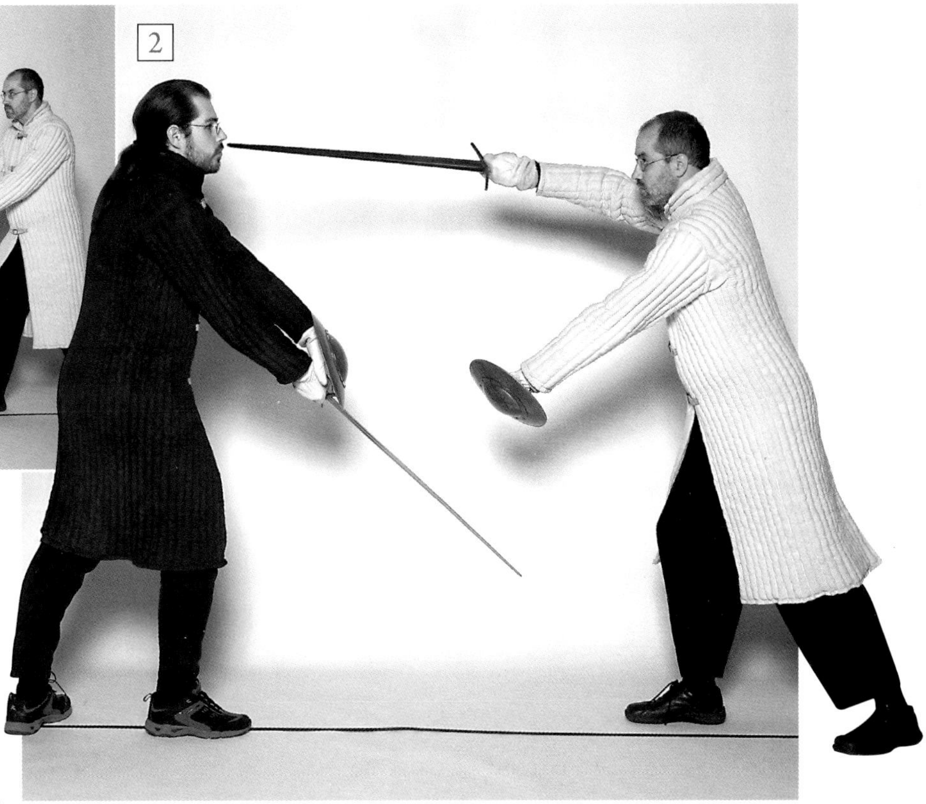

… White thrusts directly at Black's head. His buckler is shielding downward.

1

White has over-bound …

… and delivers an ascending strike on Black's arms. This opportunity is usually available to both fencers, but as a rule the under-bind is chosen.

2

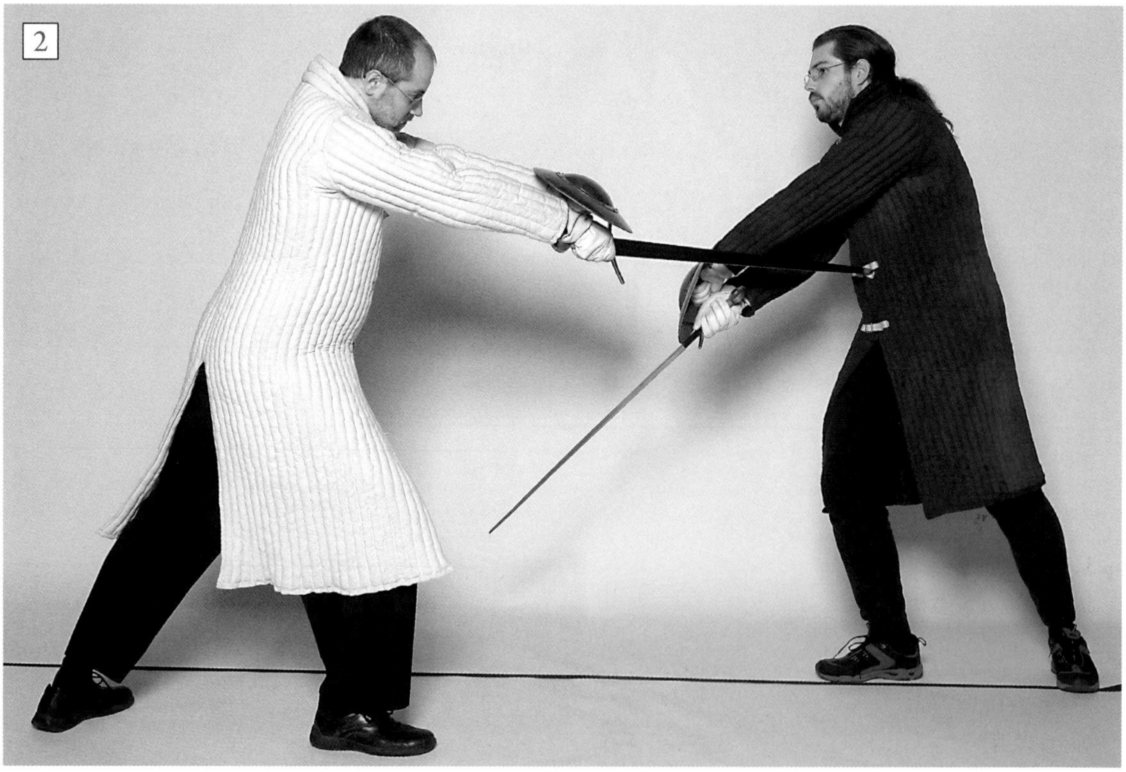

The situation offers quite different possibilities from the point of view of the fencer who is over-binding. If you are in the situation where your opponent in the Seventh Guard over-binds right then you can obviously make a shield strike. It is often the case that your opponent declines the bind and disengages. He can do that by pulling back his blade or by moving back or to the side. Liutger refers to both situations when he writes: "The one who is bound flees to the side, I attempt to follow." In this case you immediately follow your opponent's sword and thrust or strike at his openings.

2) Left Over-Bind

In principle, the left over-bind differs little from the right over-bind. As always, if you over-bind you must be sure your opponent does not make a strike or thrust at your head.

3) Left Under-Bind

The direct thrust from the bind can also be carried out from the under-bind on the left side as previously described.

White was over-bound.

White disengages the bind and tries to increase the measure. Black immediately follows up with a thrust.

In summary, you have the following possibilities:

You are standing in the Seventh Guard and are bound:
- Raise your hilt to shield and to take the opponent's arms against a shield strike.
- Thrust directly at the opponent's head.
- Thrust from the under-bind.

You have engaged the bind in response to the Seventh Guard:
- You thrust directly at the opponent's head.
- You execute a shield strike and strike at the head.
- Your opponent declines the bind and flees—you follow.
- Thrust from the under-bind.

The counter against the thrust at the head is the upper displacement that we previously learned as a counter-guard against the Second Guard. As soon as you parry the thrust with this posture, in principle you are in the same situation as in the Second Guard play against the upper displacements (section 7.2).

The Upper Long-Point as Guard
Here I will treat the Upper Long-Point as a special case because this special Long-Point is also referred to as a guard. To assume this Upper Long-Point hold the sword with the point facing up, your sword arm extended. Your buckler shields straight ahead.

You are then in a position similar to the upper displacement. This is very advantageous, because from this position you can foil an attack with a shield strike or thrust strike at any time. The only option left to your opponent is to bind your blade. Basically it is a simple and natural posture with the sword pointing up and to the right. If your opponent binds now you can simply over-bind to the right and push his blade downward. He automatically binds in your forte and you then have the advantage.

Now you again find yourself in a situation similar to the over-bound Seventh Guard. All possibilities just discussed are again open to both fencers. If the opponent attempts to flee by taking his blade back out of the bind then you simply follow with a thrust to the head.

Black is standing in the high Long-Point, White has engaged the bind.

Black over-binds.

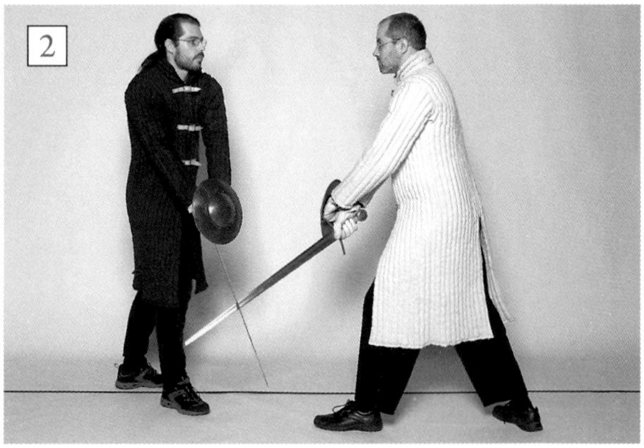

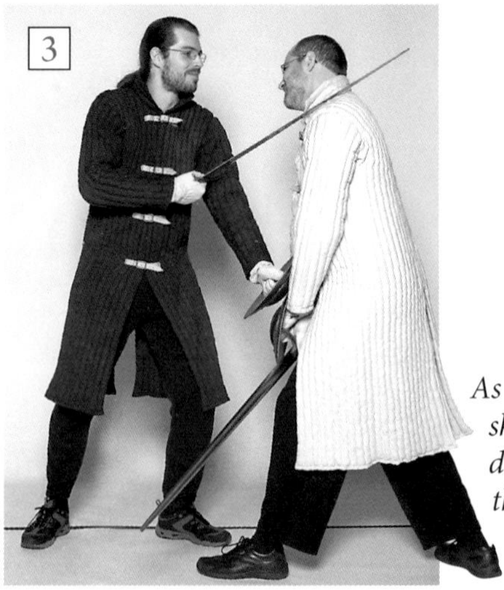

As usual, a shield strike is delivered from the bind.

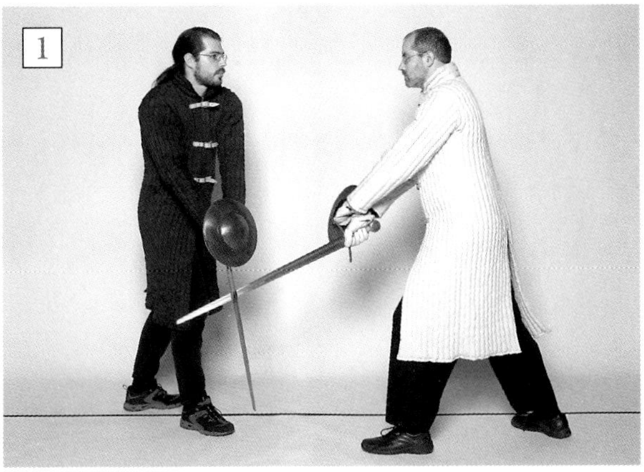

From the over-bind …

From the bind against the high Long-Point …

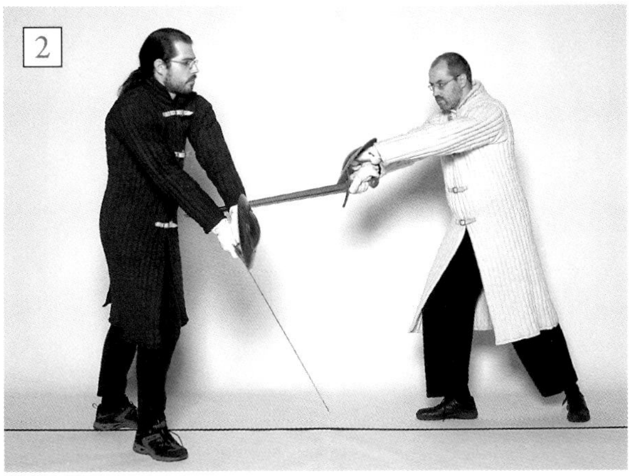

… White can of course also deliver an ascending strike.

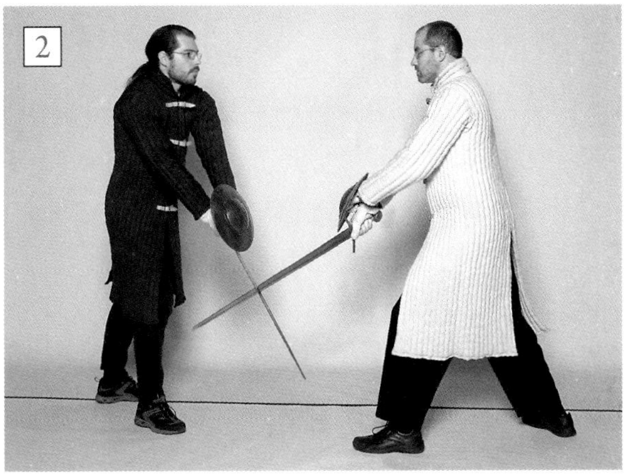

… Black over-binds.

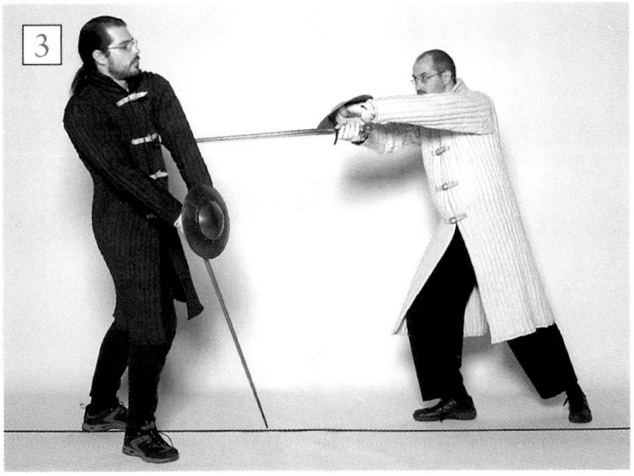

A thrust follows the strike.

White retreats and Black follows up immediately.

7.8 The Priest's Hat and its Plays

The Priest's Hat is a very versatile and particularly practical guard. It lies between the Fifth and the First Guard and offers many advantages. In particular, one can cancel (direct a blow from below against the opponent's blade to cancel their action) from it very well, even though this is not mentioned in I.33.

The Priest's Hat versus the Half-Shield
The Half-Shield is clearly the counter-guard, and here the Priest's Hat is displaced with the Half-Shield. This already moves the Priest's Hat somewhat into the attack guards and also makes clear that powerful attacks are quite possible from the Priest's Hat.

As in the First Guard, here one immediately falls under sword and shield, meaning an immediate bind. The fencer in the Half-Shield over-binds, whereupon the one coming from the Priest's Hat steps through. In this situation, the one who has been over-bound can strike upward from the Half-Shield from below to attack the hands. He also places himself in a very good thrusting position. (More on this in section 7.11 – Special Guards and their Plays.)

The Priest's Hat versus the Third Guard
The play in this case was explained in the chapter on the Third Guard (7.3).

The Priest's Hat versus the Fourth Guard
See section 7.4.

The Priest's Hat versus the Fifth Guard
See section 7.5.

The Special Priest's Hat versus the Fifth Guard
See section 7.5.

Black is standing in the Half-Shield, White in the Priest's Hat.

White falls under sword and shield. Here all of the same opportunities arise as in the First Guard against the Half-Shield.

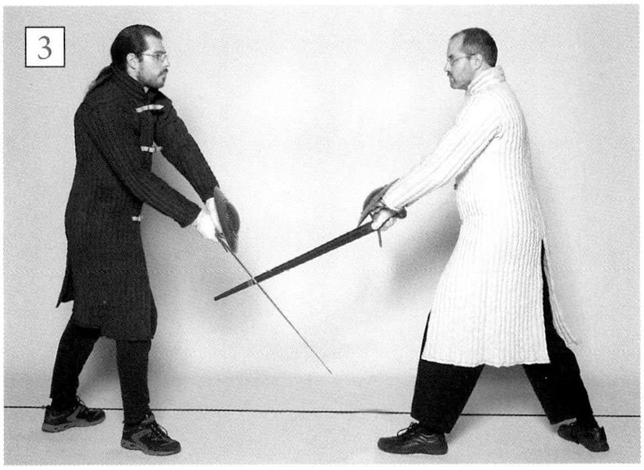

Black over-binds.

White then raises his buckler to step through.

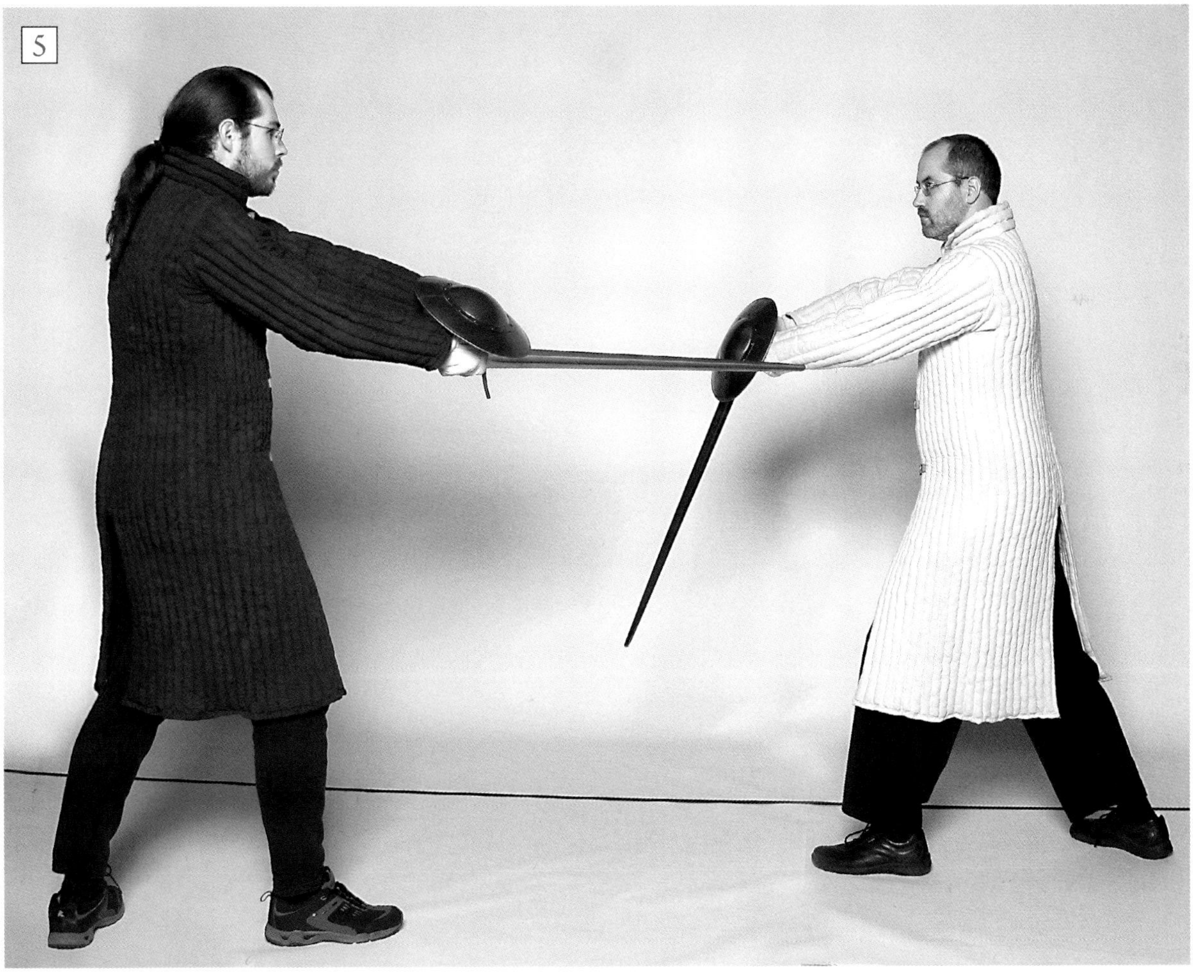

Black steps out to the side and strikes White on the hands from below.

ADDITIONAL TACTICS

You can Cancel very effectively from the Priest's Hat. This technique comes from the Liechtenauer tradition and first appeared in 1389.

You are standing in the Priest's Hat. If your opponent attacks with an over-cut make an ascending cut from the left, striking his blade with your short edge. This deflects the opponent's over-cut and you can thrust or strike at the opening. Similarly, there are many options from the Priest's Hat; for example, a parry to the right.

White is standing in the Priest's Hat, Black in the Second Guard.

If Black now attacks with an over-cut, White can strike Black's blade from below with his short edge and deflect it.

He immediately takes control with his buckler and then thrusts at the upper opening.

7.9 The Fiddle Bow and its Plays

The Fiddle Bow is a very special and versatile guard. The only disarming technique in I.33 is demonstrated from it. In practice it does not necessarily lead to disarming except with certain victory.

The Fiddle Bow is assumed in response to an over-cut from another guard. It functions very well against over-cuts when it is employed unexpectedly. For example, you can be standing in a Half-Shield and then, during the opponent's attack, change into the Fiddle Bow. If you are standing openly in a Fiddle Bow then the opponent will be reluctant to make a right over-cut.

Example: your opponent attacks with an over-cut. You immediately change your posture into a Fiddle Bow and take the opponent's blade. If the bind is securely engaged then turn your hand with the buckler outward so that you can grasp the opponent's blade. Now pull the opponent's blade back somewhat and simultaneously strike at his head. You can slice through his face from left to right or strike down at his head from the right.

FIDDLE BOW AGAINST OVER-CUT

Step 1

ARMS: The opponent's blade is resting in the "V" formed by your buckler and your sword. Now twist your buckler clockwise, so that the shield boss faces right. Grasp the flat of the opponent's blade with your four fingers; if possible do not place the thumb around the blade. Now pull the opponent's blade back and down while striking at his head or slicing through his face. In this movement you "spread out," meaning you stretch your arms apart.

BODY: Here it is important that you straighten up somewhat to muster the necessary strength in both directions simultaneously.

LEGS: After you have grasped the opponent's sword, step forward.

White in the Fiddle Bow. The Fiddle Bow is usually not assumed directly; instead, it is taken during the attack from another guard.

White takes Black's over-cut with the Fiddle Bow.

White turns his buckler and attacks Black's blade.

Close-up of grasping the blade: in this way the danger to your hands from a sharp blade is minimal.

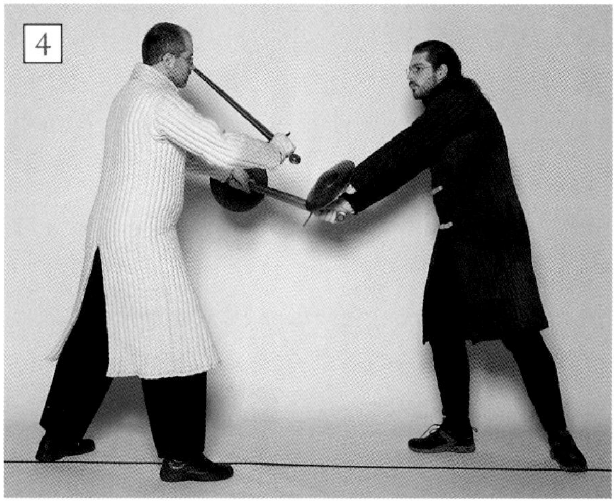

White twists the blade outward, steps forward …

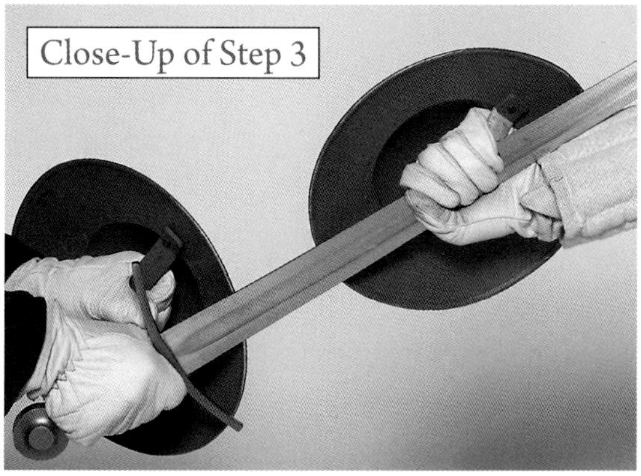

This way you have a better grip on the blade, but the danger of injury from a sharp blade is significantly greater.

… and strikes at Black's head.

White could also strike at the head from the outside.

Fiddle Bow and disarming by grasping the blade (Page 22r/43 in I.33).

If your opponent engages you in a bind (or you take his over-cut with a Fiddle Bow) then you can simply over-bind right and make a shield strike. The problematic thing about this over-binding is that the point of the opponent's sword must pass in front of your face. The whole thing takes place very quickly and if your opponent binds with a thrust then that can pose something of a danger to you.

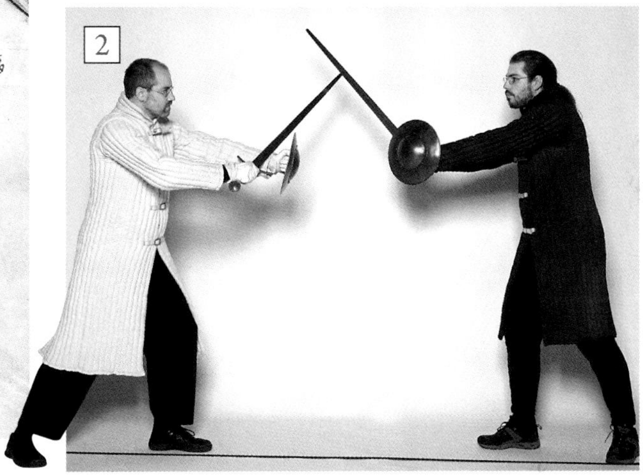

While Black attacks from the Second Guard, White changes into the Fiddle Bow.

The fencers are standing in the Half-Shield and the Second Guard.

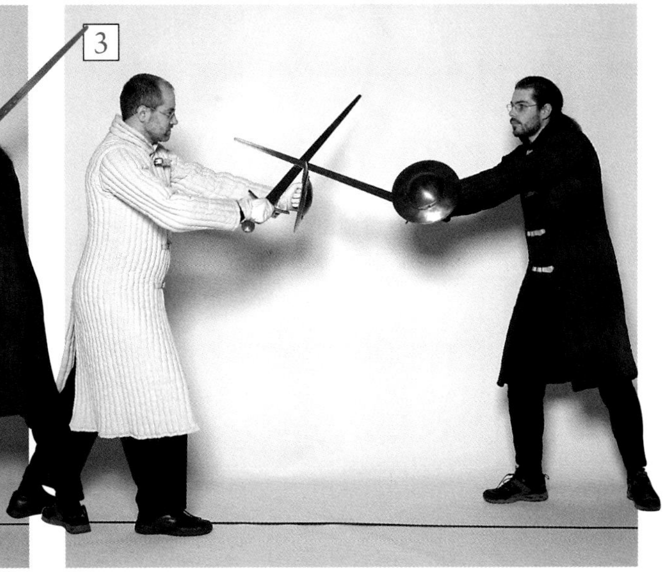

The blow is taken ...

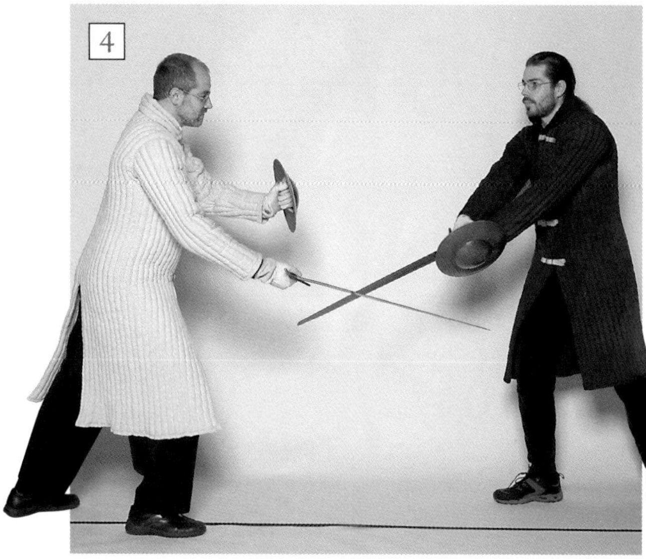

... over-bound ...

... and controlled with a shield strike.

The fight is ended with a blow to the head.

ADDITIONAL TECHNIQUES

A technique that works well from the Fiddle Bow is stepping through from the First Play. If the opposing blade is in your Fiddle Bow then simply raise the hilt and deliver a shield strike under your sword. As you do so step forward and slice through the opponent's face.

White has taken the attack with the Fiddle Bow.

White raises his hilt and thrusts his buckler forward beneath his sword hand.

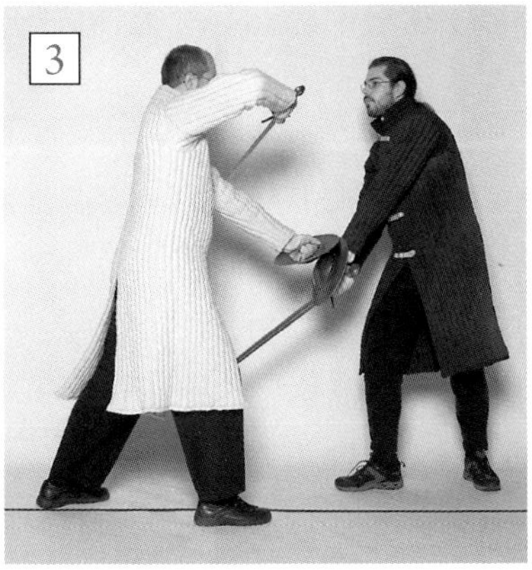

He takes control with a blow from his buckler.

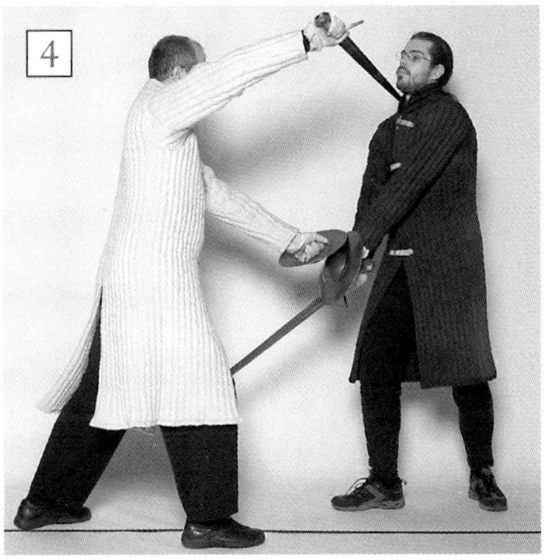

The fight is again ended with a blow to the head.

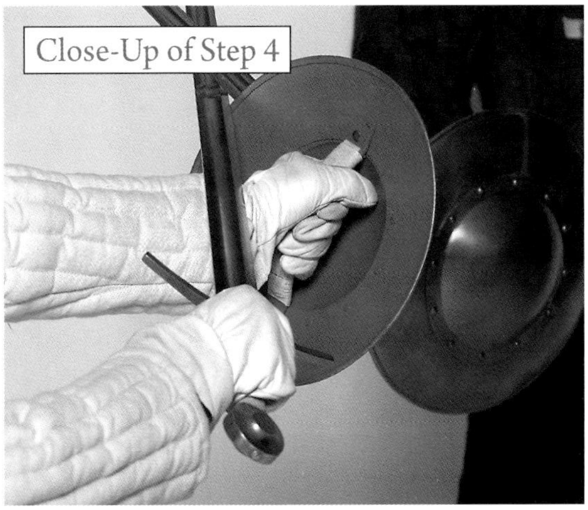

Be sure to rest the flat of the blade on your forearm. Position the blade so that its forte rests on your forearm and your point is aimed upward. This gives you the most advantageous lever effect and the best control over the opponent's blade. It also enables you to act most quickly.

7.10 The Walpurgis and its Play

On the last pages of I.33 we see Liutger fencing with a woman, Walpurgis. There has been much speculation about these pages. Why does a woman appear in this combat manual? Was it a clue that the guard was very easy to execute—even "suitable for a woman," so to speak—comparable to the Posta di Donna of the Italian Fiore dei Liberi? Is it supposed to show that it is a simple guard and requires little strength? Or was a woman really fencing at that time and taking lessons from the priest? We do not know.

The Walpurgis is a very energy-saving guard. You draw the weapon back to the body and thus take away distance. The opponent usually moves closer automatically. It is nevertheless practically impossible to directly attack an opponent standing in the Walpurgis, as he can always very easily respond with a shield strike or thrust strike.

Walpurgis versus the First Guard
A fencer is standing in the Walpurgis, his opponent in the First Guard. The fencer in the First Guard immediately changes into a middle protection, whereupon the fencer in the Walpurgis over- or outer-binds. From there he continues with a shield strike.

If you engage in a bind from the Walpurgis then you are aware that your opponent is disengaging the bind and is trying to flee. Follow immediately as per the fundamental rule: "The one who is bound flees, I attempt to follow."

Black is standing in the Walpurgis.

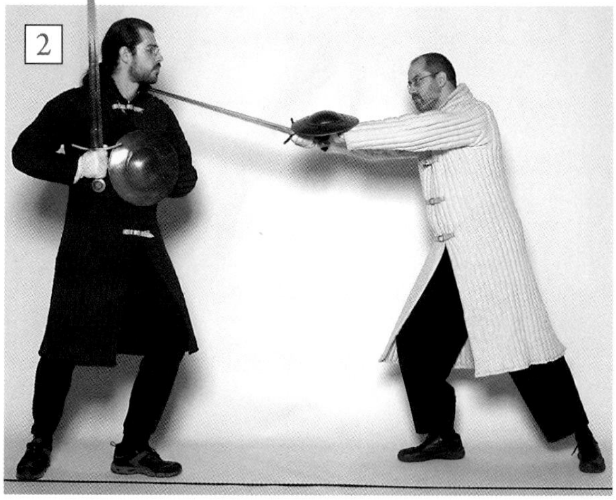

White can now attack directly.

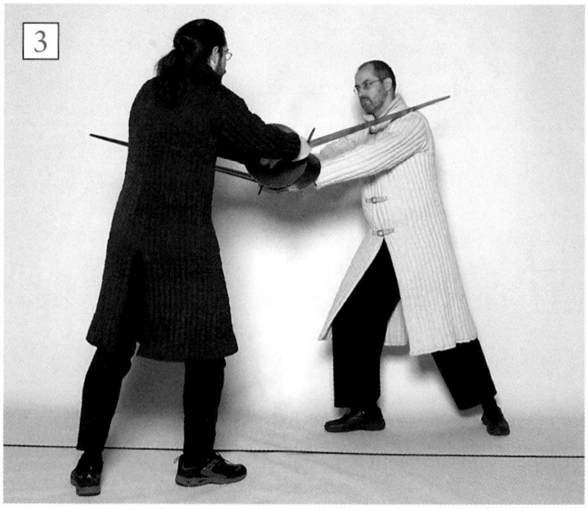

Black can easily deliver a shield strike in response. It is therefore impossible to attack the Walpurgis directly.

Black is standing in the Walpurgis, White in the First Guard.

White changes into a lower protection, as he is unable to make a direct attack.

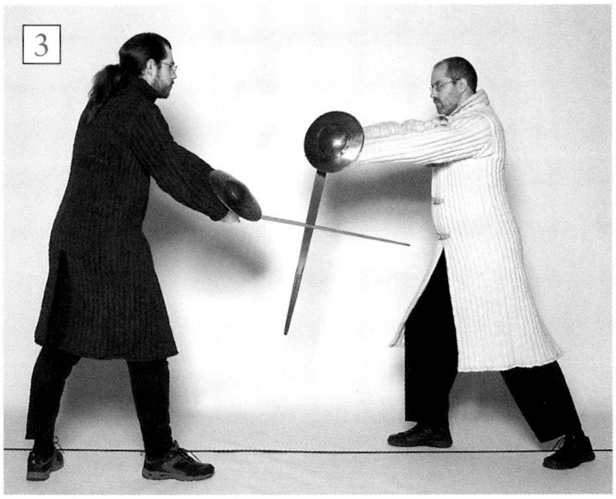

Black binds against the protection …

… and delivers a shield strike.

Once again the piece ends with a blow to the head.

The piece develops as usual from the Walpurgis Guard and the First Guard.

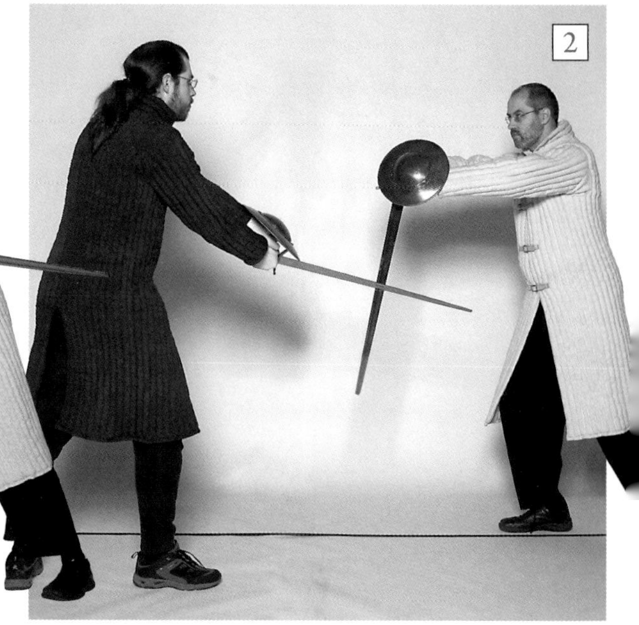

The middle protection is bound.

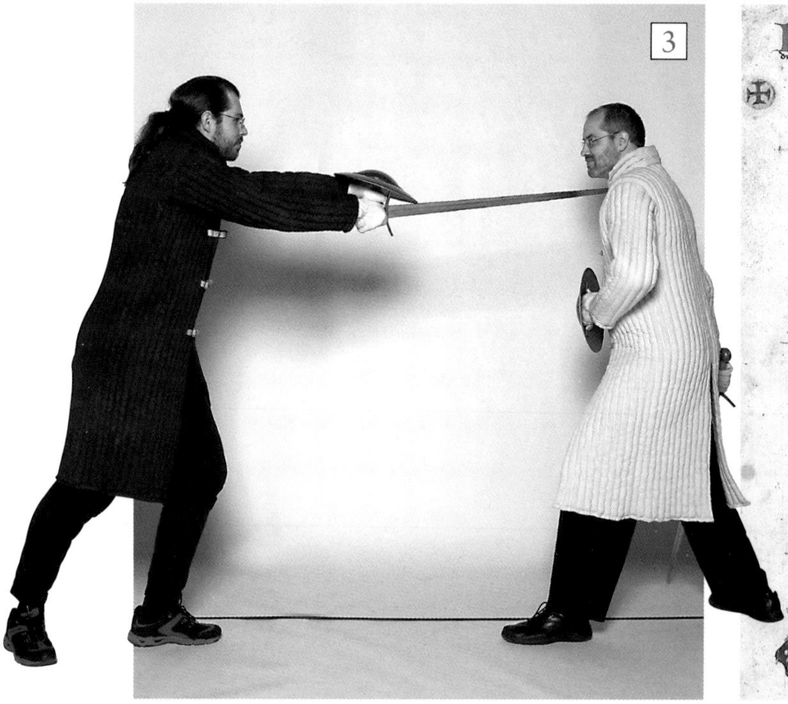

White disengages the bind and steps back, and Black pursues immediately.

Walpurgis against the priest in the First Guard (Page 32r/63 in I.33).

7.11 Special Guards and their Plays

Although most plays are linked to one of the seven guards so that one always finds a guard with its corresponding counter-guard, there are also a few guard combinations that stand outside. These are combinations of counter-guards.

PRIEST'S HAT VERSUS HALF-SHIELD
Here two of the best counter-guards meet. As always against the Half-Shield, Liutger advises to immediately fall under sword and shield from the Priest's Hat. In addition, Liutger states that one should not deliver a blow without a shield strike against the opponent's head.

Example: you fall under the sword and shield of the one standing in the Half-Shield. As per the First Play, he is over-bound. You now simply strike upward with the short edge, striking his arms. You are now also in an outstanding thrusting position. This technique was already explained in section 7.8. The step out of line is important.

Priest's Hat versus Rare Displacement
Liutger describes this rather unique combination and then uses it himself: "... one must understand that all of this can be traced back to the First Guard and to the displacement that is called Half-Shield." He then also immediately falls under the sword and shield of the Rare Displacement and directly attacks the unguarded sword hand. Afterward, the fencer in the Rare Displacement naturally over-binds and everything develops as in the First Play.

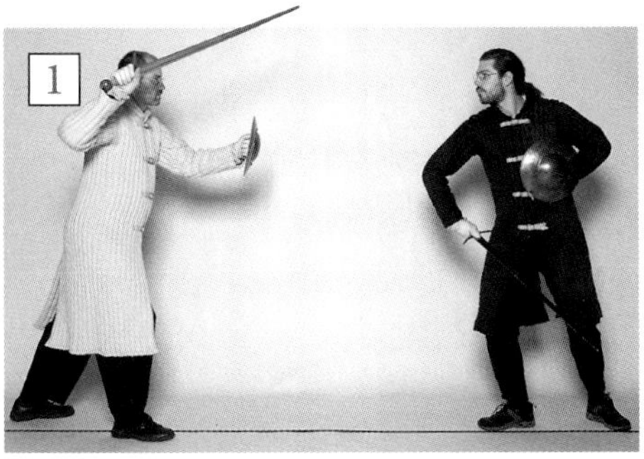

White is standing in the Rare Displacement, Black in the Priest's Hat.

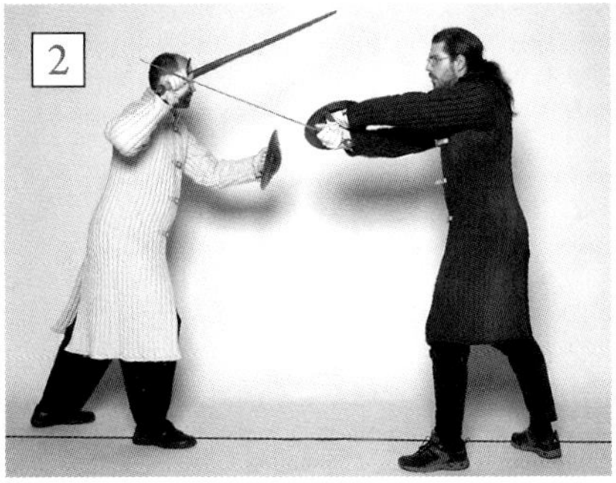

Black attacks White's unprotected sword hand.

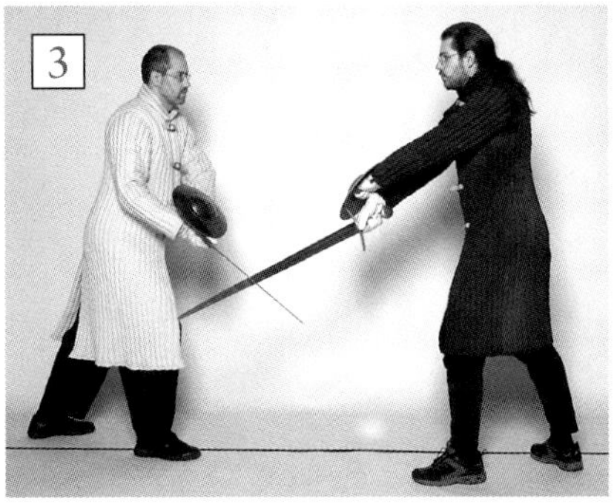

White over-binds the attack ...

... steps forward with a shield strike ...

... and ends the piece with a blow to the head.

Further Advancements: The Pieces of Later Master Fencers

After I.33 there was a rather long gap in the evolution of fencing until the beginning of the fifteenth century, when Lignitzer introduced the next techniques with the sword and buckler. Lignitzer was not the only one who described this combination of weapons, however. In the decades that followed, other master fencers wrote about the sword and buckler in their fencing manuals. They first adopted Lignitzer's pieces—in some cases almost word for word—but later they added new techniques of their own. In this chapter I will describe the pieces introduced by Lignitzer, as well as those of Hans Talhoffer and Paulus Kal (circa 1460).

Many of these pieces are identical to techniques from I.33. Some appear to have become mixed with Lignitzer's techniques, so that in later years we find a large number of techniques that are more or less old techniques in a new guise. In the explanations I use terms that are often not from these manuscripts. This is not faithful to the sources, but it does simplify the work tremendously. The terms I use are from the environment of the manuscripts: either I.33 or from the German school of the long sword according to Liechtenauer.

Unfortunately there is no explanatory text for the surviving tables by Talhoffer. This forces us to reconstruct many of these techniques using other, similar techniques. Although these techniques are also verified and in some cases were written down at the time, one can never be absolutely certain that one is on the right track.

In this sense, many of the following techniques have been tested conclusively and in free fights but are nevertheless interpolated. I therefore find it important to disassociate them from the pure interpretations like in I.33.

8.1 A Change in Concept

Lignitzer and Talhoffer developed their systems during the flowering of the German School under the influence of Liechtenauer. It should come as no surprise to us that sword fighting changed in the 150 years that separated I.33 and Talhoffer. Many techniques evolved, or were added or deleted. The entire approach appears to have changed.

In I.33, it was mainly about controlling the opponent's sword. In contrast to this, one could say that Talhoffer and especially Lignitzer stressed controlling the opponent's movements. The focus was not on binding and controlling the opposing blade; rather, it was ensuring that the opponent moved his blade as one wanted.

This is noticeable in practice, in that one seeks to create an opening which one can then attack. To achieve this one entices or forces the opponent into a certain movement. If he fails to do so or the conditions are not right then one works with the opponent's movements by attacking the openings that are created automatically and the weak points in the opponent's attack.

Another difference is the use of the buckler. While in I.33 the buckler is used almost exclusively to shield the sword hand and to control the opposing weapon, Lignitzer and Talhoffer take a completely different approach. They use the sword and buckler separate from each other. The buckler is actively used to block, parry blows, and secure lines of attack.

A third difference is the basic posture. The fencers now stand more upright. This is part of the reason why the legs suddenly become a target: they are in range. The classic concept of attacking an upper opening to then switch to a lower opening is much used here. In all, we are dealing with an entirely different system. It is not necessarily more efficient, but it is in keeping with its time.

I.33 employs a forward-leaning posture.

Later the fencer stood more upright and the legs became a target.

8.2 The Guards and Blows

The guards used by the later master fencers are roughly the same as those used with the long sword. Certain blows—in some cases similar to the master cuts of the long sword—are also necessary.

The *Zwerchhau* (Crosswise Cut) is a horizontal blow in which the thumb rests underneath, on the flat of the blade. The movements are made with the shoulder and the hip. With every blow one steps, or better springs toward the side from which the blow is made. If one strikes from the right then one steps out of line to the right.

The *Sturzhau* (Plunging Cut) is a modified over-cut. During the blow, one lets the point tilt forward and thrusts at the opening. The hilt is held high. One usually works with arms extended. A detailed description of these guards and strikes is contained in my book *Sword Fighting - An Introduction to Handling a Long Sword.*

The Fool Guard. An equivalent is found in long sword techniques.

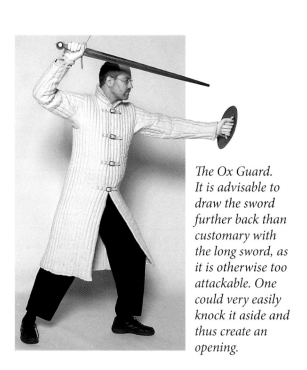

The Ox Guard. It is advisable to draw the sword further back than customary with the long sword, as it is otherwise too attackable. One could very easily knock it aside and thus create an opening.

The Plow Guard. It can vary slightly as required.

The From the Roof Guard or the Second Guard …

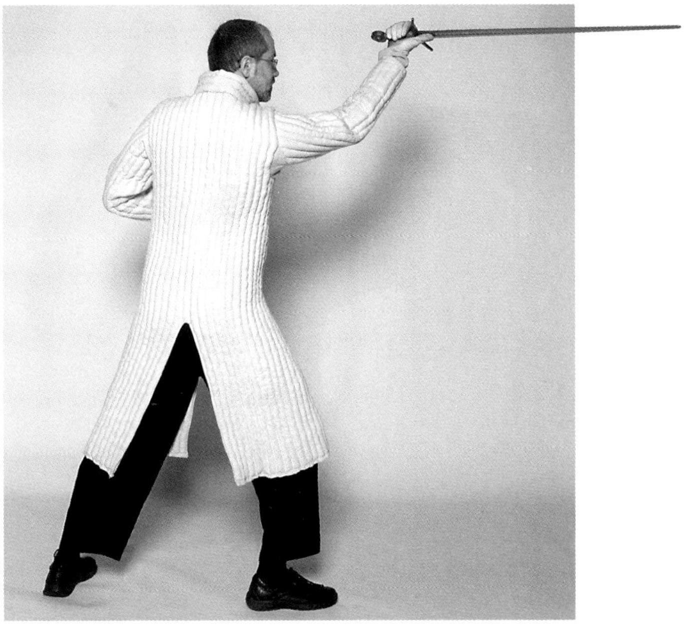

… one steps or springs to the right and delivers a horizontal blow with the short edge. The thumb rests under the flat of the blade. That is a proper Crosswise Cut.

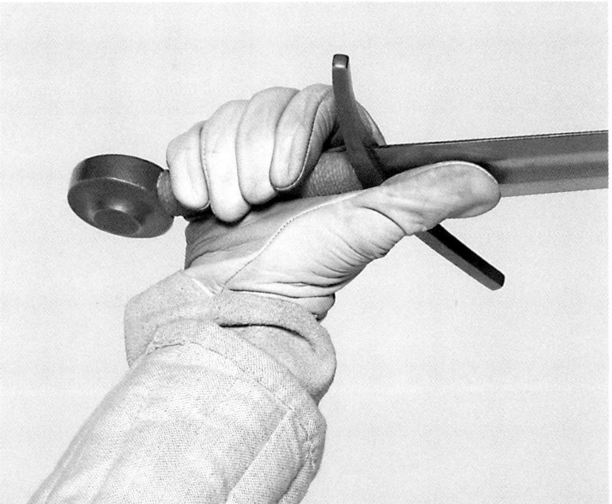

Close-up of the grip in the Crosswise Cut.

One strikes with the long edge in the right Crosswise Cut and the fencer steps out of line to the left. The hand can be more outstretched so that one gets more range.

Winding is a technique in which one pushes the opponent's sword off line and aims his own point at the opponent's openings. One usually thrusts from a Wind, but strikes and slices are also possible. In Winding, you take the opponent's foible with your forte, push his blade off line, and bring your point into line with the opponent.

The term Hang actually refers to the end position after a strike. A strike is delivered in such a way that at the end of the strike the point is aimed at the opponent. The hilt hangs down (lower hang) or the point hangs down (upper hang).

The fencers are both standing in the From the Roof on the Shoulder Guard.

White attacks with an over-cut, Black raises his buckler to parry the blow.

White then tilts his sword and thrusts over Black's buckler at the opening. This Plunging Cut is executed fluidly in a single movement.

Both fencers are in the From the Roof on the Shoulder Guard.

The fencers engage the bind.

White winds against Black's blade. Here he is in-winding or winding inward.

If Black engages strongly in the bind then White can out-wind or wind outward.

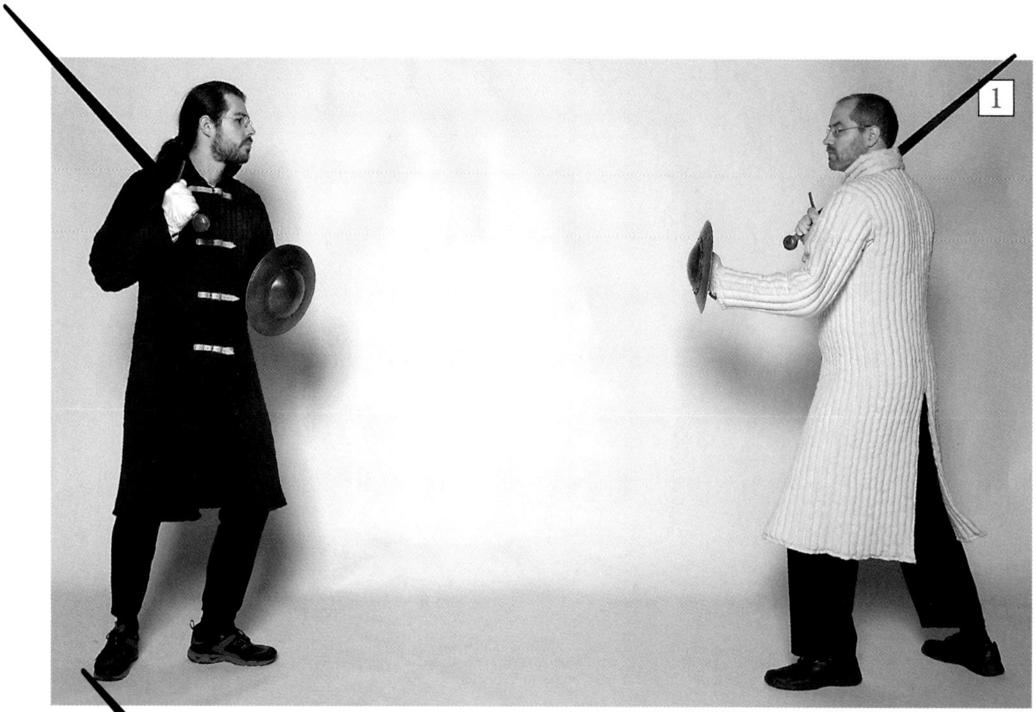

White delivers an over-cut ...

... and ends up in a lower hang.

From an under-cut …

… White ends up in an upper hang.

A New Concept: Andre Lignitzer's Set-Plays

Andre Lignitzer left us six set-plays with the buckler. As previously discussed, these six set-plays appeared in various combat manuals, in some cases word for word. I refer here to the combat manual by Peter von Danzig of 1452. The original is now found in the *Biblioteca dell'Accademia Nazionale dei Lincei e Corsiniana* in Rome under the title Cod. 44 A 8 [Cod. 1449]. With each set-play I include the original text, a corresponding modern translation, and then my own interpretation.

9.1 Lignitzer's First Set-Play

Original:
Das erst stuck mit dem pucklär aus dem oberhaw
Merck wenn dw den oberhaw treibst zw dem mann
so setz mit dem knopf dein swert inwendig auf deinen pucklär zw deinem daumen
vnd stich jm von vnden auf zw seinem gesicht
vind wind gegen seinem swert
vnd las vber Schnappen.

Translation:
When you strike at the opponent with an over-cut, hold your sword with the pommel inside your buckler against your thumb. Thrust from below at his face, wind against his sword, and snap over it.

Interpretation:
Strike an over-cut at your opponent with the intention of striking him. Be sure to have the correct measure. You do not carry the strike all the way down; instead, remain standing in the Hang position, holding your sword rather in the center position. If he holds against it wind his sword inward from the right and try to complete the thrust. The opponent will push harder outward to your right side. Then snap to the other side while blocking his arms with your buckler.

1. LIGNITZER'S FIRST PIECE

Step 1

ARMS:	Deliver a normal over-cut in such a way that your pommel is inside on your buckler hand. The buckler is thus in front of the sword and protects your sword hand.
BODY:	Remain upright, as you will need this posture to wind later.
LEGS:	As you deliver the blow, take a step forward with your right leg so that you are standing in the proper measure.

Step 2

ARMS:	Your opponent will either withdraw or parry your blow with his buckler. Despite this, pull the blow down into the Hang and from there immediately thrust into his face.
BODY:	As you do so possibly lean forward slightly.
LEGS:	Keep your right leg forward and if necessary push your right leg forward slightly.

The fencers are standing in their guards.

White strikes into the Hang. Black can either withdraw, cover with his buckler, or strike into the Bind.

Step 3

ARMS:	Your opponent will push your sword to the side. Now Wind right against the opponent's sword. Depending on the pressure, wind against his blade from the inside or outside. Often the two Winds follow one after the other.
BODY:	Turn your body slightly, depending on the direction of the Wind.
LEGS:	Continue standing with your right leg forward.

Step 4

ARMS:	Your opponent will now exert more pressure to the outside. This is what you have been waiting for. Now strike or snap around to the other side while blocking his hands with your buckler. You strike at his head from your left side with your long edge.
BODY:	Here you will turn slightly to be able to deliver the blow smoothly.
LEGS:	With the blow to the head step your left leg out and forward.

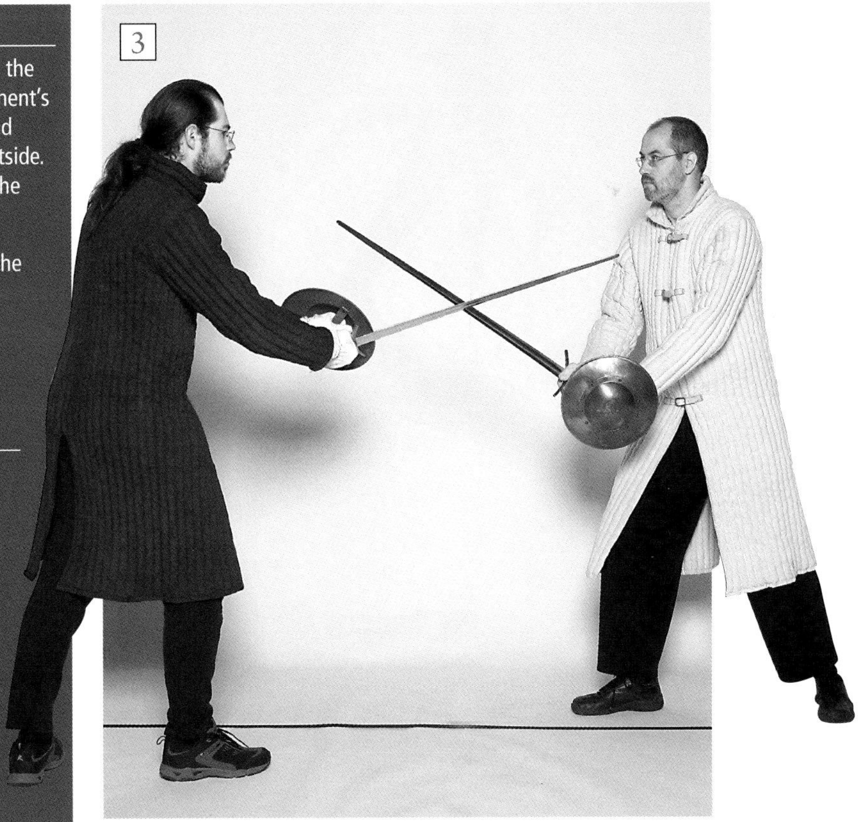

Here Black has engaged the Bind.

From the Bind or the Hang, White immediately thrusts at Black's face.

Black displaces the Bind so that White can not thrust.

White winds upward and brings the point in front of Black's face. If Black reacts too slowly then White simply thrusts at his face.

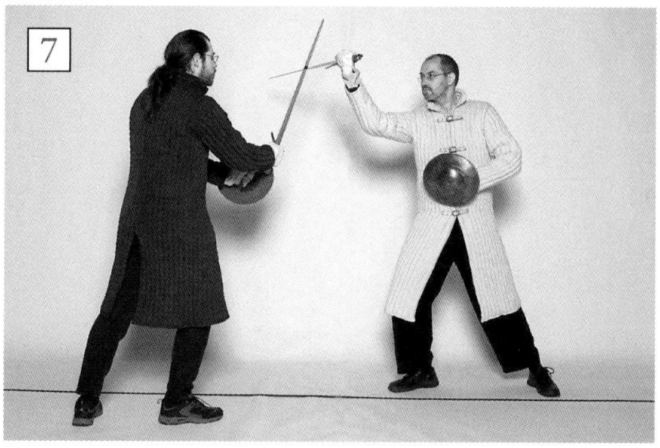

Black displaces the Wind to the right (from White's point of view).

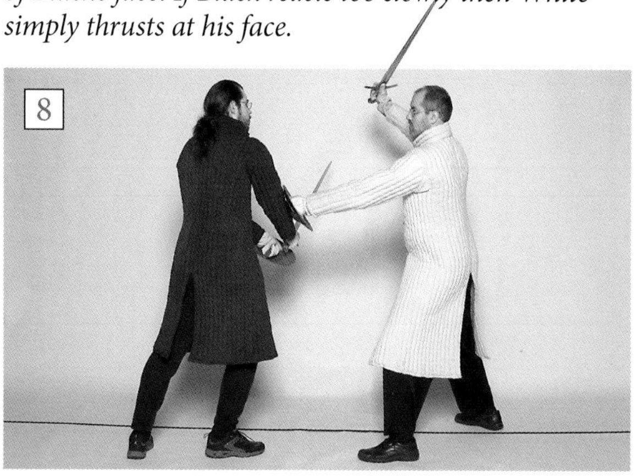

White subsequently knocks Black's arms to the side, disengages the bind ...

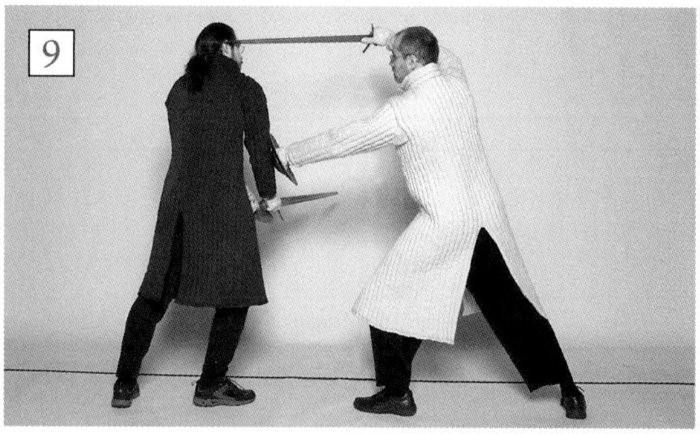

... and strikes around to the other side with a Crosswise Cut. The blow with the shield and the strike at the head take place virtually simultaneously.

9.2 Lignitzer's Second Set-Play

Original:

Das annder stuck
Item aus dem vnderhaw wenn er dir oben zwhaut
so wind gegen ÿm auf dein lincke seitten gegen deinem schilt
so so stestu ÿn zwaien schilten
so wind denn auf dein rechte seitten plos
vnd greife ÿm nach dem maul
wert er dir das vnd hebt den schilt auff
so nym das linck pain das get zw paiden seitten.

Translation:

From the under-cut: if he strikes at you from above then wind against him on your left side against your shield. This leaves you with two shields. Then wind on your right side and strike him in the mouth. If he parries that by raising his shield take his left leg. This works on both sides.

Interpretation:

Your opponent attacks with an over-cut. You respond with your sword and buckler. Without disengaging the bind, strike at his head behind his sword. In long sword techniques this action is called Doubling. If he parries this blow by pushing your blade away then block his hands with your buckler and strike at his legs.

2. LIGNITZER'S SECOND PIECE

Step 1

ARMS: Your opponent makes an over-cut. You meet him with your sword and buckler so that the opponent's blade is taken by the "V" formed by your buckler and sword.

BODY: Try to stand almost directly under the opponent's blow, giving you a stable position, but don't stand too close to him.

LEGS: As you take his blade, step your right leg forward.

Step 2

ARMS: Now Double behind your opponent's blade by striking at his head with your long edge while you push his hands down and slightly to the right with your buckler. Be certain to control his hands or his blade with your buckler.

BODY: Remain upright and work from the hips.

LEGS: As you Double step your left leg forward, practically beside the opponent's hands.

Step 3

ARMS: Should your opponent parry that, he does so only by moving his sword and buckler or his hilt up and to the right (from his perspective). You then push his hands or his blade further upward or outward with your buckler and strike at his front leg with your sword.

BODY: With the blow, possibly lean forward slightly to gain distance. Be sure not to go too low, as you do not want to give up control with the buckler too soon.

LEGS: With the blow step your left leg back to gain necessary space for the technique.

The fencers in their guards.

White begins the piece with an over-cut. Black parries with sword and buckler together.

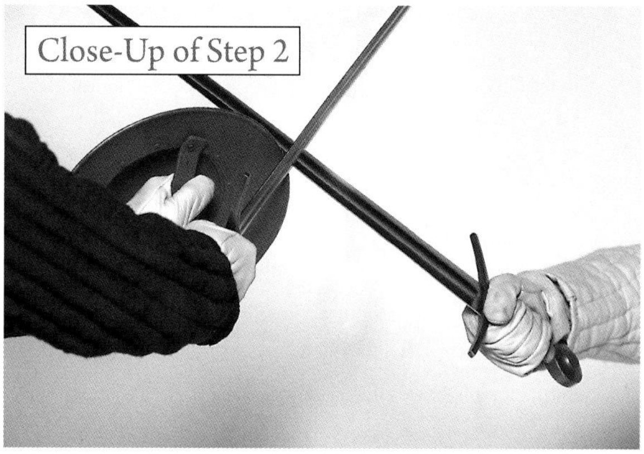

In this parry the sword and buckler form a "V" in which the blade comes to rest.

Black now strikes at the head behind White's blade, he doubles.

White covers with the buckler.

Black also covers with his buckler and strikes at his opponent's leg.

9.3 Lignitzer's Third Set-play

Original:
Das dritt stuck
Item aus dem pucklär aus dem wechselhaw
streich von der lincken seitten aus dem pucklär
vast vbersich in sein swert
vnd haw jm den von der lincken seitten zw dem haupt
vn wind plos
vnd stos ÿm nach dem maul hebt er mit schilt
vnd mit swert vnd wert das
so haw mit der langen schneid jm nach dem rechten pain
das get auch zw paiden seitten

Translation:
From the changing cut, from the left side from the buckler cancel over yourself into his sword and strike at his head from the left. Wind free and strike him in the mouth. If he parries that by raising his sword and shield strike at his right leg with the long edge. This works on both sides.

Interpretation:
Here one begins from a low guard, thus the formulation "from the buckler." One assumes a sort of Fool Guard similar to the Seventh Guard in I.33. Your opponent attacks with an over-cut. From the guard you cancel your opponent's over-cut with your short edge, knock his blade to the side, and from the left side strike at his head. Your opponent will try to parry your blow. Now draw your blade back and thrust at his face. Your opponent will raise his weapon to parry your thrust. Push his hands to the side with your buckler and strike at his leg.

3. LIGNITZER'S THIRD PIECE

Step 1

ARMS: From the low guard, cancel the opponent's over-cut with your short edge striking his blade. Here it is less about knocking away than deflecting his attack. You therefore strike his blade at an acute angle and "slice" into his blow, almost from behind. As soon as his blade is struck make a small circular movement with your wrist over your head and strike at his head from the left side. Be sure to strike in such a way that you cover your opponent's line of attack so that he cannot hit you.

BODY: Remain upright, for you need the range.

LEGS: Take a forward step to the left to avoid his blow. Be sure not to stand too far to the left; you should be able to strike your opponent well. You may have to reposition your right leg slightly.

The fencers in their guards.

Black attacks with an over-cut. White cancels from below with the short edge and forces Black's blade away.

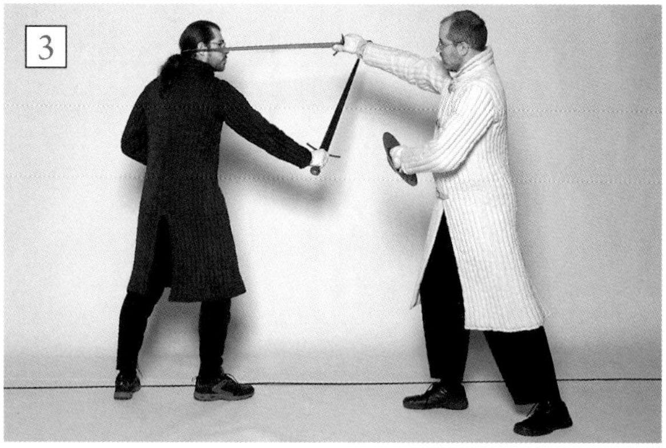

While White shields down and right with his buckler he strikes at Black's head from the left.

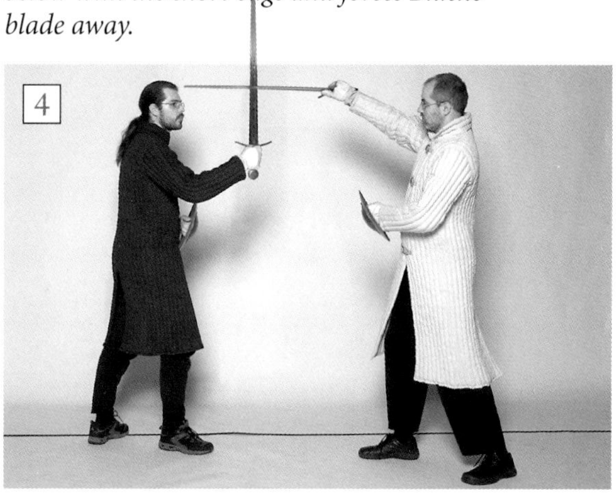

Black succeeds in parrying the attack.

White pulls his blade back, disengages the bind ...

Step 2

ARMS: Your opponent parries your blow at his head. Maintain cover with your buckler and twitch to the rear with your sword, disengaging the bind. Now immediately thrust on the opposite side of the opponent's blade at his face.

BODY: You are still standing upright so this twitch is only delivered from the arm.

LEGS: The legs move only slightly during the thrust to possibly correct the range slightly.

Step 3

ARMS: Should your opponent also succeed in parrying this thrust by pushing you to the side or upward then maintain cover with your buckler and strike at his front leg.

BODY: As you strike the blow you may have to lean forward slightly to gain the necessary range.

LEGS: As you strike at his leg you can step your left leg back. You thus gain the necessary measure for body rotation to give your blow more power.

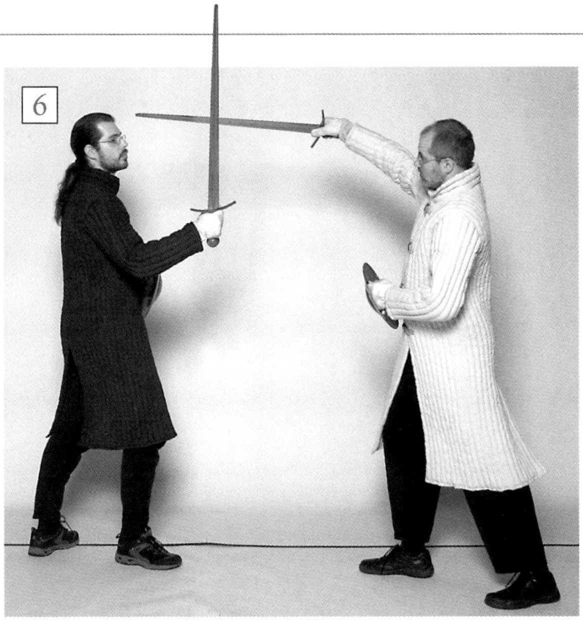

… and immediately thrust at his head.

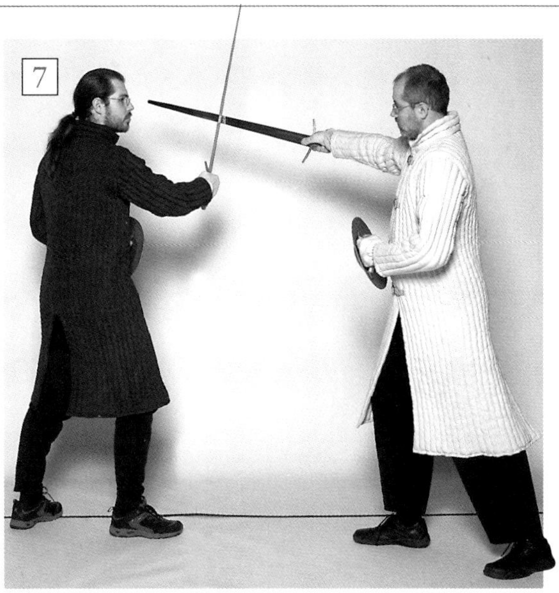

Black again succeeds in parrying the thrust.

White subsequently strikes at Black's front leg.

9.4 Lignitzer's Fourth Set-play

Original :

Das vierd stuck
Item aus dem mittelhaw
mach die twer zw paiden seitten
vnd den schaitlär mit der langen schneid
vnd stich ÿm vnden zw seinem gemächt.

Translation:

From the middle-cut: make the crosswise cut to both sides and the crown cut with the long edge and thrust at his groin.

Interpretation:

Begin your attack with a Crosswise Cut. You can also respond to an attack by your opponent with a Crosswise Cut. Then strike a Crosswise Cut on the other side. Withdraw with a Crown Cut that will force your opponent's cover upward. As you withdraw thrust at his groin or lower opening. Depending on the situation you can strike the first Crosswise Cut on the left or right side.

4. LIGNITZER'S FOURTH PIECE

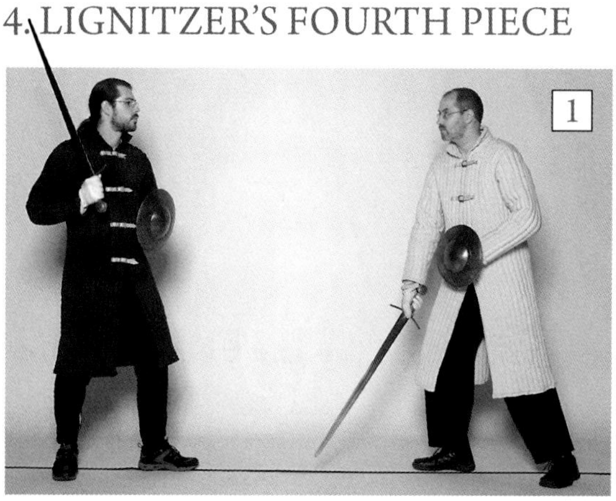

The fencers are in their guards.

White springs to the right and begins the piece with a Crosswise Cut.

Step 1

ARMS:	Attack with a Crosswise Cut or deliver a Crosswise Cut against an over-cut by your opponent. Immediately strike around to the other side with a Crosswise Cut. Keep your buckler in front of you and work with your blade over your buckler.
BODY:	Remain upright and turn with the Crosswise Cuts.
LEGS:	When you deliver the Crosswise Cut from the right step forward to the outside with your right leg. With the Crosswise Cut from the left then step to the left with your left leg.

Step 2

ARMS:	Your opponent will possibly parry the second Crosswise Cut. Then you simply make a Crown Cut at his head. You are already in a withdrawing movement, holding your buckler high.
BODY:	Stretch to achieve the correct measure for the Crown Cut.
LEGS:	You may have to step back slightly with your left leg.

Black parries this Crosswise Cut.

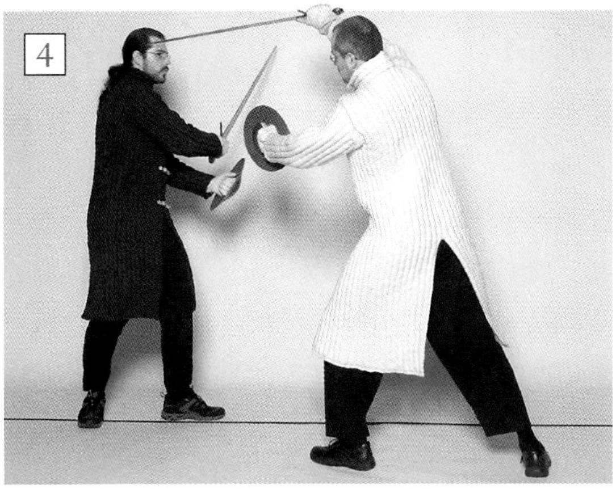

White springs to the other side and makes another Crosswise Cut, shielding right with his buckler.

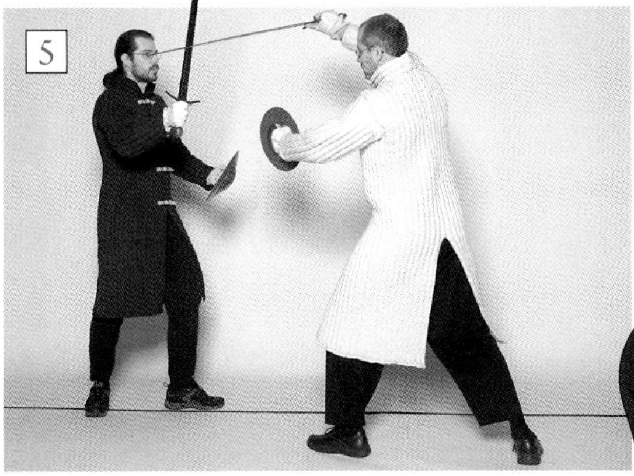

Black also parries this attack.

White subsequently makes a Crown Cut.

Step 3

ARMS: Keep your buckler high to intercept a possible blow from above. Thrust down into the opponent's genitals.

BODY: Lean forward slightly to gain range.

LEGS: It is quite likely you will have to change your measure here. Whether you move forward or not depends entirely on the situation. Personally, I tend to step my right leg forward slightly.

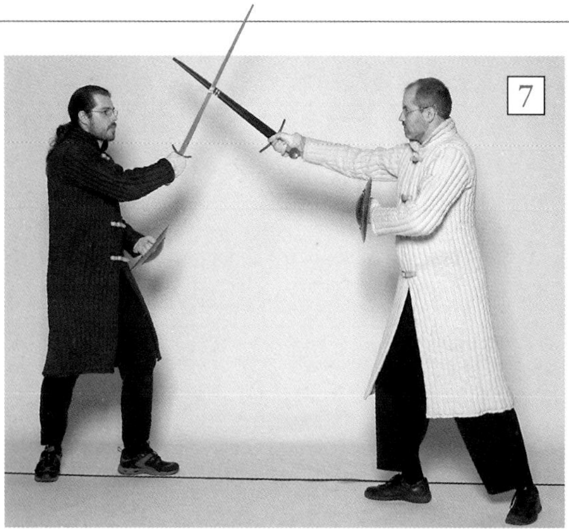

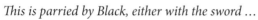

This is parried by Black, either with the sword …

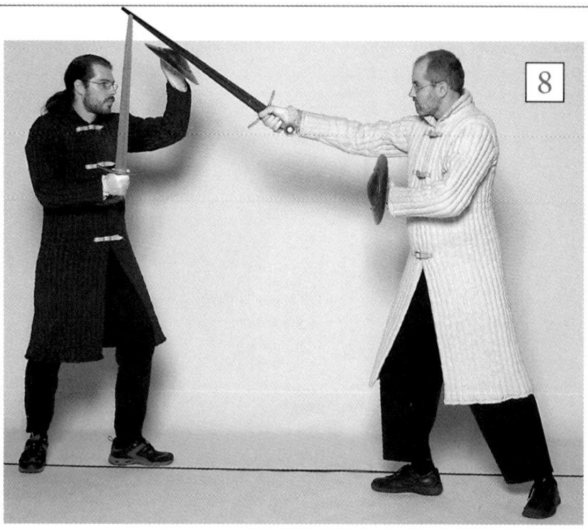

… or the buckler.

White ends the piece with a thrust to the lower opening or the genitals.

9.5 Lignitzer's Fifth Set-play

Original:
Das fünft stuck
Item aus dem sturzhaw tue sam dw jm ze der lincken seitten vber sein schilt wilt stechen
vnd var mit dein ort vnden durch
vnd stich ÿm inwendig seines schildes
vnd wind jnndes aud dein lincke seitten wert er dir das so nÿm sein rechtes pain mit der langen schneid

Translation:
From the Plunging Cut: make as if you intend to thrust over your shield from your left side, lower your point, and thrust inside his shield. Simultaneously wind on your left side. If he parries that take his right leg with the long edge.

Interpretation:
Attack with an over-cut, which in the right measure you change into a Plunging Cut. Shield to the left with your buckler. Your opponent will try to parry this with his buckler. Now move clockwise around the edge of your opponent's buckler and try to get through with a thrust. Should your opponent follow you with his buckler and make a thrust impossible then you end up in a left Ox. Take over cover with your buckler and strike at his front leg.

5. LIGNITZER'S FIFTH PIECE

Step 1

ARMS: You make an over-cut which, at the right measure, you change into a Plunging Cut. This gives you the initiative. Your opponent blocks this Plunging Cut with his buckler.

BODY: Remain upright, as you need good balance for the subsequent actions.

LEGS: Step your right leg forward with the Over-Cut/ Plunging Cut combination.

Step 2

ARMS: Now try to move clockwise around your opponent's buckler. If your opponent gives you the opportunity for a thrust then thrust immediately. You carry out this movement smoothly until you are standing in a left Ox. During the entire action cover the opponent's line of attack with your buckler.

BODY: Be sure that your stance is stable and keep your balance. The proper measure is important here.

LEGS: Keep your right leg forward; any change in measure is accomplished with the upper body.

Step 3

ARMS: From the left Ox strike the opponent's front leg with your long edge, covering his line of attack with your buckler.

BODY: Lean forward slightly to make a powerful blow.

LEGS: Take a step back with your right leg when you strike the opponent's leg.

Both fencers are standing in the From the Roof Guard.

*White begins with an over-cut,
Black raises his buckler.*

*White changes the over-cut into a Plunging Cut
and thrusts at the opening.*

*Black raises his buckler higher and parries the
Plunging Cut.*

*Moving clockwise, White now seeks an
opening to thrust.*

*Black covers his opening and follows the movement of
White's point with his buckler.*

As soon as White finds an opening …

... it is covered by Black. White seeks openings in this way until ...

... he lands in the left Ox.

Once again Black covers his opening. Black now has his weapon raised and is concentrating entirely on the upper opening. It makes no difference here whether Black covers high with his Obuckler or sword.

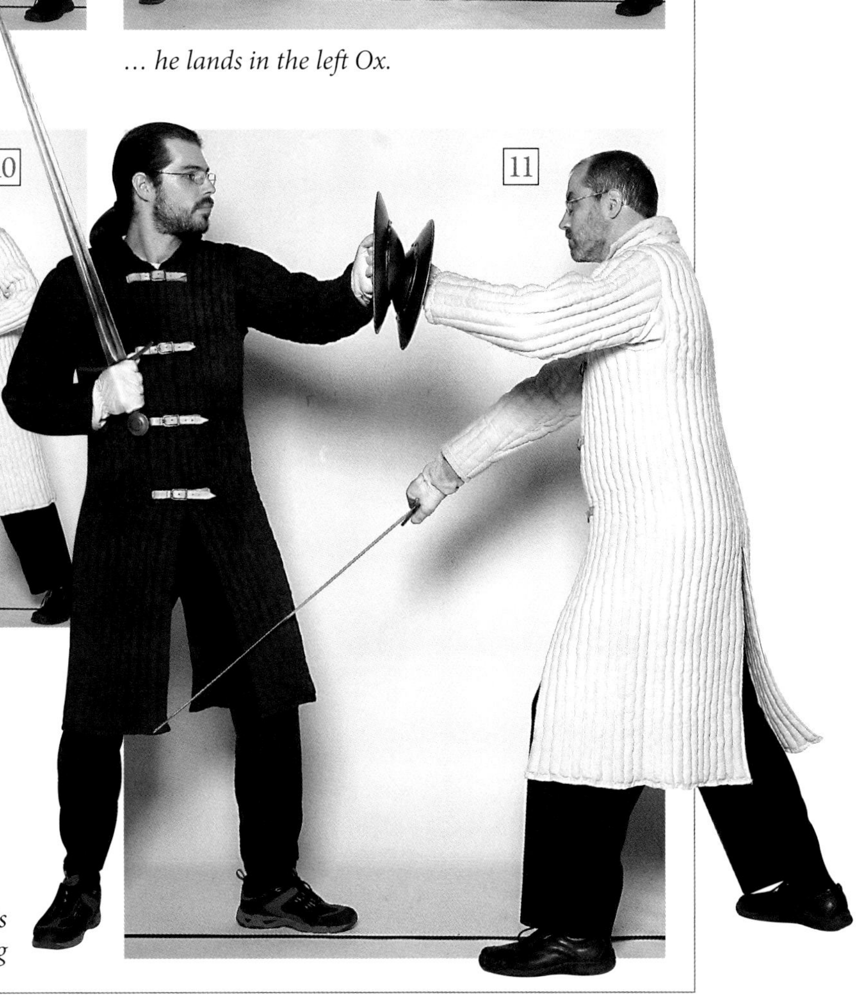

White subsequently takes cover with his buckler and strikes at Black's leg

9.6 Lignitzer's Sixth Set-play

Original:
Das sechst stuck
Item nÿm dein kling
zw dem pucklär in dein lincke hant
vnd wind gegen ÿm als mit dem halben swert
haut er order sticht er dir oben zw dem gesicht oder
vnden nach dem pain
so lass dein rechte hant varen von dem pint
vnd versetz ÿm das mit schilt vnd mit swert
vnd greiff denn mit deiner rechten hand auf sein rechte
seitten nach dem schilt wol vndersich
vnd dre in auf dein rechte seitten
so hastu ÿm den schilt genommen

Translation:
Take your blade in your left hand by your buckler and wind against him with the Half-Sword. If he strikes or thrusts high at your face or down at your leg let your

6. LIGNITZER'S SIXTH PIECE

White grasps his sword at the mid-point with his left hand. He is practically standing in the Half-Shield.

With this weapons combination he now attacks Black.

Step 1

ARMS: Take your sword in your left hand next to your buckler. Hold the blade just behind the mid-point, closer to the hilt. Wield the sword with both hands in this position and attack with a thrust or react to an attack by the opponent.

BODY: Work in an upright position and keep your center of gravity centered.

LEGS: Here I recommend advancing with your left leg so that you can later step forward with your right.

Step 2

ARMS: Deflect your opponent's attack with your sword or cross guard. You can do this safely, as your left hand has excellent protection from your buckler. Try to knock the opponent's blade to your left side.

BODY: Remain upright and move your left shoulder forward.

LEGS: Step your right leg forward as you strike his blade away.

Step 3

ARMS: Now grab the bottom edge of the opponent's buckler and quickly twist it out and to the right clockwise from his perspective. You twist the buckler from the opponent's hand and may injure his wrist. Depending on the opponent's stance and movement you can immediately thrust at his face.

BODY: Bring a body rotation into play. As you thrust try to bring your left shoulder forward.

LEGS: Possibly step forward with your left leg to support the rotation.

right hand move and parry the attack with sword and shield. Meanwhile, grasp his shield with your right hand on his right side and turn him to your right. You have thus taken his shield from him.

Interpretation:
Do not grasp the blade with your left hand quite in the middle, but rather closer to the grip. You should be able to wield sword and buckler well. React to your opponent's attack in this way or attack him. If he strikes at you, let go of the grip with your right hand, parry his attack with the sword and shield, and reach down for his buckler. Now abruptly twist the buckler out and to the right. Executed smoothly, you not only take his buckler, but you may also break his wrist. In any case it is very painful.

Black parries this thrust.

White lets go of his sword with his right hand, forces Black's blade down and left with his cross guard, and reaches for his buckler.

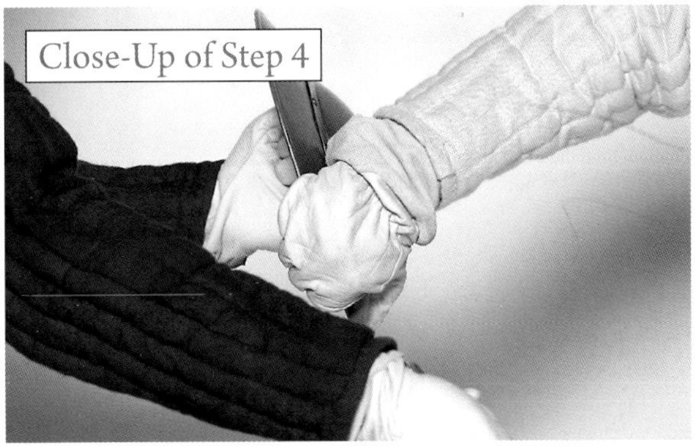

Here too the buckler is grasped by its lower left edge.

The buckler is twisted clockwise and taken.

Difficult Reconstruction: Hans Talhoffer's Set-Plays

Although the name Talhoffer is among the best known in sword fighting, this degree of fame is not entirely justified. The combat manuals written by him stand out on account of their successful representation of the fencers, but also because of a glaring absence of explanations. His representations of techniques with the sword and buckler can only loosely be combined into set-plays. There is much that must be interpolated. Generally speaking, it is only possible to confidently reconstruct snapshots.

These snapshots nevertheless offer justification for several techniques with which we are familiar from the long sword and long knife. In general, Talhoffer's version of combat with the sword and buckler is strongly influenced by the long sword and long knife. This also affects his tactical approach. Here I basically follow the 1467 edition and compare and supplement it with the 1443 and 1459 editions.

It is also interesting to note that Talhoffer attacked the uncovered sword hand but did not consistently cover it in his tables. This covering of the sword hand is typical of I.33 but later appears to have been lost.

10.1 Talhoffer's First Set-Play

The fencers begin from open postures that Talhoffer described as "stances." For the sake of simplicity I stick to the familiar term Guard. In the First Set-Play we are shown two guards that later appear even more often. Both provide high cover. The left guard is interesting, in that the fencer has his thumb on the flat of his sword. The right guard bears a slight resemblance to the Fiddle Bow, but the left hand with buckler is raised. This posture offers an excellent opportunity to begin wrestling. More on this later.

The alternative to this guard—in which the sword rests on the forearm—is the so-called Double Block, in which the attack is parried with sword and buckler. In this way one can even parry very powerful attacks safely. Immediately after parrying one reaches over the opponent's sword hand with the buckler hand and strikes at his head.

This "reaching over" is even easier to manage from the First Guard, for here the blade slides downward. From this better positioning one can grasp the buckler more quickly.

Talhoffer's two "stances" or guards (page from the Munich Talhoffer of 1467).

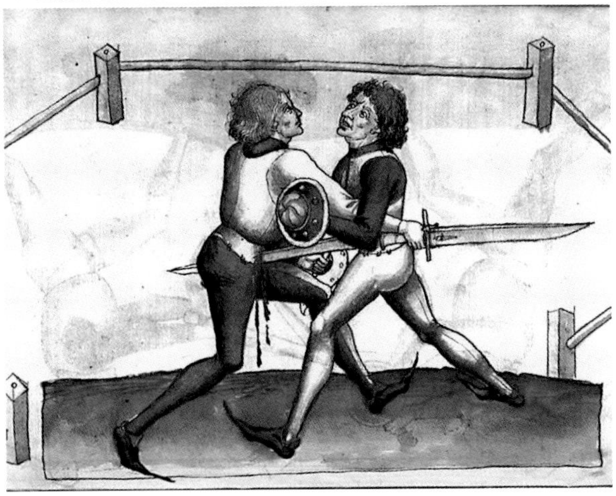

The first illustration depicts "reaching over" with a strike, the second the same maneuver with a thrust. The weapon being used is a long knife, however.

1. TALHOFFER'S FIRST SET-PLAY

The fencers are standing in their guards.

Black attacks with an over-cut, White lets the blade slide off.

Step 1

ARMS: Your opponent strikes at you with an over-cut. You parry it, either with a double block or the variant that resembles an upper Fiddle Bow.

BODY: Remain upright but lean forward slightly.

LEGS: No footwork is necessary here, as the opponent is coming toward you. Be sure to have your left leg forward.

Step 2

ARMS: Immediately after blade contact reach over the opponent's arm with your buckler and seize it in your armpit. To do so, at the beginning reach forward over the opponent's hilt. Simultaneously strike at his upper opening with your sword.

BODY: You must be flexible here to be able to correct measure discrepancies.

LEGS: With the strike, step your right leg forward. This will help you generate sufficient power for the blow.

White reaches around Black's sword hand.

White can now safely strike at Black's head.

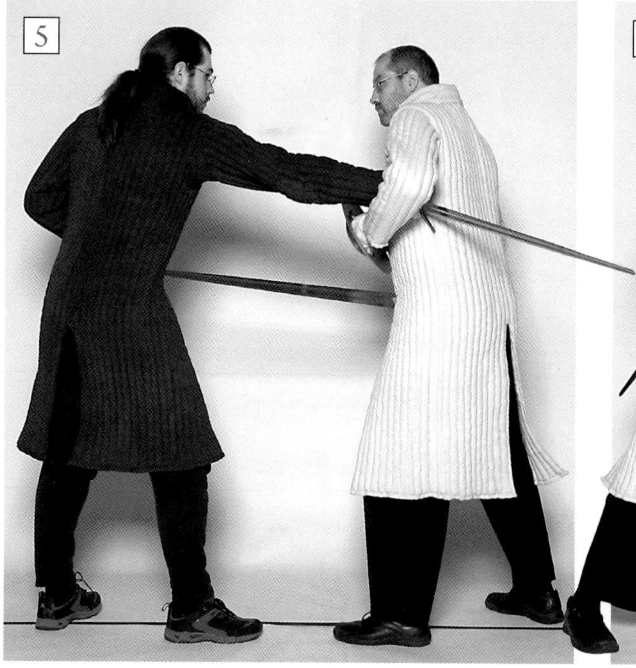

A thrust can also be made.

The thrust from the other side.

10.2 Talhoffer's Second Set-Play

From a desired guard—unfortunately we have no precise information as to which—react to an over-cut by your opponent by letting it slide off to your right side. To do this, take his blow with the flat of your blade so that the force of the blow deflects your blade to the left and past your right side. It is advisable here to place the thumb on the underside of the blade. In this technique the hilt leads—it is in front of the point. With your left—whether with or without the buckler—reach for or strike at the elbow of the opponent's sword hand and twist it to the right. You can then make a thrust or simply deliver a blow to his head. A thrust is illustrated in the manuscript, but I find a blow to the neck more effective here. Footwork is essential, as you must step out of line to the left.

2. TALHOFFER'S SECOND SET-PLAY

Step 1

ARMS:	Parry the opponent's attack by raising your hilt so that you reach forward to your left of his sword. His attack slides down the outer surface of your blade without striking you. Be absolutely sure to engage the bind with your forte against the middle of the opponent's blade. Only then are you close enough for the following techniques.
BODY:	Remain absolutely upright and stretch toward the attack. You need a solid stance for the second step.
LEGS:	As you parry step forward with your left leg, far enough that you come to be standing beside your opponent's arm. In practice you require just a single step to execute this move.

Step 2

ARMS:	Grasp (without buckler) or strike (with buckler) at the opponent's elbows. Push him outward in the direction of his blow and strike or thrust at his lower opening.
BODY:	Here you must lean forward slightly to give your push sufficient authority. If you stop pushing too soon the opponent will still be able to react.
LEGS:	You may possibly have to correct your leg positioning slightly.

The fencers in the guards.

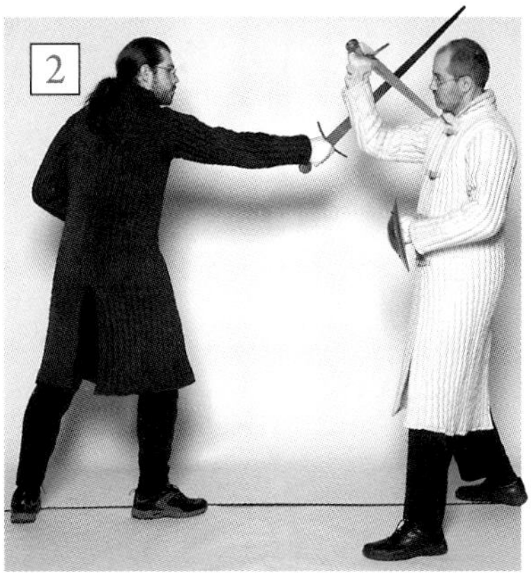

White takes Black's attack with the flat of the blade and deflects it to the right.

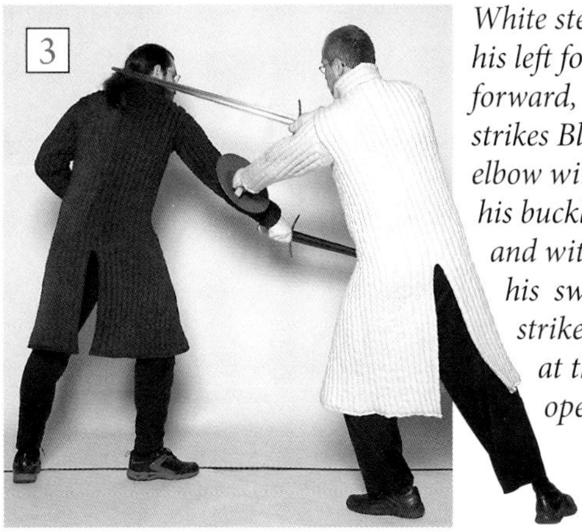

White steps his left foot forward, strikes Black's elbow with his buckler and with his sword strikes at the opening.

10.3 Talhoffer's Third Set-Play

Actually this set-play is nothing more than a reference to the fact that against a thrust one should simply attack the hand of the attacker. The possibilities for the thrust are varied so just one example of the technique will be presented here: you are standing in a guard and your opponent attacks you with a thrust. Step back, possibly slightly to the side, and make a descending cut at the opponent's forearm. You also employ your buckler.

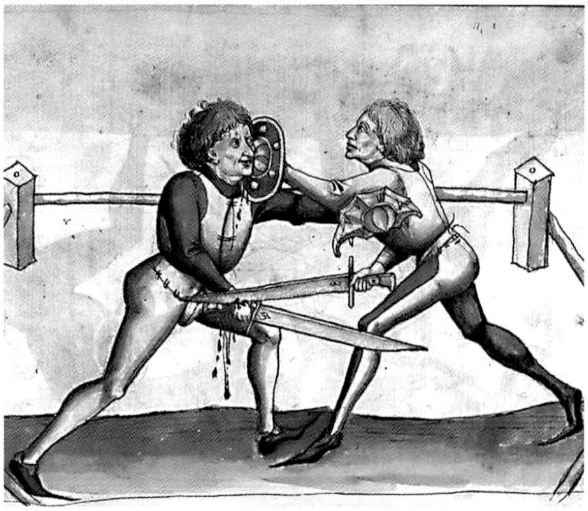

Breaking a thrust. In the illustration at the top the defender thrusts at the opening; below he attacks the sword hand.

3. TALHOFFER'S THIRD SET-PLAY

1

The fencers are standing in their guards.

2

White thrusts at the opening.

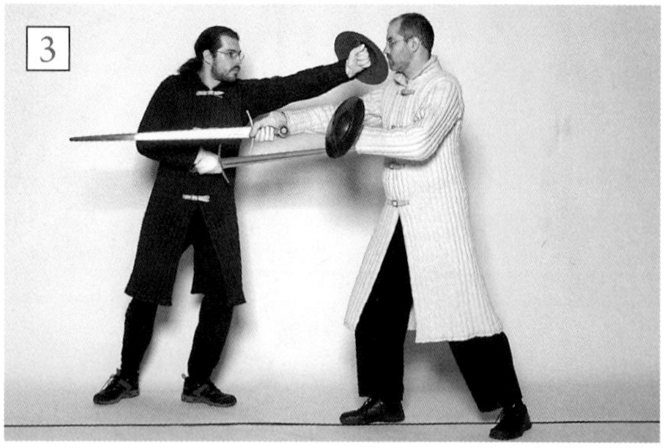

3

Black steps out of line and thrusts under White's thrust directly at the opening while striking at his face with his buckler. In the source, the thrust is made from above (see illustration left), but in practice the thrust under the sword hand has proven most effective.

The fencers are standing in their guards.

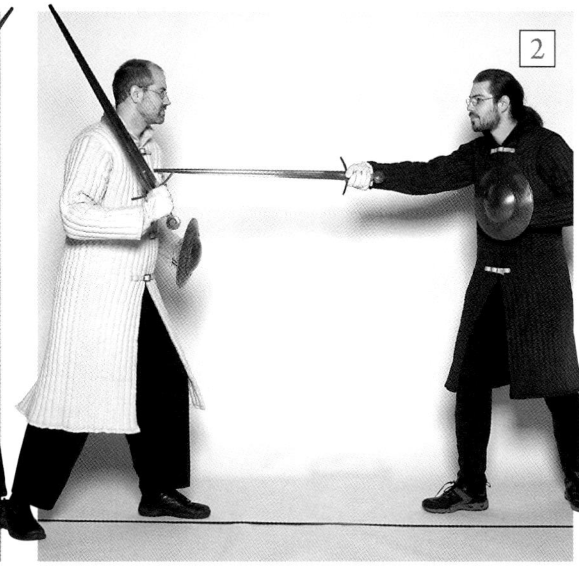

Black thrusts at the opening.

White steps out of line and strikes the unprotected sword hand.

If the measure is appropriate one can also strike with the buckler.

10.4 Talhoffer's Other Set-Plays

In two other panels Talhoffer also addresses combat against two men. Worth mentioning is the fact that in one panel he has a dagger in his buckler hand. The techniques are very unrealistic and would not be very successful in practice. In another panel he depicts a simple under-cut against the opponent's wrist in response to an over-cut. The only important thing here is to step out of line.

The fencers in their guards.

Black delivers an over-cut, White strikes from below against the unprotected sword hand. In the process he steps out of line. This strike against the wrist can also be delivered from above.

The Long Sword and Buckler: Paulus Kal's Set-Plays

Paulus Kal wrote several *Fechtbücher* between 1424 and 1462. What he left us concerning the sword and buckler cannot be characterized as overwhelming, but it is at least deserving of a closer look. The interesting thing about Kal's work is that he combines the long sword and the buckler. The weapons used are clearly long swords and the bucklers are also not normal bucklers. Kal only describes two guards taken from combat with the long sword. These two guards are the Ox and the Plow.

The bind is also very important in Kal's techniques, which is probably why he gave it its own illustration. Kal—like Lignitzer before him—also followed the path of deflecting the opponent. He created the necessary openings by parrying the opponent upward and then attacking the resulting openings.

The bind after an over-cut.

The Ox and Plow Guards.

Black is standing in the Ox Guard, White in the Plow.

11.1 Kal's First Set-Play

The attacker begins with an over-cut. The response to this is extremely simple: Kal advises you to take the attack high with your buckler and simultaneously strike low at the legs.

It may be assumed that the defender began in a kind of Second Guard or From the Roof, as he strikes his opponent's leg from the outside. Of course it is just as possible to attack his leg from the inside.

As a break Kal offers a simple and rather inelegant parry: he simply engages in a low bind against the attacker's blade. Unfortunately he says nothing about what follows.

Here the over-cut is parried with the buckler as the defender strikes at the leg.

The break to the above technique. The attack is parried with the blade.

1. KAL'S FIRST SET-PLAY

The fencers in the Ox and Plow Guards. The starting guards are of rather secondary importance here.

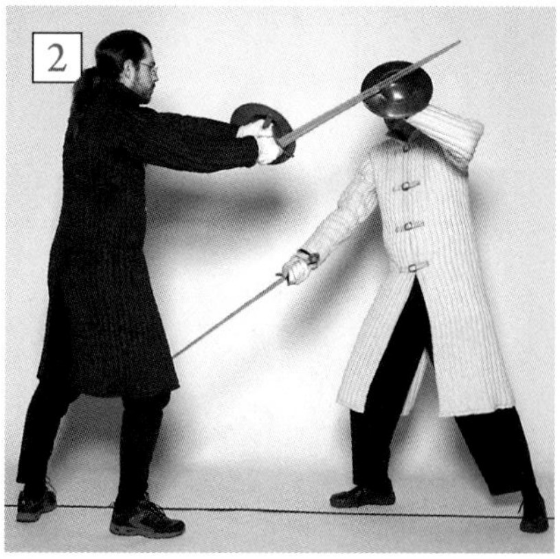

Black attacks with an over-cut and White parries the attack with his buckler and strikes at the front leg.

The break: Black parries White's attack by striking downward at the opponent's blade. From there he can continue working, depending on the pressure, measure, and balance.

As a second possibility of countering an over-cut, instead of a strike at the leg Kal simply thrusts at the lower opening. Here again the attack is begun with the buckler while simultaneously thrusting at the opening.

The over-cut is blocked with the buckler, while simultaneously striking at the opening.

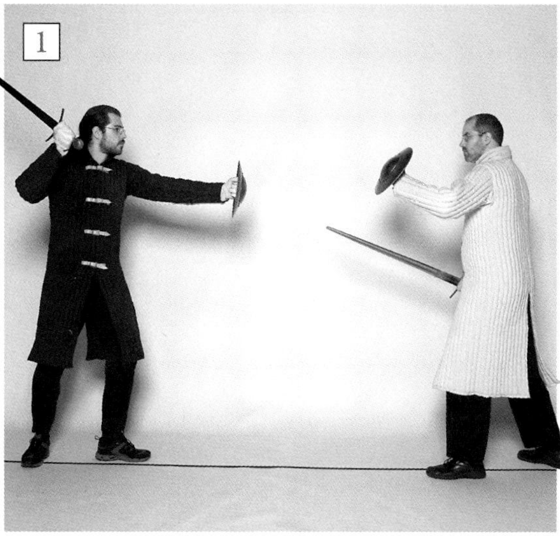

The fencers standing in their guards.

Black begins with an over-cut and White parries it with his buckler and thrusts at the opening.

11.2 Kal's Second Set-Play

The set-play begins in the bind. Immediately after engaging the bind, the fencer reaches over the opponent's hand with his pommel and wrenches it toward him and down. As he does this, he places his blade on the opponent's neck. This technique works very well, because essentially it also contains a strike should the hooking-over with the pommel not work. This works especially well with the longer grip of the long sword.

Wrenching with the pommel. The applied long edge is important here.

2. KAL'S SECOND SET-PLAY

Both fencers are standing in the From the Roof Guard.

The fencers engage the bind.

Step 1

ARMS: If you are in the bind with your forte, or at least the middle of the blade, then move your pommel over the opponent's wrist. As soon as your pommel is over his wrist wrench the opponent's hand downward and towards you while you strike at his neck with your long edge. Should your pommel slide from the opponent's hand deliver the strike anyway.

LEGS: Step your left leg forward to reach a closer measure necessary to execute this technique.

Step 2

ARMS: Pull the opponent's wrist up and back towards you while pushing his elbow down with your buckler. Increase the pressure of the blade on the opponent's neck.

LEGS: Step your right leg back slightly. This enables you to achieve a rotation in your hips that makes the techniques even more effective.

White moves his pommel over Black's hand and hooks on.

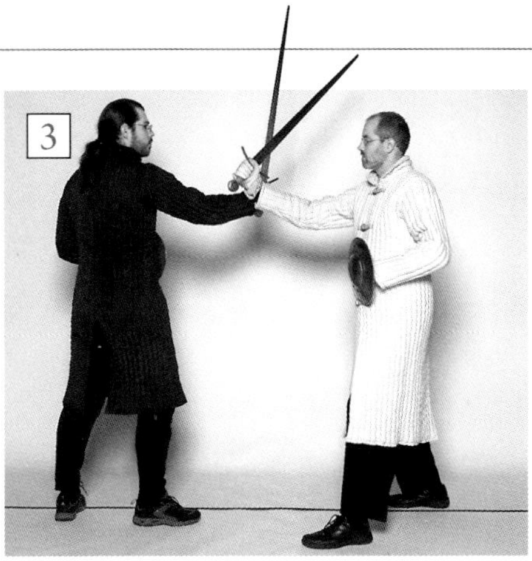

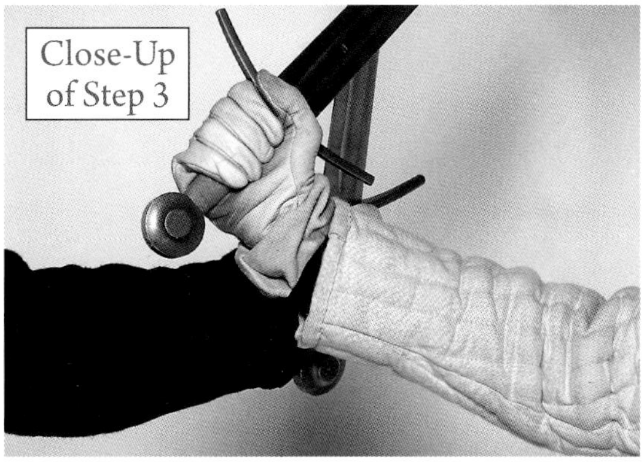

White lays his blade on Black's neck.

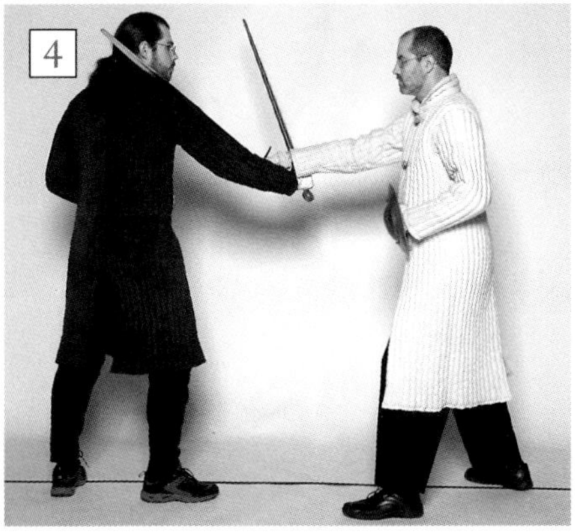

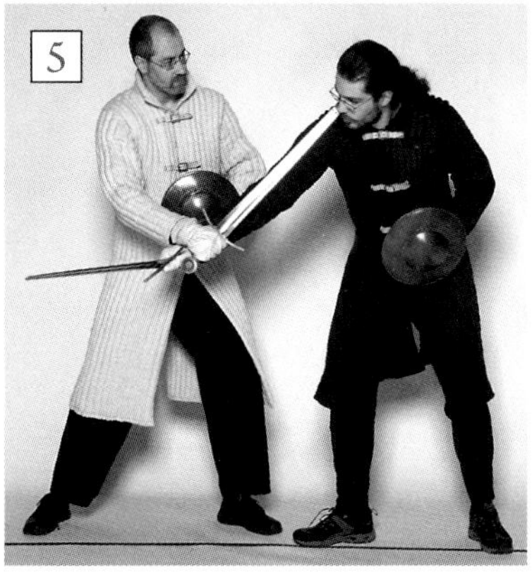

Use the pommel to grasp or hook the wrist.

Seen from the other side. White's blade is against Black's neck.

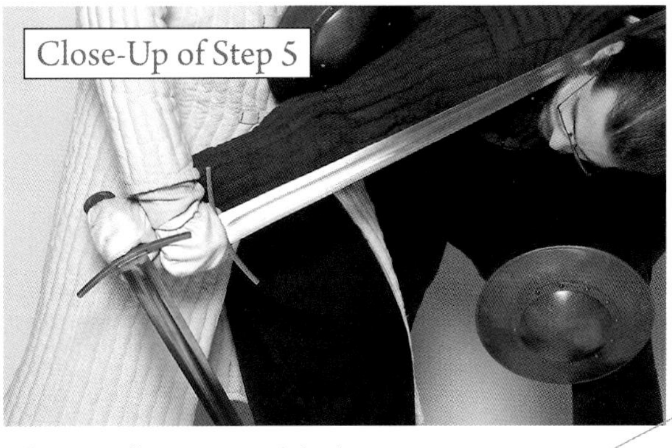

Close-up illustration of the lever.

With pressure Black is now levered. His arm is against White's hip and White pushes Black's elbow down with his buckler while pulling his wrist upward.

11.3 Kal's Third Set-Play

Here Kal illustrates the taking of the opponent's buckler as described in Lignitzer's Sixth Set-Play (section 9.6). The only difference here is how the sword is gripped.

Ideally one commences this technique from a low guard—the Plow for example. With your buckler hand, grasp the blade at the mid-point so that the point is pointing upward and take the opponent's blade with both weapons. Simultaneously, grasp the inside of the opponent's buckler (bottom right) and with a sharp clockwise twist rip it from the opponent's hand. You can subsequently hurl the buckler into the opponent's face as shown.

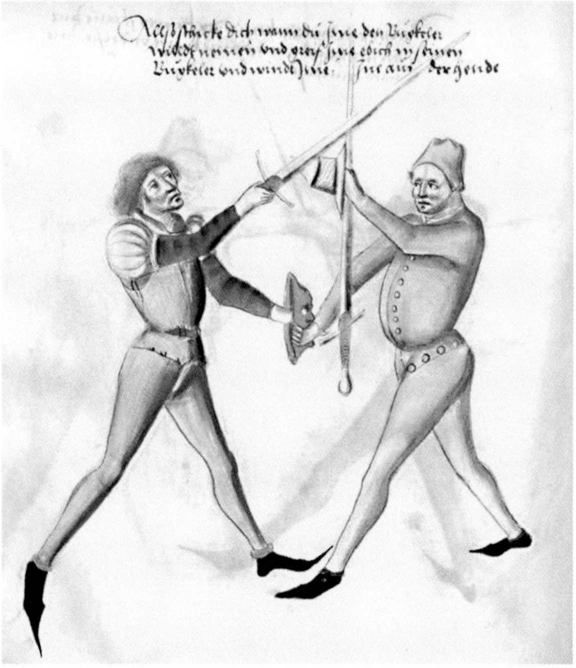

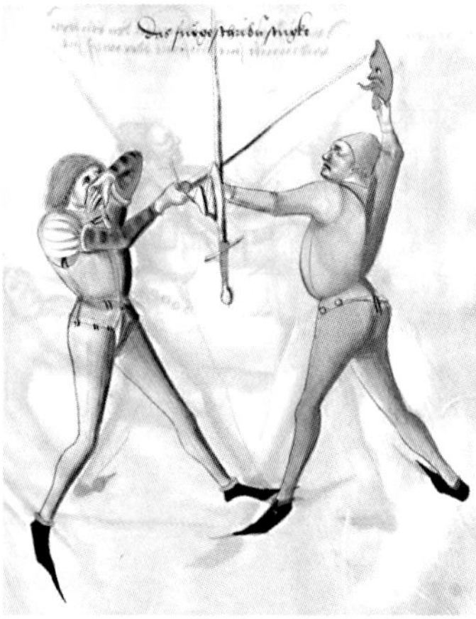

The over-cut is parried with the sword and buckler in one hand while reaching for the opponent's buckler with the other hand.

To conclude the technique the opponent's buckler is hurled into his face.

3. KAL'S THIRD SET-PLAY

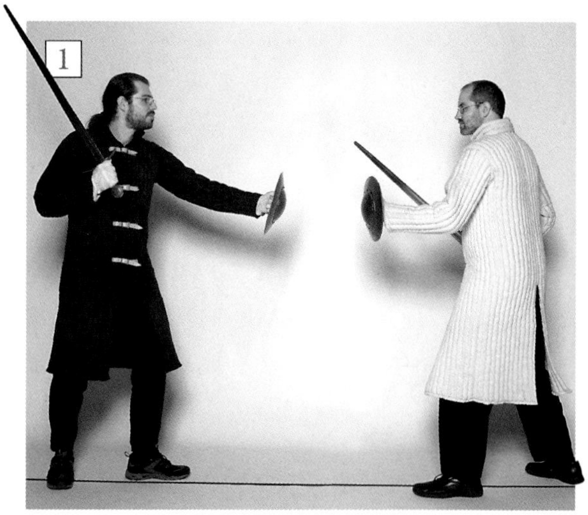

The fencers begin in the guards.

Step 1

ARMS: Grasp your blade at the mid-point as inconspicuously as possible. Turn the buckler with the front toward the opponent and take his over-cut in the "V" between your sword and buckler. Simultaneously twist the buckler out of the opponent's hand. To do this you grab the buckler at the bottom left and turn it outward in a clockwise direction.

LEGS: Step forward as you parry so that you are within reach of the opponent's buckler. Of course this technique only works if your opponent is holding his buckler in front of him.

White has grasped his blade at the mid-point, steps forward, and parries Black's over-cut. At the same time White grasps Black's buckler.

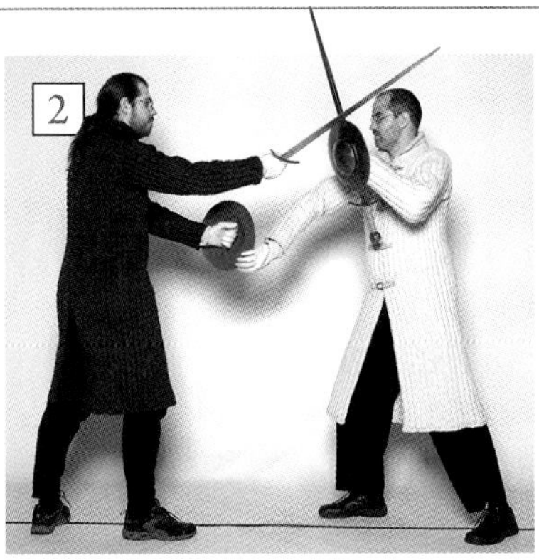

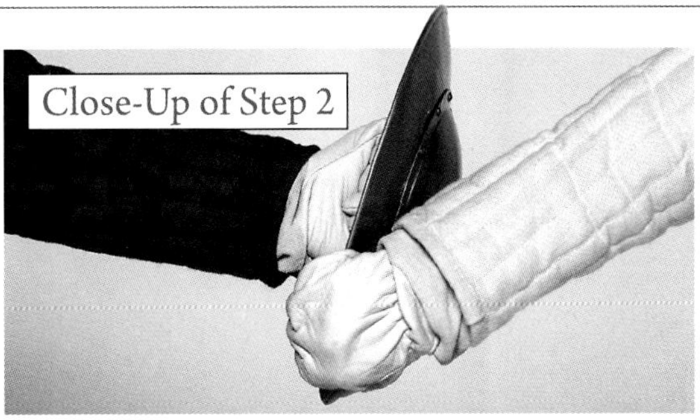

The buckler is grasped on the inside at the bottom and the back of the hand faces down and left.

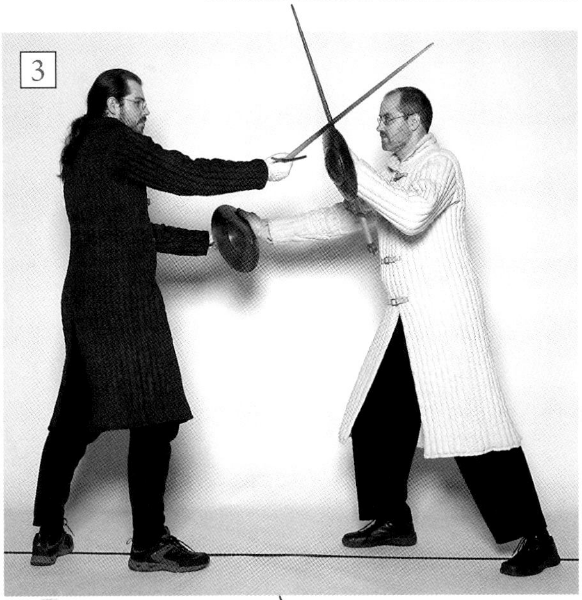

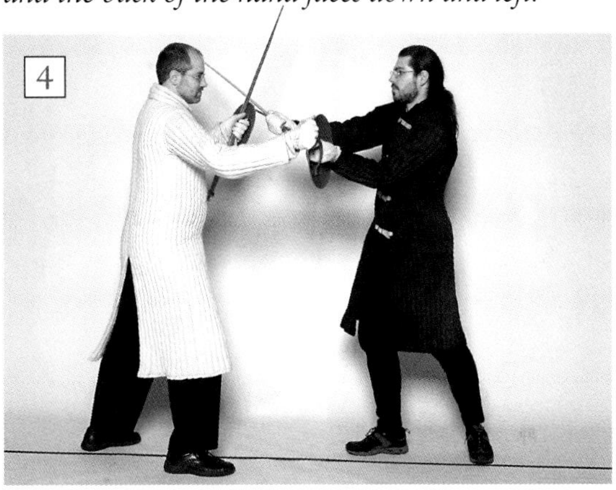

White abruptly twists the buckler outward in a clockwise direction. If Black does not let go immediately this twist is very painful.

The taking of the buckler from the other side.

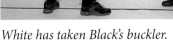

White has taken Black's buckler.

The captured buckler is used as a weapon.

11.4 Kal's Fourth Set-Play

This technique also functions as a response to an over-cut. Here the fencer attacks around the opponent's sword arm with his buckler and strikes at his head. Unfortunately, Kal does not explain how the bind was engaged. Similar techniques are described in other fencing manuals, such as the Codex Wallerstein or that of Talhoffer. If we follow these techniques, then it is probable the bind was a run-through, in which the hilt is held high to deflect the opponent's blade. Then the opponent's sword arm is attacked and a thrust made at the opening.

Kal adds that one can throw the opponent to the ground with this technique. To do this, one simply stretches out one's own buckler hand and strikes the opponent in the chest. If this is carried out smoothly with the previously mentioned step toward the opponent then it is entirely possible to throw him.

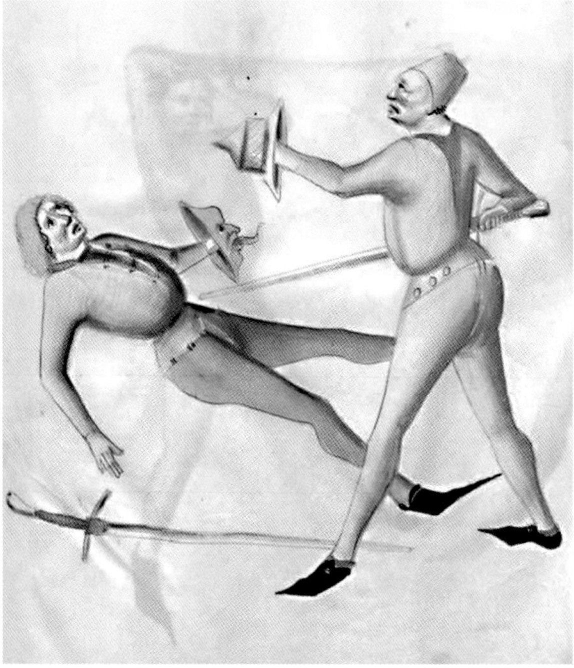

The throw at the conclusion of the Fourth Set-Play. Simply strike the opponent in the chest with your buckler.

4. KAL'S FOURTH SET-PLAY

White takes the opponent's blade with the flat and the opponent's blade slides off.

Step 1

ARMS:	Hold your buckler in front of you with your arm almost outstretched. Your sword is practically resting on your left forearm, the long edge facing forward. The hilt is held higher than your head and your point is aimed down and left. Your buckler is roughly at shoulder height or somewhat higher. Now allow the opponent's over-cut to slide left down the flat of your blade.
LEGS:	Step your left leg forward as the opponent's blade slides off.

Step 2

ARMS:	As soon as the opponent's blade slides off, with your buckler hand reach over the opponent's sword hand with a spiral motion and freeze it. You simultaneously strike at the opponent's head.

White reaches around the sword hand, freezes it …

… and ends the set-play with a thrust. Obviously he could also strike.

White now pushes Black in the chest with his buckler. The opponent can be thrown this way.

Offensive Action: Blows with the Buckler

There are several techniques that are useful in combat but are not mentioned in the fencing manuals. For a reconstruction that is faithful to the sources one must omit these techniques. Nevertheless, several of them are useful in combat.

I would not like to address all of these techniques here, as that would exceed the scope of the book. I have described important alternative techniques in the appropriate places. What is still missing is the active, offensive use of the buckler.

This is completely ignored in some sources, including I.33. In later sources we find several techniques in which the buckler is actively employed, i.e., those of Paulus Hector Mair and Wilhalm.

The buckler can definitely be used as a weapon. Blows with the buckler are powerful. Delivered properly they can have a devastating effect. Basically, blows with the buckler can be struck in two ways: with the front of the shield and the rim or edge.

The blow with the shield can only be delivered in a close measure. But this alone supplements the system wonderfully, for usually the sword is of no more use in a close measure. Often it is only possible to employ the pommel.

Here the buckler offers a real alternative. In combat one often gets so close that the blade can no longer be used. At the same time the combatants are still too far apart to grapple. It is then that the buckler comes into play.

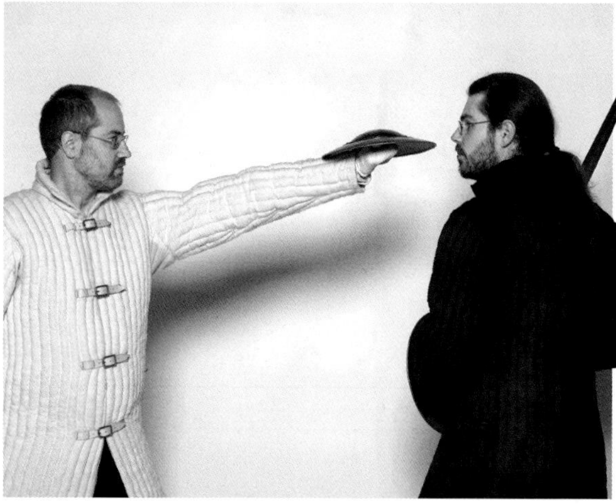

Blow with the edge of the buckler. This technique enables you to increase the range slightly. Because of the thin edge a blow with the rim of the buckler is more painful.

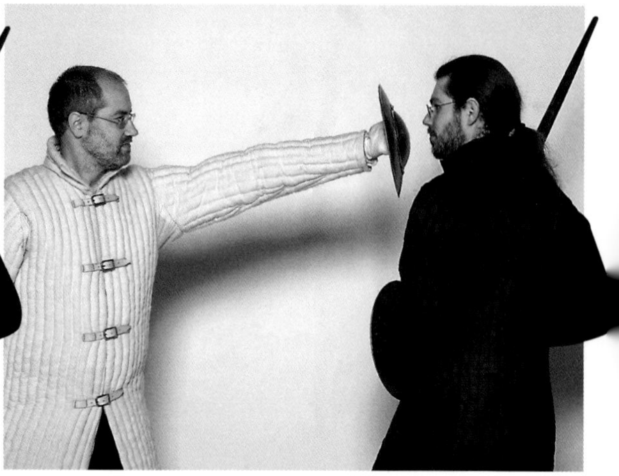

Blow with the boss. Here the range is somewhat less and the blow is not as painful, as in most cases the impact area is larger (depending on the buckler). These blows are preferable in training.

The main target of the buckler is obviously the head—particularly the face—as one can achieve the greatest effect there. In a close measure a fencer often does not cover his sword hand. In this situation a blow on the wrist with the edge of the buckler often decides the outcome. Be very careful with this in training. You can easily break bones. Exactly when the buckler is employed in this way depends on the situation and is difficult to pin down. Basically, I would casually say if it works, then do it! Do not forget that the buckler can do more than just shield, block, and deflect. The buckler is a weapon, and if properly employed a very good one.

When you strike with the buckler it is important to hold your wrist straight: your arm should take the force of the impact, not your wrist. It is necessary to adjust your grip on the buckler so that the part of the buckler you need is forward with your wrist straight. With practice this becomes automatic.

Second Guard against the Priest's Hat.

White responds to Black's over-cut by canceling from below.

Immediately after deflecting the blade White moves his pommel forward and strikes Black in the face.

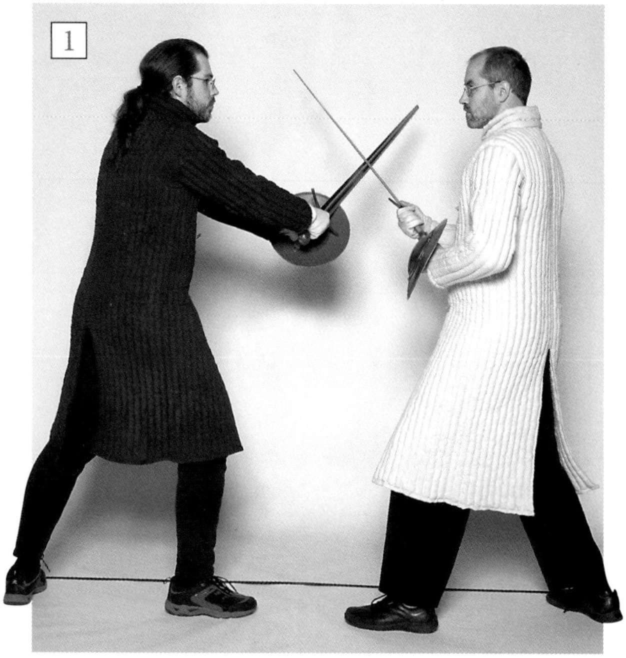

White has deflected an attack by Black but is standing in a close measure.

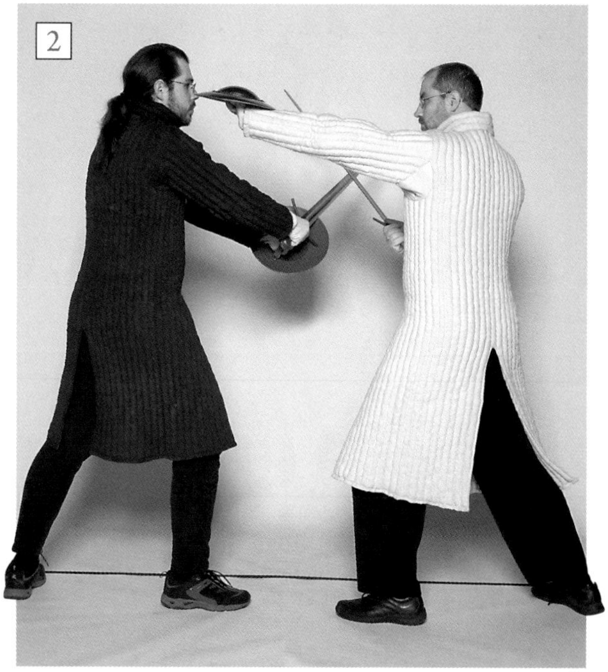

In this situation a blow with the buckler is a good alternative.

In this situation a blow with the buckler is a good alternative.

Black's over-cut is simply cancelled downward.

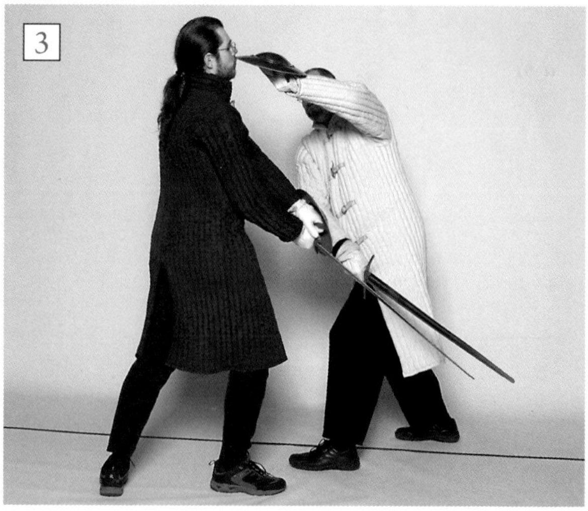

He simultaneously strikes Black in the face with his buckler.

Blow with the front side of the buckler from Jörg Wilhalm's fencing manual.

Blow with the edge of the buckler from Paulus Hector Mair's fencing manual.

A set-play from the fencing manuals of Wilhalm and Mair: White in the Long-Point and Black in the First Guard.

Black reaches for White's point, a technique with which we are familiar.

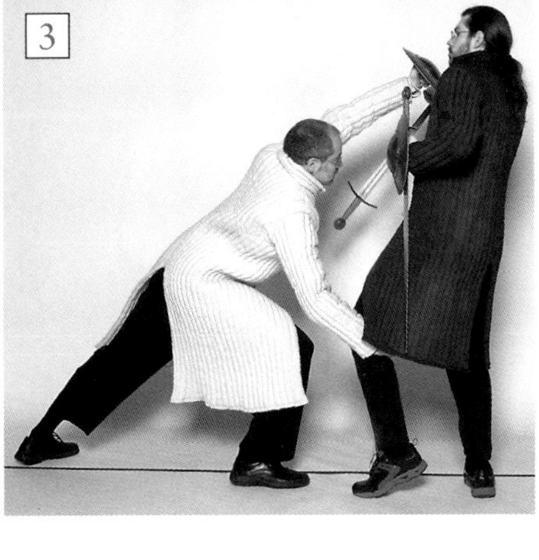

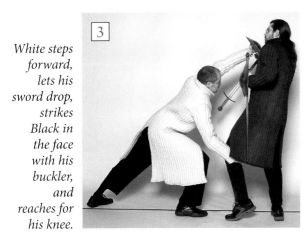

White steps forward, lets his sword drop, strikes Black in the face with his buckler, and reaches for his knee.

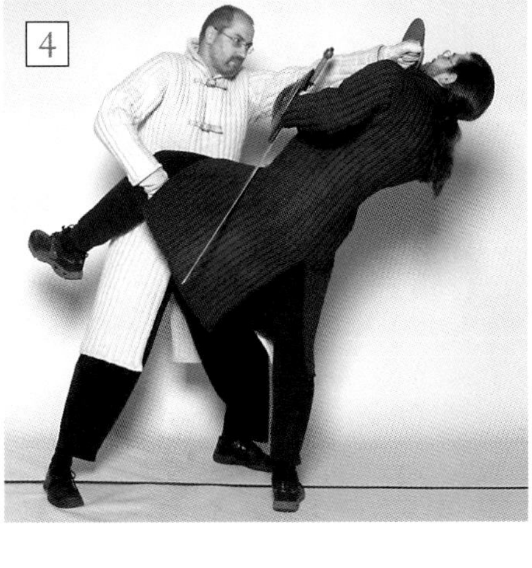

By lifting the knee and the pressure of the buckler in the face White throws Black backward.

Safety First: The Equipment

If it is pursued seriously, historical sword fighting demands that its practitioners approach the subject on a variety of levels. Every fencer wants to come as close as possible to original combat situations. On the other hand, today we must give thought to safety during training.

Safety is always in the foreground and every decision regarding equipment must be made with this in mind. The question therefore arises: which equipment enables me to achieve the highest degree of realism without endangering my partner? Even the best equipment does not provide protection against poor control.

Today the selection of swords, bucklers, and other equipment is very large. This does not make it easier to decide in favor of one or the other. Here I will illustrate and briefly describe the most important items of equipment.

13.1 The Sword

The one-handed sword is something completely different than the two-handed long sword. The two-handed sword has much greater power delivery because it is wielded with two hands. A short sword can also be very dangerous, but normally it does not deliver as much power to the blow as a long sword. With one-handed swords it is also more appropriate to use steel swords in training. Where the short sword is concerned, in my opinion many alternatives to the steel sword are not justified.

Bamboo

Bamboo swords (*shinais*) come from Japanese kendo. They must be modified somewhat for our purpose, for the original shinai has no cross guard and is too light. They are also too long, at least as a replacement for the short sword. So-called "children's shinais" have proven effective. They are meant for children and are therefore somewhat shorter. One should add some lead to the shinai to make it heavier and try to achieve a more realistic "feel." Shinais are flexible, so they bend easily in a strike. They are too rigid for a thrust, though.

The design of the shinai means that it absorbs energy in a strike. This makes them particularly well suited for free fighting. They are less well suited for training, however, as many techniques are not possible or only with difficulty. In addition, shinais can wear out very quickly. Regular maintenance can help extend the life of the bamboo sword, but this requires disassembly, which is not to everyone's taste.

Wood

Wooden swords are usually quite inexpensive to buy. They have a very wide striking edge and a thick, round tip that reduces the risk of injury. Depending on how they were made, the care they receive, and how they are used, wooden swords can last quite a long time. Unfortunately, many techniques cannot be practiced realistically with a wooden sword. They distort the feeling in the bind. Wooden swords almost never have the balance and weight of good steel swords. Wooden swords can be thoroughly recommended for beginners, especially when learning new techniques, as they are safer than steel swords when training without protective gear. But never underestimate the potential danger of the wooden sword. They are rigid in the thrust and capable of inflicting serious injuries and are therefore not suitable for free fighting.

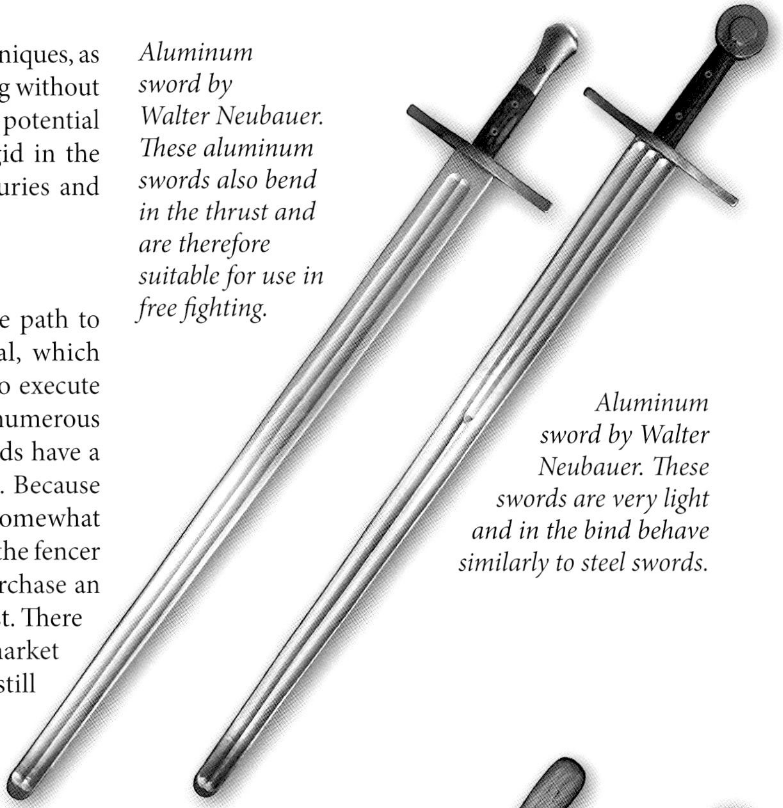

Aluminum sword by Walter Neubauer. These aluminum swords also bend in the thrust and are therefore suitable for use in free fighting.

Aluminum sword by Walter Neubauer. These swords are very light and in the bind behave similarly to steel swords.

Aluminum
Aluminum swords are the next step on the path to the proper sword. They are made of metal, which enables many techniques that are difficult to execute with bamboo or wooden swords, such as numerous techniques from the Bind. Aluminum swords have a wider striking edge than many steel swords. Because of that and their lighter weight they are somewhat safer than steel swords. They also do not tire the fencer as quickly. When shopping, be sure you purchase an aluminum sword that also bends in the thrust. There are now good aluminum swords on the market that are very light. Nevertheless, I would still recommend a steel sword.

Steel
The blunt steel sword is the best option. Ideally it has a striking edge with a thickness of about two millimeters (.08"). Balance and weight distribution should be as authentic as possible. If possible, its weight, balance, and dimensions should be no different than those of a good, sharp sword. The big difference between steel and other materials is apparent in the bind. Combat with the sword and buckler involves a great deal of work from the bind, so I would definitely recommend a steel sword combined with the necessary safety equipment.

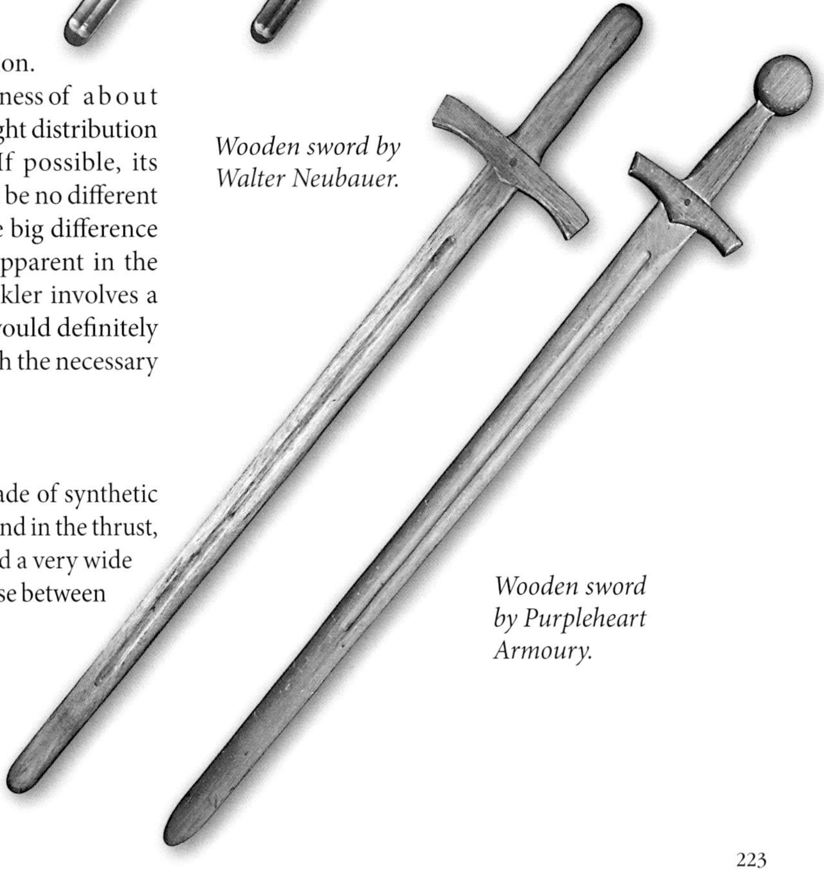

Wooden sword by Walter Neubauer.

Wooden sword by Purpleheart Armoury.

Synthetic Materials
A newcomer to the field is the sword made of synthetic materials, i.e., polyamide. These swords bend in the thrust, have a very slippery binding behavior, and a very wide striking edge. They represent a compromise between

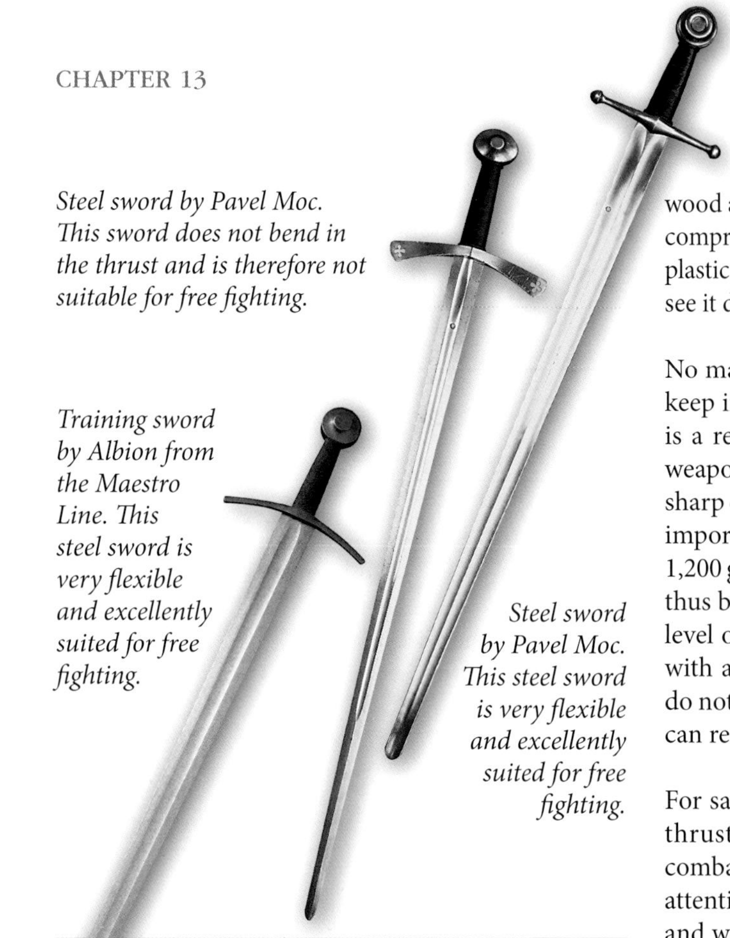

Steel sword by Pavel Moc. This sword does not bend in the thrust and is therefore not suitable for free fighting.

Training sword by Albion from the Maestro Line. This steel sword is very flexible and excellently suited for free fighting.

Steel sword by Pavel Moc. This steel sword is very flexible and excellently suited for free fighting.

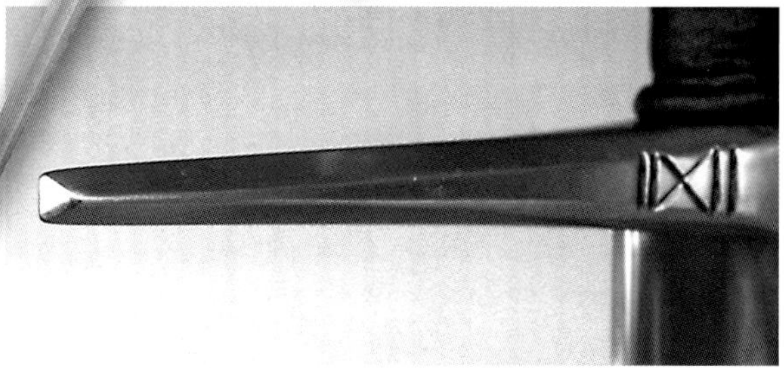

This cross guard is too thin and pointed. Painful injuries are easily possible with it.

This cross guard is absolutely safe. Round with fattened ends, not much can happen. Your training partner will be grateful for it.

wood and steel or aluminum swords. Unfortunately, this compromise has not turned out as hoped. In my view plastic swords are an experiment that failed. Other fencers see it differently, however.

No matter your ultimate decision, you should always keep in the back of your head that a training weapon is a replacement for the edged sword. This training weapon should therefore be as close as possible to the sharp original. The balance and weight are particularly important. As a rule, a sharp original weighs 1,000 to 1,200 grams (2.2–2.65lbs.). Your training sword should thus be in this weight class and have a corresponding level of balance. Weight is very important, especially with a single-handed sword. With a light sword you do not tire as quickly, are more nimble in combat, and can react with greater agility.

For safety's sake it is vital that the sword bend in the thrust. The thrust is an important component in combat with the short sword and buckler, so pay close attention to the sword's stiffness. It should bend easily and well but not be "wobbly." After a strong bend the blade should also return to a straight position.

The cross guard is also important. There are very pointed cross guards. These are perhaps justified in serious combat, but not on a training weapon. Watch out for rounded or thickened ends.

13.2 The Buckler

After the sword, the buckler is the second most important item of equipment. There are basically three kinds of buckler: wood, leather, and steel. The buckler should have a minimum diameter of 25 centimeters (9.84"), but it should also be no larger than 40 centimeters (15.75"). Pay attention to the weight: the buckler should not be heavier than the sword and should therefore weigh between 1,000 and 1,400 grams (2.2–3lbs.). Light is better here, provided the shield is robust enough.

The grip should fit the hand comfortably and allow for quick turns but also enable a sure and firm grip. It should not turn in the hand if pressure is exerted on the rim. The boss should be large enough to enable the shield to be gripped while wearing heavy gloves. The metal in the boss should have a thickness of at least 1.5 millimeters (.06").

Wood
The typical wooden buckler has a shield boss made of metal, while the shield itself is wood. As the rim of the wooden buckler wears out very quickly if used against steel swords, it is advisable to cover the shield rim with thick leather or, even better, rawhide. The wooden buckler can be used without restrictions. One should check regularly for cracks in the wood, a tight fit between the shield and boss, and looseness in the grip. Wooden bucklers generally have a limited life, but with proper manufacture and care even a wooden buckler can last a long time.

Leather
Leather bucklers are historically documented. The leather was hardened by boiling it in wax. This made the leather very stiff, comparable to modern plastics. The leather buckler's greatest advantage is its weight. Unfortunately, leather bucklers are not as durable as wooden or steel shields. The wax can also melt easily if exposed to high temperatures.

Steel
The steel buckler is the most durable version. The selection of steel bucklers is very large, but one should pay attention to different things. The buckler should not be too thin, otherwise it will not last very long, as it will become too deformed. In extreme cases it can even split open and allow a thrust to pass through, especially if the metal is already weakened. The buckler should also not be too heavy. Thick bucklers can eventually cause a fencer to tire and unnecessarily slow his movements. I personally use a buckler with a thickness of 1.5 millimeters (0.06").

Always expect to have to modify the grip of a new buckler and adapt it to meet your personal preferences. The grip can usually be modified using a variety of materials. For this reason, the grip should not be reason not to purchase if the rest of the buckler meets your needs.

As yet nothing has been done to this buckler's grip. It is uncomfortable and makes wielding the buckler difficult.

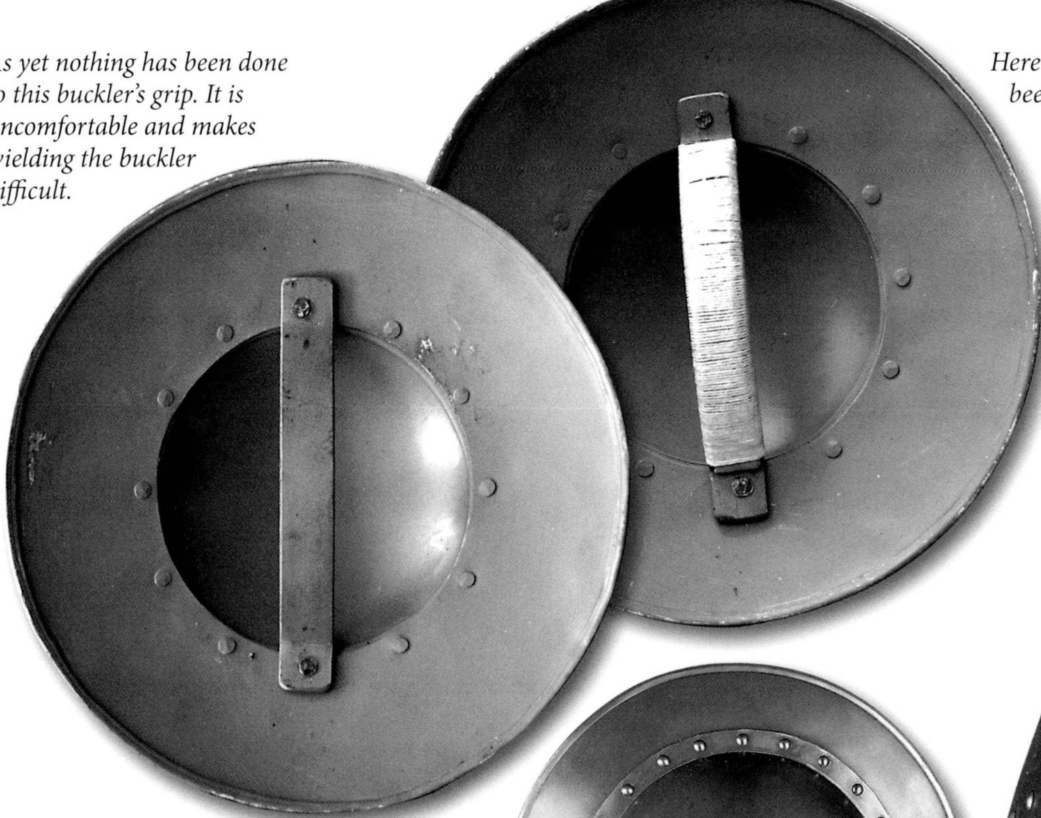

Here the grip has been lined with leather and wrapped with cord. The buckler is thus much easier to control. The grip can be made fatter or thinner according to personal preference.

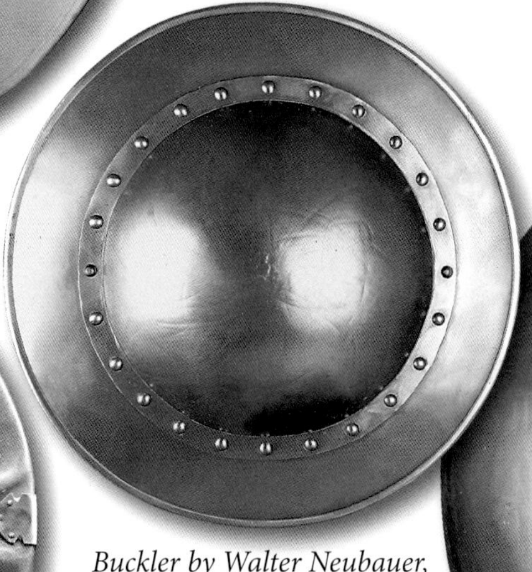

Buckler by Walter Neubauer, metal thickness 1.5 mm (0.06").

Buckler made of steel and wood by Mercenarys Tailor. Note how the rim of the shield is enclosed in rawhide.

Side view of the buckler: here the shield boss itself is rather shallow. Whether one accepts a very rounded or shallow boss is a matter of personal taste.

13.3 Protective Gear

In addition to a suitable sword and buckler, for unrestricted free fighting you also need protective gear. There are hundreds of possibilities and each fighter should choose what is best for them. Most fencers follow their own path and procure their own equipment. The motto "Anything that works is allowed" applies here. For this reason one usually finds a mix of historical and modern items of equipment.

Head
The head is best protected with a fencing mask. Fencing masks usually provide no protection for the back of the head. It is advisable to add something there yourself. Be sure that the mask is designed for a load of 1600 N. This ensures the screen is stiff and strong enough. Leather padding is also available for many fencing masks. This is highly recommended.

Neck
Here only a steel gorget can be recommended. Even thrusts against the larynx are no problem when wearing one. A good gorget also offers protection against blows on the side of the neck. The bib in front is also important, so that thrusts from below cannot slide under the neck protector. Along with the fencing mask, the gorget is one of the most important pieces of protective gear.

Joints
There are many possible ways to protect elbow, shoulder, and knee joints. Suitable protection can be obtained from ice hockey or motocross specialty stores. Other types of sport also offer good protective equipment.

Torso
The gambeson has proven most effective protecting this area. This heavily padded jacket was also used in the Middle Ages. Those who wish to can also add breast and shoulder protectors. Several companies offer good protective equipment for riot control. For combat with the short sword one can also use leather master fencer jackets, which have also proven their effectiveness.

Hands
Heavy gloves for hockey or lacrosse have now become standard. Somewhat cheaper but still very good are real fencing gloves. Good fencing gloves are not easy to obtain. As the sword and buckler were usually used in unarmored combat, pieces of armor, though contemporarily accurate, are not absolutely correct. They are also heavy and tire the fighter prematurely.

Arms and Legs
Hockey equipment provides good protection, but items used in lacrosse and in some cases motocross are also useful.

CHAPTER 14

The Most Important Part of Training: The Free Fight

The free fight is a very important part of training. It is impossible to learn how to fence without the free fight. Techniques and one's skill are put to the test in the free fight. In free fighting we frequently encounter problems that arise in fencing. Particular weaknesses should be approached regularly in free fighting to improve.

The free fight is the closest thing to real combat with sharp edges. During combat with the sword and buckler in particular, it is important to place the opponent under physical pressure and to manage the pressure that you yourself experience. This can only be practiced through free fighting. The possibility that you may hurt your partner is more than a side effect: it is an aspect that causes stress. One must learn to deal with this stress. Clear thinking and purposeful reaction under stress distinguish a good fencer.

In free fighting, the risk of injured joints, broken bones, and other serious injuries must be minimized. This can only be achieved if two things are considered: equipment and control in combat. The better the equipment, the less the risk of injury. But the less the risk of injury, the greater the readiness of the fencer to take risks that he would not take in combat with sharp weapons. Too much protective gear results in a loss of respect for the blade or the fencer becoming careless. As well, the effect of hits is often underestimated, as they are not so easily felt when wearing good equipment. For this reason you should always only wear as much protective gear as required, but not more. As the master fighters learned long ago, "*Was zehrt, das Lehrt,*" which can be loosely translated as "that which hurts, teaches," or more simply, "no pain, no gain."

Apart from the protective gear worn, one's own weapon must be kept under control at all times. If you are too tired or distracted to have sufficient concentration and control in a combat then stop it immediately. This is not only better for you, but also fair to your partner.

In free fighting blows should be struck with full speed, but not necessarily with full force. As well, you should be able to stop a strike or thrust if you see that your partner will be injured by it. With sufficient training much can be done for safety in this respect. Never forget: it is about training and learning, not just about winning. You are fighting with a partner and not an opponent.

In free fighting the objective is to defeat the opponent. All available techniques are employed, along with kicks, punches, and throws. The objective is to simulate a serious sword fight as safely and as realistically as possible. Safety is the number one requirement—but beyond that every weakness of the opponent is exploited to decide the outcome in your favor. You should also begin a free fight with this attitude. For this reason, before combat it is important to clarify what the combat is all about. For this purpose, I have established the following stages of training:

- Technique training – learning the techniques.
- Technique combat – turning the techniques into fluid, free fighting in which maximum control is exercised. The speed is less, and if possible there is no contact with the opponent.
- Training combat – free fighting with full equipment, but in which only certain previously discussed techniques are employed. This serves to test the techniques for their viability and learn them at realistic speeds.

- Free fight – combat with full equipment, in which everything is permitted (with reasonable restrictions). Here everything available to you is used to win the duel.

Several peculiarities come into play in free fighting with the sword and buckler. Free fighting with the sword and buckler is much safer compared to the long sword because the force generated by the short sword is less. With flexible steel swords thrusts are no problem. With suitable protective clothing most blows also pose no problem if the fencer has the needed control.

There is also the buckler: very effective blows can be delivered with the buckler and in particular the edge of the buckler. These should not be left out of free fighting. Most blows against the fencing mask pose no problem, but a heavy blow on the forearm or hands with the edge of the buckler can result in broken bones. Here one should either dispense with these blows or strike with the front of the buckler.

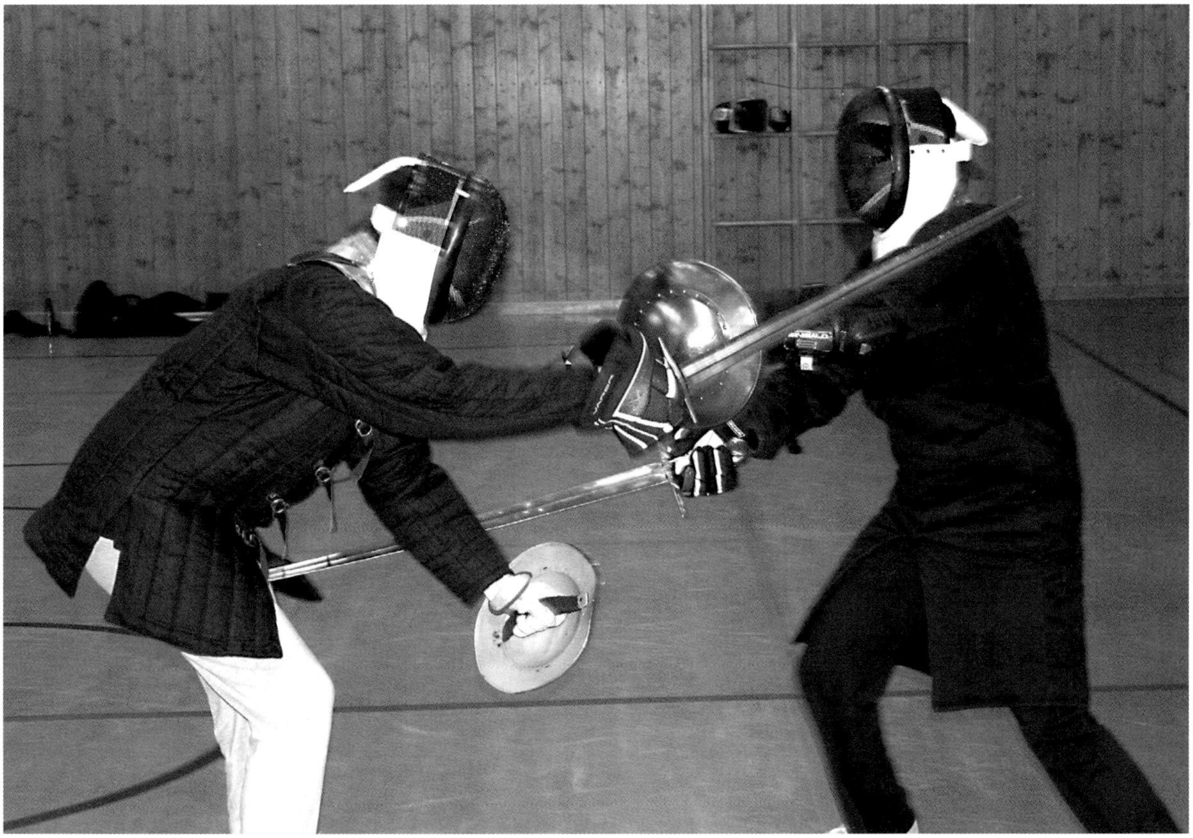

The thrust at the lower opening. Good equipment is definitely an advantage here.

Very Briefly: Tips and Tricks from Experience

During training there are always things that one should take into consideration and that repeatedly cause problems. Here are some tips on how to make your training more effective.

Guards

Regularly carry out a guard exercise, in which you assume all of the guards and counter-guards as well as the protections and constantly change between them. This will make you familiar with all the guards and with time the postures will become quite natural. Remain standing in each guard for a time and try to be relaxed but not limp. "Ready to react, but not tense" is the goal of this exercise. Then carry out every possible attack from each guard quite casually. Become familiar with attacking from the most different angles from each guard. Pay attention to proper footwork, balance, and especially clean blade control during these exercises. You should also be capable of beginning unconventional attacks from each guard.

Blows

Practice the different blows as often as possible. You should strive to execute every blow as perfectly as possible. This includes clean blade control, as well as good balance while striking and transferring power from body movement into the blow. Only a small percentage of striking power comes from the arms; the majority should come from your body. Also practice the movements of over-binding, the shield-strike, and so on. You should also practice stop-blows. These are blows delivered at a target with utmost speed and power but without hitting the target. You stop the blow just short of the target. This gives you great certainty in handling the weapon and makes training safer for your partner. Be sure to deliver the various blows from the different guards.

Thrusts

Do not ignore thrusts! Bring your entire body into play when making a thrust. Practice delivering a thrust from a great distance as quickly as possible. You should be able to thrust quickly and unexpectedly but controlled. Do not forget use of the buckler with the thrust.

Left, Right

Practice every strike, every guard, and every technique from the left and the right. As a right-hander, you should place somewhat more emphasis on your left side. The ultimate goal is the ability to execute with equal effectiveness from the right and left. You can also train effectively by consciously using your left hand more in everyday life.

Blade Follow-Up

If you are technique training, then the one who is struck should always continue wielding his blade. In real combat, a fencer will not necessarily stop an arm or hand movement just because he is struck. This follow-up with the blade also forces the fencer to pay attention to his own protection and respect the opposing blade. This will also enable you to see immediately whether or not the respective lines of attack were covered or not.

Footwork

Footwork is extremely important. Though it is different for each person, it is important that every fighter always have a stable posture from which he can act and generate power at any time.

Line of Vision

You should practice "peripheral vision"—seeing and perceiving as much as possible from the corners of the eyes. Look your opponent straight in the face, in the eyes. At the same time you should also keep his shoulders in sight. Never look at the opponent's weapon, or even worse, at the point of his weapon.

Measure

Make every attack, every strike, so that it can land. If you strike past the opponent in training, then not only are you fighting unrealistically, you are depriving your partner of the opportunity to learn the techniques properly.

Speed

Work slowly. Consciously do everything very slowly at the start. Learn the correct movements first. Soon they will become second nature and it will be easy to increase speed. It is important to learn to execute movements cleanly so that under stress they can be recalled again cleanly. This point is often overlooked.

Errors in Technique

If a technique does not work then repeat it until it does. If you cannot reach the point where the technique works then work on interpreting the technique. You can assume that the historical techniques handed down to us are correct. The mistake usually lies with oneself, so always begin there.

Clear Intentions

Tell your training partner as clearly as possible what you want to practice, how fast, and how intensely. The objective should always be clear.

Passive Partner

The training partner—who is the recipient of the technique and usually "dies" in the end—should take his role seriously. Make clean attacks, exert some force in the Bind, and alert your partner to poor balance, incorrect footwork, or other errors. At this moment you take on the role of a control mechanism and you have to assess whether the technique has functioned. Good training is only possible with a good partner.

Fooling Around

The temptation to fool around with the sword is great. Make yourself aware that most accidents occur in this situation.

Practice Frequency

Practice as often as possible, even if it is for only five minutes, during which you strike several blows.

Playing Allowed

Play with your weapon with necessary caution. Take the sword in your hands as often as possible. Become familiar with its weight, handling, and length. The more familiar you are with the weapon the better.

Results Orientation

Pay attention to the subject of your training. You will be able to do what you train for, so you should repeatedly check whether you are still on the path that you actually want to follow. This is particularly important in free fighting so you do not become "blinded by routine."

Checks by a Third Person

Ask a third training partner to observe your free fight. Not only will you receive useful feedback, but this third person will also be able to ensure that you do not exceed the previously determined speed. That is another safety aspect. It is also always helpful to record engagements with a video camera.

Appendix: Addresses, Sources, Information

Links

FIGHTING SCHOOLS AND SERIOUS SWORD FIGHTING GROUPS:

EUROPE:

HEMAC www.hemac.org

AUSTRIA:

Ars Gladii www.arsgladii.at
Dreynschlag www.dreynschlag.at
Fachverband für historisches Fechten www.historisches-fechten.at
Klingenspiel www.klingenspiel.at
Rittersporn www.rittersporn.at

GERMANY:

Ochs www.schwertkampf-ochs,de
Zornhau www.zornhau.de
Freifechter www.freifechter.de
Hammaborg www.hammaborg.de

SWITZERLAND:

Freywild www.freywild.ch

ENGLAND:

School of Traditional Medieval Fencing www.ringeck.org
Schola Gladiatoria www.fioredeiliberi.org
Boars Tooth www.boarstooth.org

FRANCE:

De Taille et d'Estoc www.detailleetdestoc.com

Other groups in Europe can be found on the map by Ars Gladii. Simply look under the heading "Left" at www.arsgladii.at. This map is updated regularly.

Internet Forums

ARS GLADII FORUM:
www.forum.arsgladii.at or on the homepage of Ars Gladii

SCHOLA GLADIATORIA FORUM:
www.fioredeiliberi.org/phpBB2/index.php

Swords and Equipment

The following is only a small selection of current manufacturers.

ALUMINUM TRAINING SWORDS:

Walter Neubauer www.trainingsschwerte.de
Walter.neubauer@freenet.de

STEEL TRAINING SWORDS:

Albion www.albion-europe.com
or www.albion-swords.com
Pavel Moc www.swords.cz
Paul Chen www.casiberia.com
Arno Eckhardt www.dietraumschmiede.de

SHARP SWORDS:

Albion www.albion-europe.com
or www.albion-swords.com
Vince Evans www.arscives.com/vevans
Arno Eckhardt www.dietraumschmiede.de

GORGETS AND OTHER ITEMS OF EQUIPMENT:

Mercenarys Tailor www.merctailor.com

Bibliography

Albrecht Dürers Fechtbuch
Hs. 26-232 / Albertina (Collection of Prints and Drawings), Wien Cod. 1246 / University of Breslau Library

CGM 558
Transcriptions by Didier de Grenier, Michael Huber, and Philippe Errard

COD. HS. 3227A
Transcription by David Lindholm

COD. 1074 NOVI von Wolfenbüttel
Transcription by Alexander Kiermayer

CODEX WALLERSTEIN
Gregorz Zabinski and Bartlomiej Walczak
Paladin Press, ISBN: 1-58160-339-8

Das Schwert (The Sword)
Thomas Laible
ISBN: 978-3-38711-05-7

Deutsches Klingenarchiv (German Blade Archive)
Dr. Heinz Huther, In-House Publisher

Egenolph 1529
Transcription by Alexander Kiermayer

Gladiatoria
KK5013 / MS. germ. quart 16 / Cod. Guelf. 78.2 Aug 2° Transcription by Carsten Lorbeer, Pragmatische Schriftlichkeit

Hans von Speyer
M.I.29 University Library Salzburg

HS.BEST.7020
Historical Archive Cologne, Transcription by Andreas Meier, Marita Wiedner, Pragmatische Schriftlichkeit

Jakob Sutor's *Künstliches Fechtbuch*
ISBN: 3-937188-26-6
VRZ Verlag

Journal of the Armour Research Society
Volume 1, 2005, ISSN 1557-1297
Armour Research Society

Jude Lew COD. I.6.4°.3
University Library Salzburg,
Transcription by Grzegorz Zabinski

Meister Johannes Liechtenauers *Kunst des Fechtens*
Martin Wierschin,
C.D. Beck Verlag, Munich

P 5126
(incomplete copy, late fifteenth century)
Art History Museum Vienna, Manuscript Chart. B1021, 1542 / Research Library Gotha, Castle Friedenstein

Paulus Hector Mair
Codex Vindobonensis Palatinus 10.825
Austrian National Library, Vienna

Paulus Kal
Cgm 1507, circa 1460
Bavarian State Library Munich

Peter von Danzig
Cod. 44 A 8 (Cod. 1449) 1452, Bibliotheca dell'Academica Nazinale dei Lincei e Corsiniana, transcription by Grzegorz Zabinski

Records of the Medieval Sword
Ewart Oakeshott
ISBN: 0-85115-566-9
Boydell & Brewer LTD

Sigmund Ringeck
Manuscript Dresd. C487
Saxony Regional Library / Dresden
Transcription by Martin Wierschin

Solothurner Fechtbuch 1506 – 1514
Central Library Solothurn

Swords of the Viking Age
Ian Pierce
ISBN: 1-84383-089-2
Boydell Press

The Martial Arts of Renaissance Europe
Sydney Anglo
ISBN: 0-300-08352-1
Yale University Press

The Medieval Art of Swordmanship
Jeffrey L. Forgeng
ISBN: 1-891448-38-2
Chivalry Bookshelf

The Secret History of the Sword
J. Christopher Amberger
ISBN: 1-892515-04-0
Multi-Media Books

The Sword in the Age of Chivalry
Ewart Oakeshott
ISBN: 0-85115-362-3
Boydell Press

Würgegriff und Mordschlag
Hanz Czynner, Ute Bergner and Johannes Giessauf
ISBN: 10-3-201-01855-4
Adeva Verlag

List of Guards

A tabular listing of the guards and counter-guards inclusive of the pages of Manuscript I.33 on which they appear. All seven guards are also found on 1r/1 and 1v/2.

GUARD	DISPLACED WITH
1st Guard	
2r/3	Half-Shield
3r/5	Half-Shield
4r/7	Crutch
5r/9	Crutch
5v/10	Crutch
6v/12	Long-Point
7v/14	Long-Point
8v/16	Half-Shield
11v/22	Half-Shield
15r/29	Fourth Guard
15r/29	Half-Shield
16r/31	Long-Point
32r/61	Walpurgis
2nd Guard	
9r/17	Upper Protection
10r/19	Upper Protection
10v/20	Half-Shield
3rd Guard	
12r/23	Middle Protection
12v/24	Middle Protection
13r/25	Half-Shield
14r/27	Long-Point
26r/51	Priest's Hat
4th Guard	
14v/28	Half-Shield
15r/29	First Guard
56v/52	Priest's Hat
30r/59	Priest's Hat
31r/61	Priest's Hat
5th Guard	
27r/53	Priest's Hat
27v/54	Half-Shield
28r/55	Half-Shield
29r/57	Special Priest's Hat

GUARD	DISPLACED WITH
6th Guard	
17r/33	
7th Guard	
17v/34	Bind
19r/37	Bind
20r/39	Bind
20v/40	Bind
23r/45	Thrust
Crutch	
4r/7	First Guard
5r/9	First Guard
5v/10	First Guard
Fiddle Bow	
22r/43	
22v/44	
Half-Shield	
2r/3	First Guard
3r/5	First Guard
8v/16	First Guard
10v/20	Second Guard
11v/22	First Guard
13r/25	Third Guard
14v/28	Fourth Guard
15r/29	First Guard
23v/46	Priest's Hat
24v/48	Priest's Hat
27v/54	Fifth Guard
28r/55	Fifth Guard
Take the Arm	
4v/8	
12v/24	
18v/36	
19r/37	

GUARD	DISPLACED WITH
Long-Point	
6v/12	First Guard
7v/14	First Guard
14r/27	Third Guard
16r/31	First Guard
Priest's Hat	
23v/46	Half-Shield
24v/48	Half-Shield
25r/49	Rare Displacement
26r/51	Third Guard
26v/52	Fourth Guard
27r/53	Fifth Guard
30r/59	Fourth Guard
31r/61	Fourth Guard
Special Priest's Hat	
29r/57	Fifth Guard
Upper Protection	
9r/17	Second Guard
10r/19	Second Guard
Middle Protection	
12r/23	Third Guard
12v/24	Third Guard
Lower Protection	
32r/63	Walpurgis
25r/50	Priest's Hat
Walpurgis	
32r/63	First Guard

Glossary (German-English)

A

Abnehmen: To move away or free yourself from a bind or begin an attack from a bind.

Abreissen: To follow the opponent's weapon or hands, usually with the hilt downward. Push the opponent's weapon or hands down with the hilt.

Abschneiden (Slice Off): To slice across the opponent's hands from below or above.

Abschnappen (Snap Off): To disengage from a bind by sliding or batting the blade away with a strong blow.

Absetzen (Set Aside): To simultaneously parry the opponent's blade while making a thrust, usually from the Ox or Plow.

Abziehen (Withdraw): To disengage from the opponent and move out of range of his weapon. Usually after the combat has ended.

Alber (Fool): One of the six guards. The sword is held downward, and the point is held in front of you, pointing diagonally at the ground.

Am Schwert (On the Sword): To execute an attack from a bind. You work "on the sword."

Anbinden (Crossing of the Blades): The engaged position with weapons crossed in which the weapons come together at the moment of contact. A distinction is made between "being hard on the sword" or "soft on the sword."

Ansetzen (Place): An attack aimed at a certain body part.

B

Band (Bind): The moment of contact between two weapons and the actual contact of two weapons.

Blösse (Openings): The opponent's four openings: the first is his right side above the belt, the second is his left above the belt, the third is his right side below the belt, and the fourth is his left below the belt. Also called *Fenster* (Windows).

Brentschirn: A state of "battle" in which the edges of the swords rub together in the binding position. From this position you try to take the opponent's sword.

Bruch (Break): The counter to a certain technique. The break foils a technique.

Buckler: Small round hand shield, also called a fist shield.

Büffel (Buffalo): Disparaging term for a fighter who relies solely on his strength and aggression.

D

Drei Häue (Three Blows): Three blows in succession—an under-cut from the right and an under-cut from the left, followed by a powerful Crown Cut.

Drei Wunder (Three Wonders): The three components of sword fighting: the cut, the thrust, and the slice.

Duplieren (Doubling): To strike the opponent from a binding position. Your own blade often comes between the opponent's sword and the opponent, making a defense almost impossible.

Durchlaufen (Running Through): The attempt to pass the opponent's weapon and reach his back.

Durchsetzen (Push Through): A timed thrust whose target is between the opponent's hands and body.

Durchstreichen (Striking Through): To carry through a blow from below against the opponent's blade to the point that you separate from the bind and thrust at another opening.

Durchwechseln (Changing Through): Avoiding contact with the opponent's blade and seeking another opening, usually with a thrust from the Ox. Can also happen from a bind.

E

Einhorn (Unicorn): The Unicorn is an end position after an under-cut with the point aimed high. In the right Unicorn the arms are crossed.

Einlaufen (Running In): To change from a near to a close measure. Usually followed by wrestling and/or throws. Running In is the beginning of wrestling on the sword.

Eisenpforte (Iron Gate): A guard in which the point is placed on the ground in front of you. Similar to the Barrier or Fool Guard.

F

Fehler (Feint): A feint. It is carried out as if you are about to attack a certain opening to attack another vulnerable opening.

Fläche (Flat): The flat, or broad side, of the blade.

Fühlen (To Feel): While in a binding position, to sense whether the enemy is hard or soft in the bind. Sense his intentions.

G

Gehilz (Hilt): The grip of the sword, including cross guard, grip, and pommel. *Gehilz* also sometimes refers to the cross guard.

Geschränkter Ort: A thrust in which the hands are held crossed over, the left hand under right.

Gewappnet Stehen: A stance where the sword becomes a barrier in front of the body, with the left hand grasping the middle of the blade and the hilt in the right hand.

H

Halbschwert (Half-Sword): A technique in which you grip your sword with the left hand in order to achieve a more precise thrust. Used mainly in armed combat.

Handarbeit (Handwork): The combat itself between the approach and withdrawal. The actual sword fight occurs during Handwork.

Hängen (Hanging): Stance in which the point or the pommel "hangs" downward.

Hängetort (Hanging Point): Position in which the point hangs downward. The hilt is held over the head. If you are in a right Hanging Point, the point hangs down to the left.

Huten (Guards): The basic stances. According to Liechtenauer there are four different guards, while Ringeck names six. They are: Fool, Plow, Ox, From the Roof, Barrier, and Tail Guards. In many combat manuals there are even more, though most are variations of Ringeck's six basic guards.

I

Indes (Meanwhile): Not "Before" or "After," but "Meanwhile" or "at the same time." The most important tempo in sword fighting because it is the only safe one.

K

Krauthacke (Garden Hoe): A swift sequence of vertical blows to the upper and lower openings during which you step toward the opponent.

Kreuz (Cross): The cross formed by the cross guard and the blade. Sometimes also a synonym for cross guard.

Krieg (War): Winding, mutating, doubling, binding, etc.—all the techniques that take place at relatively close quarters. The point is mainly used in the War position.

Kron (Crown): Defensive technique in which you lift your sword and deflect the opponent's blade with your cross guard or forte.

Krumphau (Crooked Cut): Technique in which the arms are crossed, for example, countering an over-cut with the short edge from a right Plow and ending in a left Plow. When executing a Crooked Cut you step toward the opponent with a cross step.

Kurze Schneide (Short Edge): Also called the "false edge." The edge of the sword that normally points toward the fighter when holding the sword normally in front of him.

L

Lange Schneide (Long Edge): The edge of the sword that strikes the target in a normal blow. The edge that points away from the fighter when holding the sword normally in front of him.

Langort (Long Point): Also called "Long Guard." An additional guard with the blade horizontal and the arms extended straight forward. The hands and blade form a line.

Leger/Läger (Position): To assume a position.

Leichmeister (Dance Master): Dance master, especially for arms-dance and arms-plays. A derogatory term.

Linke Klinge: Short edge.

M

Meisterhau (Master Cut): According to Ringeck there are five Master Cuts: Crooked Cut, Wrath Cut, Crosswise Cut, Crown Cut, and Squinting Cut.

Mensur (Measure): Distance. The term refers to the various distances between fighters during combat.

Mittelhau (Middle-Cut): A left-to-right horizontal side cut at medium height.

Mordschlag (Death Blow): A technique in which you hold the blade with both hands and strike with the hilt.

Mordstück (Death Device): A device that ends in the death of one or both fighters.

Mutieren (Mutate): A Winding technique in which you thrust from the Ox position past the opponent's hands to his lower openings without losing blade contact.

N

Nach (After): When the opponent attacks you end up in the "After" (by merely parrying). In the "After" you only react to the opponent.

Natternzunge (Viper Tongue): A rapidly repeated sequence of thrusts over the opponent's hilt during which a change through movement is repeatedly indicated but never carried out until the opponent becomes confused and leaves an opening for a thrust. The movement resembles the flicking tongue of a viper.

Nebenhut (Tail Guard): One of the six guards. The sword is held with the cross guard at hip level; the point is aimed down and back.

O

Ochs (Ox): One of the six guards. The sword is held with the cross guard at eye level or higher, the point aimed at the opponent's face. Optimally place the thumb on the blade.

Oberhau (Over-Cut): Every blow that is struck from above.

Ort (Point): The tip of the sword.

P

Pflug (Plow): One of the six guards. The sword is held with the grip at hip level and the point is aimed up and forward, toward the opponent.

R

Rauschen (Swoosh): To attack with a rapid succession of blows.

Redel (Wheel): To hold the sword with an outstretched right arm and execute a swift circular motion of the blade in front.

S

Scheitelhau (Crown Cut): One of the Master Cuts. A vertical downward blow from the "crown."

Schielhau (Squinting Cut): One of the Master Cuts. A downward cut with the short edge at the opponent's shoulder or neck.

Schlüssel (Key): A guard in which the hilt is held far back. The blade rests on the left arm, pointing forward. The hilt is held roughly in front of the right breast.

Schrankhut (Barrier Guard): One of the six guards. The sword is held in front of you, with the point aimed at the ground. The Barrier can be executed with the blade held vertically or diagonally in front of you.

Schwäche (Foible): The first third of the blade beginning at the point and extending to the middle.

Schnappen (Snap): To execute a sudden movement of the blade from the bind and immediately strike the side of the opponent's blade. During the movement the pommel snaps forward and back.

Sprechfenster (Talking Window): The blades are in a strong bind and you wait for or determine the opponent's intentions.

Stärke (Forte): The last third of the blade from the cross guard to the middle.

Streichen (Cancel): To direct a blow from below against the opponent's blade to cancel their action.

Stücke (Device): Also known as a "fighting trick." Techniques or attack combinations designed to get past an opponent's defenses.

Sturzhau (Plunging Cut): A powerful strike in which you advance and simultaneously strike from above with the short edge with crossed hands.

U

Überlaufen (Overrunning): A blow that reaches the opponent before his reaches you. For example, a Crown Cut against the legs.

Umschlagen (Strike Around): To pull away after a blow for another to the opposite side.

Unterhau (Under-Cut): Every blow that is struck from below.

V

Verkehrer: A technique in which, from a strong bind, the opponent is thrown with the help of his elbow.

Versatzungen (Displacements): There are four Displacements and they describe the breaks for the four basic guards: Crooked Cut breaks Ox, Crown Cut breaks Fool, Crosswise Cut breaks From the Roof, and Squinting Cut breaks Plow.

Versetzen (Displace): Deflect an attack with your own attack/blow so that it misses its target.

Verzucken (Twitch): Suddenly and abruptly change the direction of attack.

Vom Tag (From the Roof): One of the six guards. The sword is held with the cross guard at chin height or over the head. The point is aimed upward or slightly to the rear.

Vor (Before): If you are fighting in the "Before" then you retain the initiative and the opponent reacts to your attacks.

W

Wechsel (Change): A guard similar to the Tail Guard, with the long edge facing down.

Wechselhau (Changing Cut): If a strike misses and you withdraw the blade along the same attacking plane to strike with the short edge it is called a Changing Cut.

Weckmeister: An upward thrust at the opponent's face made after an attack from the Plow has been parried.

Winden (Winding): Any turning of the blade while pressing on the opponent's blade to bring one end or the other of your sword (point or pommel) against him. There are a total of twenty-four Winds (1 x 2 x 3 x 4 = 24): "One winding from two sides with three attacks to the four openings."

Z

Zecken (Tick): A light strike with the weapon.

Zornhau (Wrath Cut): One of the Master Cuts. An over-cut that is struck with great force, either from the right or from above

Zucken (Drawing): An abrupt disengagement from the bind downward and to the rear, immediately followed by a thrust. Can also be executed without binding.

Zufechten (Approach): The part of the combat before you reach striking distance. In the approach neither opponent can reach the other with his sword.

Zwerchhau (Crosswise Cut): One of the Master Cuts. A blow that is struck more or less on the horizontal plane (from the side), in contrast to an over-cut, for example. The Crosswise Cut is not a middle-cut.

ENGLISH

A

After: When the opponent attacks you end up in the "After" (by merely parrying). In the "After" you only react to the opponent.

B

Barrier Guard: One of the six guards. The sword is held in front of you, with the point aimed at the ground. The Barrier can be executed with the blade held vertically or diagonally in front of you.

Before: If you are fighting in the "Before" then you retain the initiative and the opponent reacts to your attacks.

Bind: The moment of contact between two weapons and the actual contact of two weapons.

Break: The counter to a certain technique. The break foils a technique.

Buckler: Small round hand shield, also called a fist shield.

Buffalo: Disparaging term for a fighter who relies solely on his strength and aggression.

C

Cancel: To direct a blow from below against the opponent's blade to cancel their action.

Change: A guard similar to the Tail Guard, with the long edge facing down.

Changing Cut: If a strike misses and you withdraw the blade along the same attacking plane to strike with the short edge it is called a Changing Cut.

Changing Through: Avoiding contact with the opponent's blade and seeking another opening, usually with a thrust from the Ox. Can also happen from a bind.

Crooked Cut: Technique in which the arms are crossed, for example, countering an over-cut with the short edge from a right Plow and ending in a left Plow. When executing a Crooked Cut you step toward the opponent with a cross step.

Cross: The cross formed by the cross guard and the blade. Sometimes also a synonym for cross guard.

Crossing of the Blades: The engaged position with weapons crossed in which the weapons come together at the moment of contact. A distinction is made between "being hard on the sword" or "soft on the sword."

Crown: Defensive technique in which you lift your sword and deflect the opponent's blade with your cross guard or forte.

Crown Cut: One of the Master Cuts. A vertical downward blow from the "crown."

D

Death Blow: A technique in which you hold the blade with both hands and strike with the hilt.

Death Device: A device which ends in the death of one or both fighters.

Device: Also known as a "fighting trick." Techniques or attack combinations designed to get past an opponent's defenses.

Displace: Deflect an attack with your own attack/blow so that it misses its target.

Displacements: There are four Displacements and they describe the breaks for the four basic guards: Crooked Cut breaks Ox, Crown Cut breaks Fool, Crosswise Cut breaks From the Roof, and Squinting Cut breaks Plow.

Doubling: To strike the opponent from a binding position. Your own blade often comes between the opponent's sword and the opponent, making a defense almost impossible.

F

Feint: It is carried out as if you are about to attack a certain opening to attack another vulnerable opening.

Feel: While in a binding position, to sense whether the enemy is hard or soft in the bind. Sense his intentions.

Flat: The flat, or broad side, of the blade.

Foible: The first third of the blade, beginning at the point and extending to the middle.

Fool: One of the six guards. The sword is held downward and the point is held in front of you, pointing diagonally at the ground.

Forte: The last third of the blade from the cross guard to the middle.

From the Roof: One of the six guards. The sword is held with the cross guard at chin height or over the head. The point is aimed upward or slightly to the rear.

G

Garden Hoe: A swift sequence of vertical blows to the upper and lower openings during which you step toward the opponent.

Guards: The basic stances. According to Liechtenauer there are four different guards, while Ringeck names six. They are: Fool, Plow, Ox, From the Roof, Barrier, and Tail Guards. In many combat manuals there are even more, though most are variations of Ringeck's six basic guards.

H

Handwork: The combat itself between the approach and withdrawal. The actual sword fight occurs during Handwork.

Hanging: Stance in which the point or the pommel "hangs" downward.

Hilt: The grip of the sword, including cross guard, grip, and pommel.

I

Iron Gate: A guard in which the point is placed on the ground in front of you. Similar to the Barrier or Fool Guard.

K

Key: A guard in which the hilt is held far back. The blade rests on the left arm, pointing forward. The hilt is held roughly in front of the right breast.

L

Long Edge: The edge of the sword that strikes the target in a normal blow. The edge that points away from the fighter when holding the sword normally in front of him.

Long Point: Also called "Long Guard." An additional guard with the blade horizontal and the arms extended straight forward. The hands and blade form a line.

M

Master Cut: According to Ringeck there are five Master Cuts: Crooked Cut, Wrath Cut, Crosswise Cut, Crown Cut, and Squinting Cut.

Meanwhile: Not "Before" or "After," but "Meanwhile" or "at the same time." The most important tempo in sword fighting because it is the only safe one.

Measure: Distance. The term refers to the various distances between fighters during combat.

Middle-Cut: A left-to-right horizontal side cut at medium height.

Mutate: A Winding technique in which you thrust from the Ox position past the opponent's hands to his lower openings without losing blade contact.

O

On the Sword: To execute an attack from a bind. You work "on the sword."

Openings: The opponent's four openings. The first is his right side above the belt, the second is his left above the belt, the third is his right side below the belt, and the fourth is his left below the belt. Also called Windows.

Over-Cut: Every blow that is struck from above.

Overrunning: A blow that reaches the opponent before his reaches you. For example, a Crown Cut against the legs.

Ox: One of the six guards. The sword is held with the cross guard at eye level or higher with the point aimed at the opponent's face. Optimally place the thumb on the blade.

P

Place: An attack aimed at a certain body part.

Plow: One of the six guards. The sword is held with the grip at hip level and the point is aimed up and forward, toward the opponent.

Plunging Cut: A powerful strike in which you advance and simultaneously strike from above with the short edge with crossed hands.

Point: The tip of the sword.

Push Through: A timed thrust whose target is between the opponent's hands and body.

R

Running In: To change from a near to a close measure. Usually followed by wrestling and/or throws. Running In is the beginning of wrestling on the sword.

Running Through: The attempt to pass the opponent's weapon and reach his back.

S

Set Aside: To simultaneously parry the opponent's blade while making a thrust, usually from the Ox or Plow.

Short Edge: Also called the "false edge." The edge of the sword that normally points toward the fighter when holding the sword normally in front of him.

Slice Off: To slice across the opponent's hands from below or above.

Snap: To execute a sudden movement of the blade from the bind and immediately strike the side of the opponent's blade. During the movement the pommel snaps forward and back.

Snap Off: To disengage from a bind by sliding or batting the blade away with a strong blow.

Squinting Cut: One of the Master Cuts. A downward cut with the short edge at the opponent's shoulder or neck.

Strike Around: To pull away after a blow for another to the opposite side.

Striking Through: To carry through a blow from below against the opponent's blade to the point that you separate from the bind and thrust at another opening.

T

Tail Guard: One of the six guards. The sword is held with the cross guard at hip level while the point is aimed down and back.

Talking Window: The blades are in a strong bind and you wait for or determine the opponent's intentions.

Three Blows: Three blows in succession: an under-cut from the right and an under-cut from the left, followed by a powerful Crown Cut.

Three Wonders: The three components of sword fighting: the cut, the thrust, and the slice.

Tick: A light strike with the weapon.

Twitch: Suddenly and abruptly change the direction of attack.

U

Under-Cut: Every blow that is struck from below.

Unicorn: The Unicorn is an end position after an under-cut with the point aimed high. In the right Unicorn the arms are crossed.

V

Viper Tongue: A rapidly repeated sequence of thrusts over the opponent's hilt, during which a change through movement is repeatedly indicated but never carried out until the opponent becomes confused and leaves an opening for a thrust. The movement resembles the flicking tongue of a viper.

W

War: Winding, mutating, doubling, binding, etc.—all the techniques that take place at relatively close quarters. The point is mainly used in the War position.

Wheel: To hold the sword with an outstretched right arm and execute a swift circular motion of the blade in front.

Winding: Any turning of the blade while pressing on the opponent's blade to bring one end or the other of your sword (point or pommel) against him. There are a total of twenty-four Winds (1 x 2 x 3 x 4 = 24): "One winding from two sides with three attacks to the four openings."

Withdraw: To disengage from the opponent and move out of range of his weapon. Usually after the combat has ended.